Praise for *Fundamentals of Data Visualization*

Wilke has written the rare data visualization book that will help you move beyond the standard line, bar, and pie charts that you know and use. He takes you through the conceptual underpinnings of what makes an effective visualization and through a library of different graphs that anyone can utilize. This book will quickly become a go-to reference for anyone working with and visualizing data.

—*Jonathan Schwabish, Senior Fellow, Urban Institute*

In this well-illustrated view of what it means to clearly visualize data, Claus Wilke explains his rationale for why some graphs are effective and others are not. This incredibly useful guide provides clear examples that beginners can emulate as well as explanations for stylistic choices so experts can learn what to modify.

—*Steve Haroz, Research Scientist, Inria*

Wilke's book is the best practical guide to visualization for anyone with a scientific disposition. This clear and accessible book is going to live at arm's reach on lab tables everywhere.

—*Scott Murray, Lead Program Manager, O'Reilly Media*

Fundamentals of Data Visualization

A Primer on Making Informative and Compelling Figures

Claus O. Wilke

Beijing · Boston · Farnham · Sebastopol · Tokyo

Fundamentals of Data Visualization

by Claus O. Wilke

Published by O'Reilly Media, Inc., 1005 Gravenstein Highway North, Sebastopol, CA 95472.

O'Reilly books may be purchased for educational, business, or sales promotional use. Online editions are also available for most titles (*http://oreilly.com*). For more information, contact our corporate/institutional sales department: 800-998-9938 or *corporate@oreilly.com*.

Editors: Mike Loukides and Melissa Potter
Production Editor: Kristen Brown
Copyeditor: Rachel Head
Proofreader: James Fraleigh

Indexer: Ellen Troutman-Zaig
Interior Designer: David Futato
Cover Designer: Karen Montgomery
Illustrator: Claus Wilke

March 2019:   First Edition

Revision History for the First Edition
2019-03-15:   First Release
2019-05-03:   Second Release
2019-06-07:   Third Release
2020-03-27:   Fourth Release

See *http://oreilly.com/catalog/errata.csp?isbn=9781492031086* for release details.

978-1-492-03108-6

[LSI]

Table of Contents

Part II.   Principles of Figure Design

Preface

If you are a scientist, an analyst, a consultant, or anybody else who has to prepare technical documents or reports, one of the most important skills you need to have is the ability to make compelling data visualizations, generally in the form of figures. Figures will typically carry the weight of your arguments. They need to be clear, attractive, and convincing. The difference between good and bad figures can be the difference between a highly influential or an obscure paper, a grant or contract won or lost, a job interview gone well or poorly. And yet, there are surprisingly few resources to teach you how to make compelling data visualizations. Few colleges offer courses on this topic, and there are not that many books on this topic either. (Some exist, of course.) Tutorials for plotting software typically focus on how to achieve specific visual effects rather than explaining why certain choices are preferred and others not. In your day-to-day work, you are simply expected to know how to make good figures, and if you're lucky you have a patient adviser who teaches you a few tricks as you're writing your first scientific papers.

In the context of writing, experienced editors talk about "ear," the ability to hear (internally, as you read a piece of prose) whether the writing is any good. I think that when it comes to figures and other visualizations, we similarly need "eye," the ability to look at a figure and see whether it is balanced, clear, and compelling. And just as is the case with writing, the ability to see whether a figure works or not can be learned. Having eye means primarily that you are aware of a larger collection of simple rules and principles of good visualization, and that you pay attention to little details that other people might not.

In my experience, again just as in writing, you don't develop eye by reading a book over the weekend. It is a lifelong process, and concepts that are too complex or too subtle for you today may make much more sense five years from now. I can say for myself that I continue to evolve in my understanding of figure preparation. I routinely try to expose myself to new approaches, and I pay attention to the visual and design choices others make in their figures. I'm also open to changing my mind. I might today consider a given figure great, but next month I might find a reason to criticize it. So with this in mind, please don't take anything I say as gospel. Think critically about my reasoning for certain choices and decide whether you want to adopt them or not.

While the materials in this book are presented in a logical progression, most chapters can stand on their own, and there is no need to read the book cover to cover. Feel free to skip around, to pick out a specific section that you're interested in at the moment, or one that covers a particular design choice you're pondering. In fact, I think you will get the most out of this book if you don't read it all at once, but rather read it piecemeal over longer stretches of time, try to apply just a few concepts from the book in your figuremaking, and come back to read about other concepts or reread sections on concepts you learned about a while back. You may find that the same chapter tells you different things if you reread it after a few months have passed.

Even though nearly all of the figures in this book were made with R and ggplot2, I do not see this as an R book. I am talking about general principles of figure preparation. The software used to make the figures is incidental. You can use any plotting software you want to generate the kinds of figures I'm showing here. However, ggplot2 and similar packages make many of the techniques I'm using much simpler than other plotting libraries. Importantly, because this is not an R book, I do not discuss code or programming techniques anywhere in this book. I want you to focus on the concepts and the figures, not on the code. If you are curious about how any of the figures were made, you can check out the book's source code at its GitHub repository (*https://github.com/clauswilke/dataviz*).

Thoughts on Graphing Software and Figure-Preparation Pipelines

I have over two decades of experience preparing figures for scientific publications and have made thousands of figures. If there has been one constant over these two decades, it's been the change in figure preparation pipelines. Every few years, a new plotting library is developed or a new paradigm arises, and large groups of scientists switch over to the hot new toolkit. I have made figures using gnuplot, Xfig, Mathematica, Matlab, matplotlib in Python, base R, ggplot2 in R, and possibly others I can't currently remember. My current preferred approach is ggplot2 in R, but I don't expect that I'll continue using it until I retire.

This constant change in software platforms is one of the key reasons why this book is not a programming book and why I have left out all code examples. I want this book to be useful to you regardless of which software you use, and I want it to remain valuable even once everybody has moved on from ggplot2 and is using the next new thing. I realize that this choice may be frustrating to some ggplot2 users who would like to know how I made a given figure. However, anybody who is curious about my coding techniques can read the source code of the book. It is available. Also, in the future I may release a supplementary document focused just on the code.

One thing I have learned over the years is that automation is your friend. I think figures should be autogenerated as part of the data analysis pipeline (which should also be automated), and they should come out of the pipeline ready to be sent to the printer, with no manual post-processing needed. I see a lot of trainees autogenerate rough drafts of their figures, which they then import into Illustrator for sprucing up. There are several reasons why this is a bad idea. First, the moment you manually edit a figure, your final figure becomes irreproducible. A third party cannot generate the exact same figure you did. While this may not matter much if all you did was change the font of the axis labels, the lines are blurry, and it's easy to cross over into territory where things are less clear-cut. As an example, let's say you want to manually replace cryptic labels with more readable ones. A third party may not be able to verify that the label replacement was appropriate. Second, if you add a lot of manual post-processing to your figure-preparation pipeline, then you will be more reluctant to make any changes or redo your work. Thus, you may ignore reasonable requests for change made by collaborators or colleagues, or you may be tempted to reuse an old figure even though you've actually regenerated all the data. Third, you may yourself forget what exactly you did to prepare a given figure, or you may not be able to generate a future figure on new data that exactly visually matches your earlier figure. These are not made-up examples. I've seen all of them play out with real people and real publications.

For all these reasons, interactive plot programs are a bad idea. They inherently force you to manually prepare your figures. In fact, it's probably better to autogenerate a figure draft and spruce it up in Illustrator than to make the entire figure by hand in some interactive plot program. Please be aware that Excel is an interactive plot program as well and is not recommended for figure preparation (or data analysis).

One critical component in a book on data visualization is the feasibility of the proposed visualizations. It's nice to invent some elegant new type of visualization, but if nobody can easily generate figures using this visualization then there isn't much use to it. For example, when Tufte first proposed sparklines nobody had an easy way of making them. While we need visionaries who move the world forward by pushing the envelope of what's possible, I envision this book to be practical and directly applicable to working data scientists preparing figures for their publications. Therefore, the visualizations I propose in the subsequent chapters can be generated with a few lines of R code via ggplot2 and readily available extension packages. In fact, nearly every figure in this book, with the exception of a few figures in Chapters 26, 27, and 28, was autogenerated exactly as shown.

Conventions Used in This Book

The following typographical conventions are used in this book:

Italic
> Indicates new terms, URLs, email addresses, filenames, and file extensions.

`Constant width`
> Used to refer to program elements such as variable or function names, statements, and keywords.

 This element signifies a tip or suggestion.

 This element signifies a general note.

 This element indicates a warning or caution.

Using Code Examples

Supplemental material is available for download at *https://github.com/clauswilke/dataviz*.

This book is here to help you get your job done. In general, if example code is offered with this book, you may use it in your programs and documentation. You do not need to contact us for permission unless you're reproducing a significant portion of the code. For example, writing a program that uses several chunks of code from this book does not require permission. Selling or distributing a CD-ROM of examples from O'Reilly books does require permission. Answering a question by citing this book and quoting example code does not require permission. Incorporating a significant amount of example code from this book into your product's documentation does require permission.

We appreciate, but do not require, attribution. An attribution usually includes the title, author, publisher, and ISBN. For example: "*Fundamentals of Data Visualization by Claus O. Wilke* (O'Reilly). Copyright 2019 Claus O. Wilke, 978-1-492-03108-6."

You may find that additional uses fall within the scope of fair use (for example, reusing a few figures from the book). If you feel your use of code examples or other content falls outside fair use or the permission given above, feel free to contact us at *permissions@oreilly.com*.

O'Reilly Online Learning

 For almost 40 years, *O'Reilly Media* has provided technology and business training, knowledge, and insight to help companies succeed.

Our unique network of experts and innovators share their knowledge and expertise through books, articles, conferences, and our online learning platform. O'Reilly's online learning platform gives you on-demand access to live training courses, in-depth learning paths, interactive coding environments, and a vast collection of text and video from O'Reilly and 200+ other publishers. For more information, please visit *http://oreilly.com*.

How to Contact Us

Please address comments and questions concerning this book to the publisher:

O'Reilly Media, Inc.
1005 Gravenstein Highway North
Sebastopol, CA 95472
800-998-9938 (in the United States or Canada)
707-829-0515 (international or local)
707-829-0104 (fax)

We have a web page for this book, where we list errata, examples, and any additional information. You can access this page at *http://bit.ly/fundamentals-of-data-visualization*.

To comment or ask technical questions about this book, send email to *bookquestions@oreilly.com*.

For more information about our books, courses, conferences, and news, see our website at *http://www.oreilly.com*.

Find us on Facebook: *http://facebook.com/oreilly*

Follow us on Twitter: *http://twitter.com/oreillymedia*

Watch us on YouTube: *http://www.youtube.com/oreillymedia*

Acknowledgments

This project would not have been possible without the fantastic work the RStudio team has put into turning the R universe into a first-rate publishing platform. In particular, I have to thank Hadley Wickham for creating ggplot2, the plotting software that was used to make all the figures throughout this book. I would also like to thank Yihui Xie for creating R Markdown and for writing the `knitr` and `bookdown` packages. I don't think I would have started this project without these tools ready to go. Writing R Markdown files is fun, and it's easy to collect material and gain momentum. Special thanks go to Achim Zeileis and Reto Stauffer for `colorspace`, Thomas Lin Pedersen for `ggforce` and `gganimate`, Kamil Slowikowski for `ggrepel`, Edzer Pebesma for `sf`, and Claire McWhite for her work on `colorspace` and `colorblindr` to simulate color-vision deficiency in assembled R figures.

Several people have provided helpful feedback on draft versions of this book. Most importantly, Mike Loukides, my editor at O'Reilly, and Steve Haroz have both read and commented on every chapter. I also received helpful comments from Carl Bergstrom, Jessica Hullman, Matthew Kay, Tristan Mahr, Edzer Pebesma, Jon Schwabish, and Hadley Wickham. Len Kiefer's blog and Kieran Healy's book and blog postings have provided numerous inspirations for figures to make and datasets to use. A number of people pointed out minor issues or typos, including Thiago Arrais, Malcolm Barrett, Jessica Burnett, Jon Calder, Antônio Pedro Camargo, Daren Card, Kim Cressman, Akos Hajdu, Thomas Jochmann, Andrew Kinsman, Will Koehrsen, Alex Lalejini, John Leadley, Katrin Leinweber, Mikel Madina, Claire McWhite, S'busiso Mkhondwane, Jose Nazario, Steve Putman, Maëlle Salmon, Christian Schudoma, James Scott-Brown, Enrico Spinielli, Wouter van der Bijl, and Ron Yurko.

I would also more broadly like to thank all the other contributors to the tidyverse and the R community in general. There truly is an R package for any visualization challenge one may encounter. All these packages have been developed by an extensive community of thousands of data scientists and statisticians, and many of them have in some form contributed to the making of this book.

Finally, I would like to thank my wife Stefania for patiently enduring many evenings and weekends during which I spent hours in front of the computer writing ggplot2 code, obsessing over minute details of certain figures, and fleshing out chapter details.

## CHAPTER 1

Introduction

Data visualization is part art and part science. The challenge is to get the art right without getting the science wrong, and vice versa. A data visualization first and foremost has to accurately convey the data. It must not mislead or distort. If one number is twice as large as another, but in the visualization they look to be about the same, then the visualization is wrong. At the same time, a data visualization should be aesthetically pleasing. Good visual presentations tend to enhance the message of the visualization. If a figure contains jarring colors, imbalanced visual elements, or other features that distract, then the viewer will find it harder to inspect the figure and interpret it correctly.

In my experience, scientists frequently (though not always!) know how to visualize data without being grossly misleading. However, they may not have a well-developed sense of visual aesthetics, and they may inadvertently make visual choices that detract from their desired message. Designers, on the other hand, may prepare visualizations that look beautiful but play fast and loose with the data. It is my goal to provide useful information to both groups.

This book attempts to cover the key principles, methods, and concepts required to visualize data for publications, reports, or presentations. Because data visualization is a vast field, and in its broadest definition could include topics as varied as schematic technical drawings, 3D animations, and user interfaces, I necessarily had to limit my scope. I am specifically covering the case of static visualizations presented in print, online, or as slides. The book does not cover interactive visuals or movies, except in one brief section in Chapter 16. Therefore, throughout this book, I will use the words "visualization" and "figure" somewhat interchangeably. The book also does not provide any instruction on *how* to make figures with existing visualization software or programming libraries. The annotated bibliography at the end of the book includes pointers to appropriate texts covering these topics.

The book is divided into three parts. The first, "From Data to Visualization," describes different types of plots and charts, such as bar graphs, scatterplots, and pie charts. Its primary emphasis is on the science of visualization. In this part, rather than attempting to provide encyclopedic coverage of every conceivable visualization approach, I discuss a core set of visuals that you will likely encounter in publications and/or need in your own work. In organizing this part, I have attempted to group visualizations by the type of message they convey rather than by the type of data being visualized. Statistical texts often describe data analysis and visualization by type of data, organizing the material by number and type of variables (one continuous variable, one discrete variable, two continuous variables, one continuous and one discrete variable, etc.). I believe that only statisticians find this organization helpful. Most other people think in terms of a message, such as how large something is, how it is composed of parts, how it relates to something else, and so on.

The second part, "Principles of Figure Design," discusses various design issues that arise when assembling data visualizations. Its primary but not exclusive emphasis is on the aesthetic aspect of data visualization. Once we have chosen the appropriate type of plot or chart for our dataset, we have to make aesthetic choices about the visual elements, such as colors, symbols, and font sizes. These choices can affect both how clear a visualization is and how elegant it looks. The chapters in this second part address the most common issues that I have seen arise repeatedly in practical applications.

The third part, "Miscellaneous Topics," covers a few remaining issues that didn't fit into the first two parts. It discusses file formats commonly used to store images and plots, provides thoughts about the choice of visualization software, and explains how to place individual figures into the context of a larger document.

Ugly, Bad, and Wrong Figures

Throughout this book, I frequently show different versions of the same figures, some as examples of how to make a good visualization and some as examples of how not to. To provide a simple visual guideline of which examples should be emulated and which should be avoided, I am labeling problematic figures as "ugly," "bad," or "wrong" (Figure 1-1):

Ugly
    A figure that has aesthetic problems but otherwise is clear and informative

Bad
    A figure that has problems related to perception; it may be unclear, confusing, overly complicated, or deceiving

Wrong
    A figure that has problems related to mathematics; it is objectively incorrect

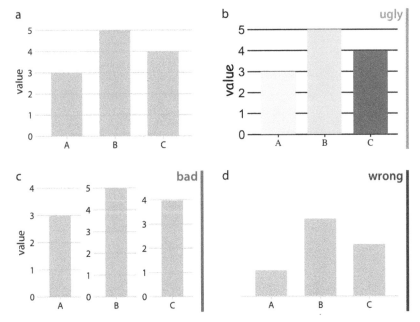

Figure 1-1. Examples of ugly, bad, and wrong figures. (a) A bar plot showing three values (A = 3, B = 5, and C = 4). This is a reasonable visualization with no major flaws. (b) An ugly version of part (a). While the plot is technically correct, it is not aesthetically pleasing. The colors are too bright and not useful. The background grid is too prominent. The text is displayed using three different fonts in three different sizes. (c) A bad version of part (a). Each bar is shown with its own y axis scale. Because the scales don't align, this makes the figure misleading. One can easily get the impression that the three values are closer together than they actually are. (d) A wrong version of part (a). Without an explicit y axis scale, the numbers represented by the bars cannot be ascertained. The bars appear to be of lengths 1, 3, and 2, even though the values displayed are meant to be 3, 5, and 4.

I am not explicitly labeling good figures. Any figure that isn't labeled as flawed should be assumed to be at least acceptable. It is a figure that is informative, looks appealing, and could be printed as is. Note that among the good figures, there will still be differences in quality, and some good figures will be better than others.

I generally provide my rationale for specific ratings, but some are a matter of taste. In general, the "ugly" rating is more subjective than the "bad" or "wrong" rating. Moreover, the boundary between "ugly" and "bad" is somewhat fluid. Sometimes poor design choices can interfere with human perception to the point where a "bad" rating is more appropriate than an "ugly" rating. In any case, I encourage you to develop your own eye and to critically evaluate my choices.

## PART I

From Data to Visualization

## CHAPTER 2

Visualizing Data: Mapping Data onto Aesthetics

Whenever we visualize data, we take data values and convert them in a systematic and logical way into the visual elements that make up the final graphic. Even though there are many different types of data visualizations, and on first glance a scatterplot, a pie chart, and a heatmap don't seem to have much in common, all these visualizations can be described with a common language that captures how data values are turned into blobs of ink on paper or colored pixels on a screen. The key insight is the following: all data visualizations map data values into quantifiable features of the resulting graphic. We refer to these features as *aesthetics*.

Aesthetics and Types of Data

Aesthetics describe every aspect of a given graphical element. A few examples are provided in Figure 2-1. A critical component of every graphical element is of course its *position*, which describes where the element is located. In standard 2D graphics, we describe positions by an x and y value, but other coordinate systems and one- or three-dimensional visualizations are possible. Next, all graphical elements have a *shape*, a *size*, and a *color*. Even if we are preparing a black-and-white drawing, graphical elements need to have a color to be visible: for example, black if the background is white or white if the background is black. Finally, to the extent we are using lines to visualize data, these lines may have different widths or dash–dot patterns. Beyond the examples shown in Figure 2-1, there are many other aesthetics we may encounter in a data visualization. For example, if we want to display text, we may have to specify font family, font face, and font size, and if graphical objects overlap, we may have to specify whether they are partially transparent.

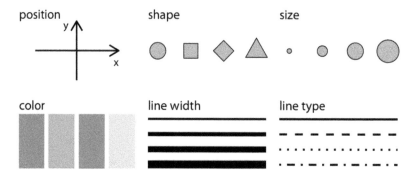

Figure 2-1. Commonly used aesthetics in data visualization: position, shape, size, color, line width, line type. Some of these aesthetics can represent both continuous and discrete data (position, size, line width, color), while others can usually only represent discrete data (shape, line type).

All aesthetics fall into one of two groups: those that can represent continuous data and those that cannot. Continuous data values are values for which arbitrarily fine intermediates exist. For example, time duration is a continuous value. Between any two durations, say 50 seconds and 51 seconds, there are arbitrarily many intermediates, such as 50.5 seconds, 50.51 seconds, 50.50001 seconds, and so on. By contrast, number of persons in a room is a discrete value. A room can hold 5 persons or 6, but not 5.5. For the examples in Figure 2-1, position, size, color, and line width can represent continuous data, but shape and line type can usually only represent discrete data.

Next we'll consider the types of data we may want to represent in our visualization. You may think of data as numbers, but numerical values are only two out of several types of data we may encounter. In addition to continuous and discrete numerical values, data can come in the form of discrete categories, in the form of dates or times, and as text (Table 2-1). When data is numerical we also call it *quantitative* and when it is categorical we call it *qualitative*. Variables holding qualitative data are *factors*, and the different categories are called *levels*. The levels of a factor are most commonly without order (as in the example of *dog, cat, fish* in Table 2-1), but factors can also be ordered, when there is an intrinsic order among the levels of the factor (as in the example of *good, fair, poor* in Table 2-1).

Table 2-1. Types of variables encountered in typical data visualization scenarios.

Type of variable	Examples	Appropriate scale	Description
Quantitative/ numerical continuous	1.3, 5.7, 83, 1.5 × 10⁻²	Continuous	Arbitrary numerical values. These can be integers, rational numbers, or real numbers.
Quantitative/ numerical discrete	1, 2, 3, 4	Discrete	Numbers in discrete units. These are most commonly but not necessarily integers. For example, the numbers 0.5, 1.0, 1.5 could also be treated as discrete if intermediate values cannot exist in the given dataset.
Qualitative/ categorical unordered	dog, cat, fish	Discrete	Categories without order. These are discrete and unique categories that have no inherent order. These variables are also called *factors*.
Qualitative/ categorical ordered	good, fair, poor	Discrete	Categories with order. These are discrete and unique categories with an order. For example, "fair" always lies between "good" and "poor." These variables are also called *ordered factors*.
Date or time	Jan. 5 2018, 8:03am	Continuous or discrete	Specific days and/or times. Also generic dates, such as July 4 or Dec. 25 (without year).
Text	The quick brown fox jumps over the lazy dog.	None, or discrete	Free-form text. Can be treated as categorical if needed.

To examine a concrete example of these various types of data, take a look at Table 2-2. It shows the first few rows of a dataset providing the daily temperature normals (average daily temperatures over a 30-year window) for four US locations. This table contains five variables: month, day, location, station ID, and temperature (in degrees Fahrenheit). Month is an ordered factor, day is a discrete numerical value, location is an unordered factor, station ID is similarly an unordered factor, and temperature is a continuous numerical value.

Table 2-2. First 8 rows of a dataset listing daily temperature normals for four weather stations. Data source: National Oceanic and Atmospheric Administration (NOAA).

Month	Day	Location	Station ID	Temperature (°F)
Jan	1	Chicago	USW00014819	25.6
Jan	1	San Diego	USW00093107	55.2
Jan	1	Houston	USW00012918	53.9
Jan	1	Death Valley	USC00042319	51.0
Jan	2	Chicago	USW00014819	25.5
Jan	2	San Diego	USW00093107	55.3
Jan	2	Houston	USW00012918	53.8
Jan	2	Death Valley	USC00042319	51.2

Scales Map Data Values onto Aesthetics

To map data values onto aesthetics, we need to specify which data values correspond to which specific aesthetics values. For example, if our graphic has an x axis, then we need to specify which data values fall onto particular positions along this axis. Similarly, we may need to specify which data values are represented by particular shapes or colors. This mapping between data values and aesthetics values is created via *scales*. A scale defines a unique mapping between data and aesthetics (Figure 2-2). Importantly, a scale must be one-to-one, such that for each specific data value there is exactly one aesthetics value and vice versa. If a scale isn't one-to-one, then the data visualization becomes ambiguous.

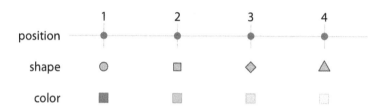

Figure 2-2. Scales link data values to aesthetics. Here, the numbers 1 through 4 have been mapped onto a position scale, a shape scale, and a color scale. For each scale, each number corresponds to a unique position, shape, or color, and vice versa.

Let's put things into practice. We can take the dataset shown in Table 2-2, map temperature onto the y axis, day of the year onto the x axis, and location onto color, and visualize these aesthetics with solid lines. The result is a standard line plot showing the temperature normals at the four locations as they change during the year (Figure 2-3).

Figure 2-3 is a fairly standard visualization for a temperature curve and likely the visualization most data scientists would intuitively choose first. However, it is up to us which variables we map onto which scales. For example, instead of mapping temperature onto the y axis and location onto color, we can do the opposite. Because now the key variable of interest (temperature) is shown as color, we need to show sufficiently large colored areas for the colors to convey useful information [Stone, Albers Szafir, and Setlur 2014]. Therefore, for this visualization I have chosen squares instead of lines, one for each month and location, and I have colored them by the average temperature normal for each month (Figure 2-4).

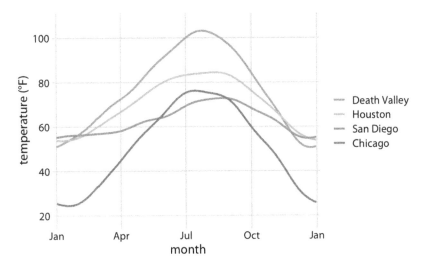

Figure 2-3. Daily temperature normals for four selected locations in the US. Temperature is mapped to the y axis, day of the year to the x axis, and location to line color. Data source: NOAA.

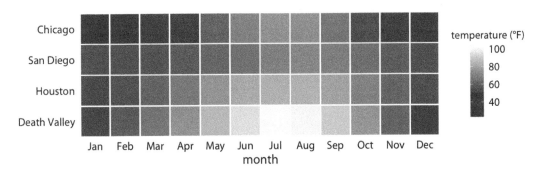

Figure 2-4. Monthly normal mean temperatures for four locations in the US. Data source: NOAA.

I would like to emphasize that Figure 2-4 uses two position scales (month along the *x* axis and location along the *y* axis), but neither is a continuous scale. Month is an ordered factor with 12 levels and location is an unordered factor with 4 levels. Therefore, the two position scales are both discrete. For discrete position scales, we generally place the different levels of the factor at an equal spacing along the axis. If the factor is ordered (as is here the case for month), then the levels need to be placed in the appropriate order. If the factor is unordered (as is here the case for location), then the order is arbitrary, and we can choose any order we want. I have ordered the locations from overall coldest (Chicago) to overall hottest (Death Valley) to generate a pleasant staggering of colors. However, I could have chosen any other order and the figure would have been equally valid.

Both Figures 2-3 and 2-4 used three scales in total, two position scales and one color scale. This is a typical number of scales for a basic visualization, but we can use more than three scales at once. Figure 2-5 uses five scales—two position scales, one color scale, one size scale, and one shape scale—and each scale represents a different variable from the dataset.

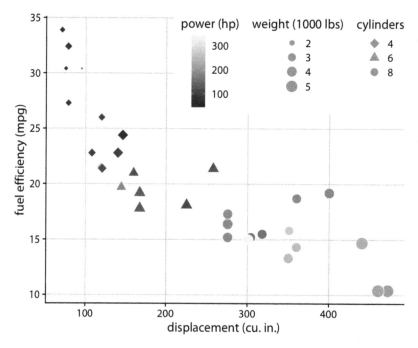

Figure 2-5. Fuel efficiency versus displacement, for 32 cars (1973–74 models). This figure uses five separate scales to represent data: (i) the x axis (displacement); (ii) the y axis (fuel efficiency); (iii) the color of the data points (power); (iv) the size of the data points (weight); and (v) the shape of the data points (number of cylinders). Four of the five variables displayed (displacement, fuel efficiency, power, and weight) are numerical continuous. The remaining one (number of cylinders) can be considered to be either numerical discrete or qualitative ordered. Data source: Motor Trend, 1974.

CHAPTER 3

Coordinate Systems and Axes

To make any sort of data visualization, we need to define position scales, which determine where in a graphic different data values are located. We cannot visualize data without placing different data points at different locations, even if we just arrange them next to each other along a line. For regular 2D visualizations, two numbers are required to uniquely specify a point, and therefore we need two position scales. These two scales are usually but not necessarily the *x* and *y* axes of the plot. We also have to specify the relative geometric arrangement of these scales. Conventionally, the *x* axis runs horizontally and the *y* axis vertically, but we could choose other arrangements. For example, we could have the *y* axis run at an acute angle relative to the *x* axis, or we could have one axis run in a circle and the other run radially. The combination of a set of position scales and their relative geometric arrangement is called a *coordinate system*.

Cartesian Coordinates

The most widely used coordinate system for data visualization is the 2D *Cartesian coordinate system*, where each location is uniquely specified by an *x* and a *y* value. The *x* and *y* axes run orthogonally to each other, and data values are placed in an even spacing along both axes (Figure 3-1). The two axes are continuous position scales, and they can represent both positive and negative real numbers. To fully specify the coordinate system, we need to specify the range of numbers each axis covers. In Figure 3-1, the *x* axis runs from –2.2 to 3.2 and the *y* axis runs from –2.2 to 2.2. Any data values between these axis limits are placed at the appropriate respective location in the plot. Any data values outside the axis limits are discarded.

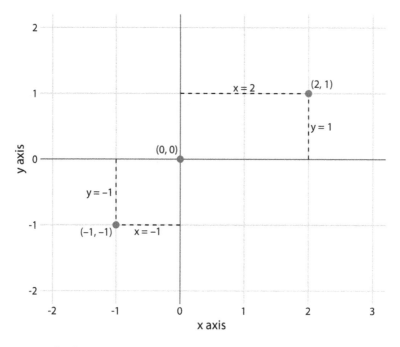

Figure 3-1. Standard Cartesian coordinate system. The horizontal axis is conventionally called x and the vertical axis y. The two axes form a grid with equidistant spacing. Here, both the x and the y grid lines are separated by units of one. The point (2, 1) is located two x units to the right and one y unit above the origin (0, 0). The point (−1, −1) is located one x unit to the left and one y unit below the origin.

Data values usually aren't just numbers, however. They come with units. For example, if we're measuring temperature, the values may be measured in degrees Celsius or Fahrenheit. Similarly, if we're measuring distance, the values may be measured in kilometers or miles, and if we're measuring duration, the values may be measured in minutes, hours, or days. In a Cartesian coordinate system, the spacing between grid lines along an axis corresponds to discrete steps in these data units. In a temperature scale, for example, we may have a grid line every 10 degrees Fahrenheit, and in a distance scale, we may have a grid line every 5 kilometers.

A Cartesian coordinate system can have two axes representing two different units. This situation arises quite commonly whenever we're mapping two different types of variables to x and y. For example, in Figure 2-3, we plotted temperature versus days of the year. The y axis of Figure 2-3 is measured in degrees Fahrenheit, with a grid line every at 20 degrees, and the x axis is measured in months, with a grid line at the first of every third month. Whenever the two axes are measured in different units, we can stretch or compress one relative to the other and maintain a valid visualization of the data (Figure 3-2). Which version is preferable may depend on the story we want to convey. A tall and narrow figure emphasizes change along the *y* axis and a short and wide figure does the opposite. Ideally, we want to choose an aspect ratio that ensures that any important differences in position are noticeable.

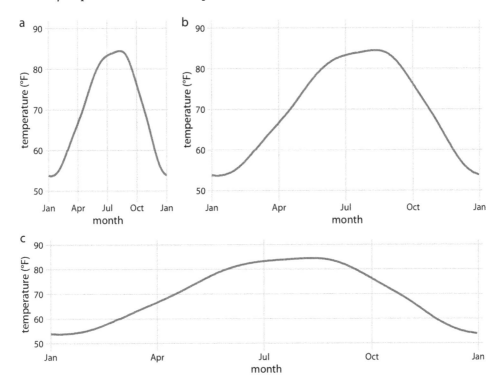

Figure 3-2. Daily temperature normals for Houston, TX. Temperature is mapped to the y *axis and day of the year to the* x *axis. Parts (a), (b), and (c) show the same figure in different aspect ratios. All three parts are valid visualizations of the temperature data. Data source: NOAA.*

On the other hand, if the *x* and *y* axes are measured in the same units, then the grid spacings for the two axes should be equal, such that the same distance along the *x* or *y* axis corresponds to the same number of data units. As an example, we can plot the temperature in Houston, TX, against the temperature in San Diego, CA, for every day of the year (Figure 3-3a). Since the same quantity is plotted along both axes, we need to make sure that the grid lines form perfect squares, as is the case in Figure 3-3a.

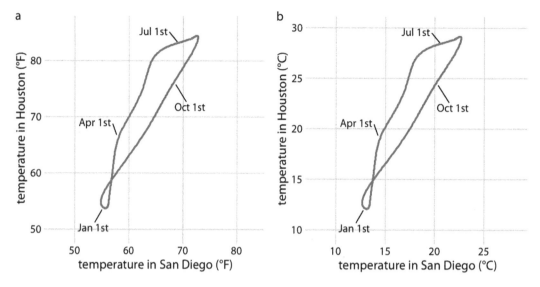

Figure 3-3. Daily temperature normals for Houston, TX, plotted versus the respective temperature normals of San Diego, CA. The first days of the months January, April, July, and October are highlighted to provide a temporal reference. (a) Temperatures are shown in degrees Fahrenheit. (b) Temperatures are shown in degrees Celsius. Data source: NOAA.

You may wonder what happens if you change the units of your data. After all, units are arbitrary, and your preferences might be different from somebody else's. A change in units is a linear transformation, where we add or subtract a number to or from all data values and/or multiply all data values with another number. Fortunately, Cartesian coordinate systems are invariant under such linear transformations. Therefore, you can change the units of your data and the resulting figure will not change as long as you change the axes accordingly. As an example, compare Figures 3-3a and 3-3b. Both show the same data, but in part (a) the temperature units are degrees Fahrenheit and in part (b) they are degrees Celsius. Even though the grid lines are in different locations and the numbers along the axes are different, the two data visualizations look exactly the same.

Nonlinear Axes

In a Cartesian coordinate system, the grid lines along an axis are spaced evenly both in data units and in the resulting visualization. We refer to the position scales in these coordinate systems as *linear*. While linear scales generally provide an accurate representation of the data, there are scenarios where nonlinear scales are preferred. In a nonlinear scale, even spacing in data units corresponds to uneven spacing in the visualization, or conversely even spacing in the visualization corresponds to uneven spacing in data units.

The most commonly used nonlinear scale is the *logarithmic scale,* or *log scale* for short. Log scales are linear in multiplication, such that a unit step on the scale corresponds to multiplication with a fixed value. To create a log scale, we need to log-transform the data values while exponentiating the numbers that are shown along the axis grid lines. This process is demonstrated in Figure 3-4, which shows the numbers 1, 3.16, 10, 31.6, and 100 placed on linear and log scales. The numbers 3.16 and 31.6 may seem like strange choices, but they were selected because they are exactly half-way between 1 and 10 and between 10 and 100 on a log scale. We can see this by observing that $10^{0.5} = \sqrt{10} \approx 3.16$, and equivalently $3.16 \times 3.16 \approx 10$. Similarly, $10^{1.5} = 10 \times 10^{0.5} \approx 31.6$.

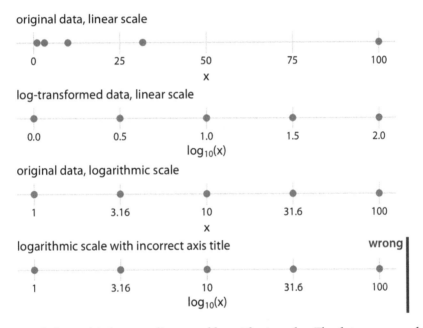

Figure 3-4. Relationship between linear and logarithmic scales. The dots correspond to the data values 1, 3.16, 10, 31.6, and 100, which are evenly spaced numbers on a logarithmic scale. We can display these data points on a linear scale, we can log-transform them and then show them on a linear scale, or we can show them on a logarithmic scale. Importantly, the correct axis title for a logarithmic scale is the name of the variable shown, not the logarithm of that variable.

Mathematically, there is no difference between plotting the log-transformed data on a linear scale or plotting the original data on a logarithmic scale (Figure 3-4). The only difference lies in the labeling for the individual axis ticks and for the axis as a whole.

In most cases, the labeling for a logarithmic scale is preferable, because it places less mental burden on the reader to interpret the numbers shown as the axis tick labels. There is also less of a risk of confusion about the base of the logarithm. When working with log-transformed data, we can get confused about whether the data was transformed using the natural logarithm or the logarithm to base 10. And it's not uncommon for labeling to be ambiguous—e.g., $\log(x)$, which doesn't specify a base at all. I recommend that you always verify the base when working with log-transformed data. When plotting log-transformed data, always specify the base in the labeling of the axis.

Because multiplication on a log scale looks like addition on a linear scale, log scales are the natural choice for any data that has been obtained by multiplication or division. In particular, ratios should generally be shown on a log scale. As an example, I have taken the number of inhabitants in each county in Texas and divided it by the median number of inhabitants across all Texas counties. The resulting ratio is a number that can be larger or smaller than 1. A ratio of exactly 1 implies that the corresponding county has the median number of inhabitants. When visualizing these ratios on a log scale, we can see that the population numbers in Texas counties are symmetrically distributed around the median, and that the most populous counties have over 100 times more inhabitants than the median while the least populous counties have over 100 times fewer inhabitants (Figure 3-5).

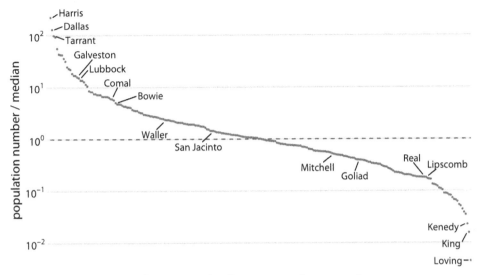

Texas counties, from most to least populous

Figure 3-5. Population numbers of Texas counties relative to their median value. Select counties are highlighted by name. The dashed line indicates a ratio of 1, corresponding to a county with median population number. The most populous counties have approximately 100 times more inhabitants than the median county, and the least populous counties have approximately 100 times fewer inhabitants than the median county. Data source: 2010 US Decennial Census.

By contrast, for the same data, a linear scale obscures the differences between a county with median population number and a county with a much smaller population number than median (Figure 3-6).

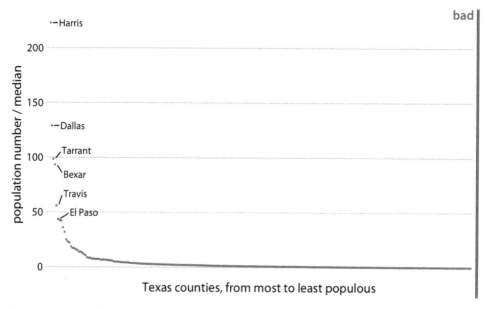

Figure 3-6. Population sizes of Texas counties relative to their median value. By display-ing a ratio on a linear scale, we have overemphasized ratios > 1 and have obscured ratios < 1. As a general rule, ratios should not be displayed on a linear scale. Data source: 2010 US Decennial Census.

On a log scale, the value 1 is the natural midpoint, similar to the value 0 on a linear scale. We can think of values greater than 1 as representing multiplications and values less than 1 divisions. For example, we can write $10 = 1 \times 10$ and $0.1 = 1/10$. The value 0, on the other hand, can never appear on a log scale. It lies infinitely far from 1. One way to see this is to consider that $\log(0) = -\infty$. Or, alternatively, consider that to go from 1 to 0, it takes either an infinite number of divisions by a finite value (e.g., $1/10/10/10/10/10/10 \cdots = 0$) or one division by infinity (i.e., $1/\infty = 0$).

Log scales are frequently used when the dataset contains numbers of very different magnitudes. For the Texas counties shown in Figures 3-5 and 3-6, the most populous one (Harris) had 4,092,459 inhabitants in the 2010 US Census while the least popu-lous one (Loving) had 82. So, a log scale would be appropriate even if we hadn't divi-ded the population numbers by their median to turn them into ratios. But what would we do if there was a county with 0 inhabitants? This county could not be shown on the logarithmic scale, because it would lie at minus infinity. In this situa-tion, the recommendation is sometimes to use a *square-root scale*, which uses a square-root transformation instead of a log transformation (Figure 3-7). Just like a log scale, a square-root scale compresses larger numbers into a smaller range, but unlike a log scale, it allows for the presence of 0.

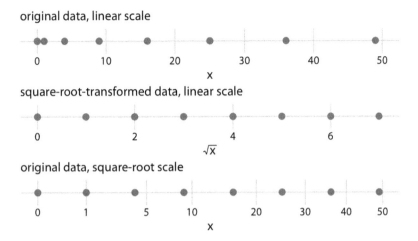

Figure 3-7. Relationship between linear and square-root scales. The dots correspond to the data values 0, 1, 4, 9, 16, 25, 36, and 49, which are evenly spaced numbers on a square-root scale, since they are the squares of the integers from 0 to 7. We can display these data points on a linear scale, we can square-root-transform them and then show them on a linear scale, or we can show them on a square-root scale.

I see two problems with square-root scales. First, while on a linear scale one unit step corresponds to addition or subtraction of a constant value, and on a log scale it corresponds to multiplication with or division by a constant value, no such rule exists for a square-root scale. The meaning of a unit step on a square-root scale depends on the scale value at which we're starting. Second, it is unclear how to best place axis ticks on a square-root scale. To obtain evenly spaced ticks, we would have to place them at squares, but axis ticks at, for example, positions 0, 4, 25, 49, and 81 (every second square) would be unintuitive. Alternatively, we could place them at linear intervals (10, 20, 30, etc.), but this would result in either too few axis ticks near the low end of the scale or too many near the high end. In Figure 3-7, I have placed the axis ticks at positions 0, 1, 5, 10, 20, 30, 40, and 50 on the square-root scale. These values are arbitrary but provide a reasonable covering of the data range.

Despite these problems with square-root scales, they are valid position scales and I do not discount the possibility that they have appropriate applications. For example, just like a log scale is the natural scale for ratios, one could argue that the square-root scale is the natural scale for data that comes in squares. One scenario in which data is naturally squares is in the context of geographic regions. If we show the areas of geographic regions on a square-root scale, we are highlighting the regions' linear extent from east to west or north to south. These extents could be relevant, for example, if we were wondering how long it might take to drive across a region. Figure 3-8 shows the areas of states in the US Northeast on both a linear and a square-root scale. Even though the areas of these states are quite different (Figure 3-8a), the relative time it will take to drive across each state is more accurately represented by the figure on the square-root scale (Figure 3-8b) than the figure on the linear scale (Figure 3-8a).

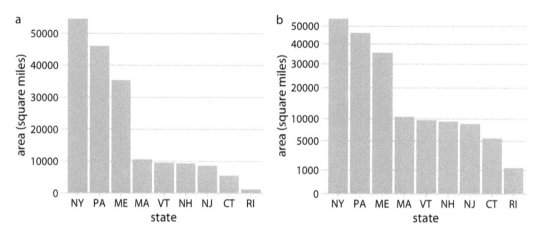

Figure 3-8. Areas of northeastern US states. (a) Areas shown on a linear scale. (b) Areas shown on a square-root scale. Data source: Google.

Coordinate Systems with Curved Axes

All the coordinate systems we have encountered so far have used two straight axes positioned at a right angle to each other, even if the axes themselves established a nonlinear mapping from data values to positions. There are other coordinate systems, however, where the axes themselves are curved. In particular, in the *polar* coordinate system, we specify positions via an angle and a radial distance from the origin, and therefore the angle axis is circular (Figure 3-9).

Polar coordinates can be useful for data of a periodic nature, such that data values at one end of the scale can be logically joined to data values at the other end. For example, consider the days in a year. December 31st is the last day of the year, but it is also one day before the first day of the year. If we want to show how some quantity varies over the year, it can be appropriate to use polar coordinates with the angle coordinate specifying each day. Let's apply this concept to the temperature normals of Figure 2-3. Because temperature normals are average temperatures that are not tied to any specific year, Dec. 31st can be thought of as 366 days later than Jan. 1st (temperature normals include Feb. 29th) and also 1 day earlier.

By plotting the temperature normals in a polar coordinate system, we emphasize this cyclical property they have (Figure 3-10). In comparison to Figure 2-3, the polar version highlights how similar the temperatures are in Death Valley, Houston, and San Diego from late fall to early spring. In the Cartesian coordinate system, this fact is obscured because the temperature values in late December and in early January are shown in opposite parts of the figure and therefore don't form a single visual unit.

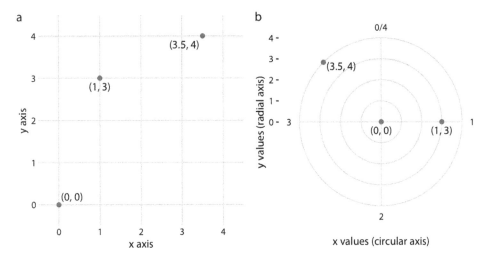

Figure 3-9. Relationship between Cartesian and polar coordinates. (a) Three data points shown in a Cartesian coordinate system. (b) The same three data points shown in a polar coordinate system. We have taken the x coordinates from part (a) and used them as angular coordinates and the y coordinates from part (a) and used them as radial coordinates. The circular axis runs from 0 to 4 in this example, and therefore x = 0 and x = 4 are the same locations in this coordinate system.

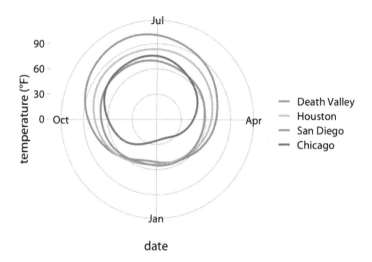

Figure 3-10. Daily temperature normals for four selected locations in the US, shown in polar coordinates. The radial distance from the center point indicates the daily temperature in Fahrenheit, and the days of the year are arranged counterclockwise starting with Jan. 1st at the 6:00 position. Data source: NOAA.

A second setting in which we encounter curved axes is in the context of geospatial data, i.e., maps. Locations on the globe are specified by their longitude and latitude. But because the earth is a sphere, drawing latitude and longitude as Cartesian axes is misleading and not recommended (Figure 3-11). Instead, we use various types of nonlinear projections that attempt to minimize artifacts and that strike different balances between conserving areas or angles relative to the true shape lines on the globe (Figure 3-11).

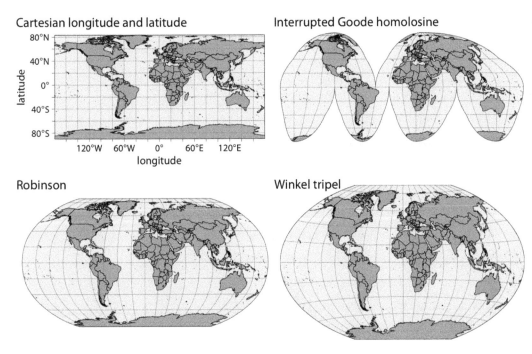

Figure 3-11. Map of the world, shown in four different projections. The Cartesian longitude and latitude system maps the longitude and latitude of each location onto a regular Cartesian coordinate system. This mapping causes substantial distortions in both areas and angles relative to their true values on the 3D globe. The interrupted Goode homolosine projection perfectly represents true surface areas, at the cost of dividing some land masses into separate pieces, most notably Greenland and Antarctica. The Robinson projection and the Winkel tripel projection both strike a balance between angular and area distortions, and they are commonly used for maps of the entire globe.

## CHAPTER 4

Color Scales

There are three fundamental use cases for color in data visualizations: we can use color to distinguish groups of data from each other, to represent data values, and to highlight. The types of colors we use and the way in which we use them are quite different for these three cases.

Color as a Tool to Distinguish

We frequently use color as a means to distinguish discrete items or groups that do not have an intrinsic order, such as different countries on a map or different manufacturers of a certain product. In this case, we use a *qualitative* color scale. Such a scale contains a finite set of specific colors that are chosen to look clearly distinct from each other while also being equivalent to each other. The second condition requires that no one color should stand out relative to the others. Also, the colors should not create the impression of an order, as would be the case with a sequence of colors that get successively lighter. Such colors would create an apparent order among the items being colored, which by definition have no order.

Many appropriate qualitative color scales are readily available. Figure 4-1 shows three representative examples. In particular, the ColorBrewer project provides a nice selection of qualitative color scales, including both fairly light and fairly dark colors [Brewer 2017].

Okabe Ito

ColorBrewer Dark2

ggplot2 hue

Figure 4-1. Example qualitative color scales. The Okabe Ito scale is the default scale used throughout this book [Okabe and Ito 2008]. The ColorBrewer Dark2 scale is provided by the ColorBrewer project [Brewer 2017]. The ggplot2 hue scale is the default qualitative scale in the widely used plotting software ggplot2.

As an example of how we use qualitative color scales, consider Figure 4-2. It shows the percent population growth from 2000 to 2010 in US states. I have arranged the states in order of their population growth, and I have colored them by geographic region. This coloring highlights that states in the same regions have experienced similar population growth. In particular, states in the West and the South have seen the largest population increases, whereas states in the Midwest and the Northeast have grown much less.

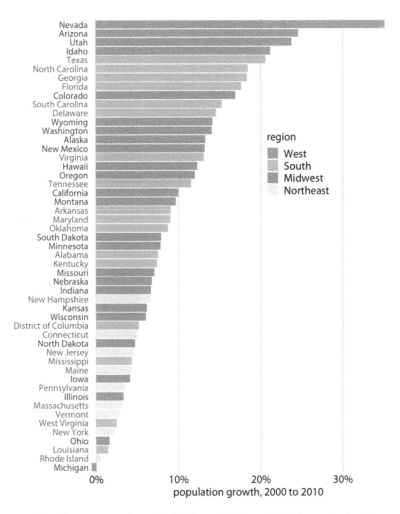

Figure 4-2. Population growth in the US from 2000 to 2010. States in the West and South have seen the largest increases, whereas states in the Midwest and Northeast have seen much smaller increases (or even, in the case of Michigan, a decrease). Data source: US Census Bureau.

Color to Represent Data Values

Color can also be used to represent quantitative data values, such as income, temperature, or speed. In this case, we use a *sequential* color scale. Such a scale contains a sequence of colors that clearly indicate which values are larger or smaller than which other ones, and how distant two specific values are from each other. The second point implies that the color scale needs to be perceived to vary uniformly across its entire range.

Sequential scales can be based on a single hue (e.g., from dark blue to light blue) or on multiple hues (e.g., from dark red to light yellow) (Figure 4-3). Multihue scales tend to follow color gradients that can be seen in the natural world, such as dark red, green, or blue to light yellow, or dark purple to light green. The reverse (e.g., dark yellow to light blue) looks unnatural and doesn't make a useful sequential scale.

Figure 4-3. Example sequential color scales. The ColorBrewer Blues scale is a monochromatic scale that varies from dark to light blue. The Heat and Viridis scales are multihue scales that vary from dark red to light yellow and from dark blue via green to light yellow, respectively.

Representing data values as colors is particularly useful when we want to show how the data values vary across geographic regions. In this case, we can draw a map of the geographic regions and color them by the data values. Such maps are called *choropleths*. Figure 4-4 shows an example where I have mapped annual median income within each county in Texas onto a map of those counties.

In some cases, we need to visualize the deviation of data values in one of two directions relative to a neutral midpoint. One straightforward example is a dataset containing both positive and negative numbers. We may want to show those with different colors, so that it is immediately obvious whether a value is positive or negative as well as how far in either direction it deviates from zero. The appropriate color scale in this situation is a *diverging* color scale. We can think of a diverging scale as two sequential scales stitched together at a common midpoint, which usually is represented by a light color (Figure 4-5). Diverging scales need to be balanced, so that the progression from light colors in the center to dark colors on the outside is approximately the same in either direction. Otherwise, the perceived magnitude of a data value would depend on whether it fell above or below the midpoint value.

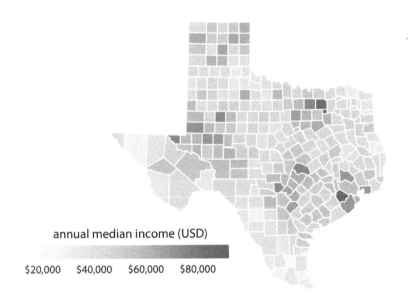

annual median income (USD)

$20,000 $40,000 $60,000 $80,000

Figure 4-4. Median annual income in Texas counties. The highest median incomes are seen in major Texas metropolitan areas, in particular near Houston and Dallas. No median income estimate is available for Loving County in West Texas, and therefore that county is shown in gray. Data source: 2015 Five-Year American Community Survey.

CARTO Earth

ColorBrewer PiYG

Blue-Red

Figure 4-5. Example diverging color scales. Diverging scales can be thought of as two sequential scales stitched together at a common midpoint color. Common color choices for diverging scales include brown to greenish blue, pink to yellow-green, and blue to red.

As an example application of a diverging color scale, consider Figure 4-6, which shows the percentage of people identifying as white in Texas counties. Even though percentage is always a positive number, a diverging scale is justified here, because 50% is a meaningful midpoint value. Numbers above 50% indicate that whites are in the majority and numbers below 50% indicate the opposite. The visualization clearly shows in which counties whites are in the majority, in which they are in the minority, and in which whites and nonwhites occur in approximately equal proportions.

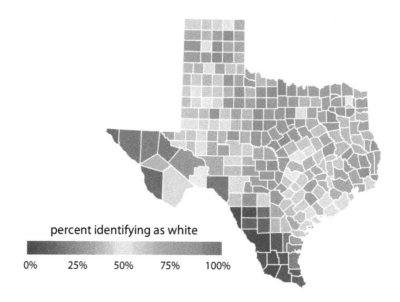

Figure 4-6. Percentage of people identifying as white in Texas counties. Whites are in the majority in North and East Texas but not in South or West Texas. Data source: 2010 US Decennial Census.

Color as a Tool to Highlight

Color can also be an effective tool to highlight specific elements in the data. There may be specific categories or values in the dataset that carry key information about the story we want to tell, and we can strengthen the story by emphasizing the relevant figure elements to the reader. An easy way to achieve this emphasis is to color these figure elements in a color or set of colors that vividly stand out against the rest of the figure. This effect can be achieved with *accent* color scales, which are color scales that contain both a set of subdued colors and a matching set of stronger, darker, and/or more saturated colors (Figure 4-7).

Figure 4-7. Example accent color scales, each with four base colors and three accent colors. Accent color scales can be derived in several different ways: (top) we can take an existing color scale (e.g., the Okabe Ito scale, Figure 4-1) and lighten and/or partially desaturate some colors while darkening others; (middle) we can take gray values and pair them with colors; (bottom) we can use an existing accent color scale (e.g., the one from the ColorBrewer project).

As an example of how the same data can support differing stories with different coloring approaches, I have created a variant of Figure 4-2 where now I highlight two specific states, Texas and Louisiana (Figure 4-8). Both states are in the South, they are immediate neighbors, and yet one state (Texas) was the fifth fastest growing state within the US from 2000 to 2010 whereas the other was the third slowest growing.

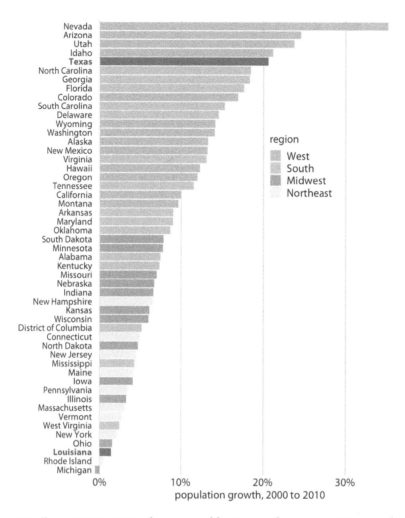

Figure 4-8. From 2000 to 2010, the two neighboring southern states, Texas and Louisiana, experienced among the highest and lowest population growth across the US. Data source: US Census Bureau.

When working with accent colors, it is critical that the baseline colors do not compete for attention. Notice how drab the baseline colors are in Figure 4-8, yet they work well to support the accent color. It is easy to make the mistake of using baseline colors that are too colorful, so that they end up competing for the reader's attention against the accent colors. There is an easy remedy, however: just remove all color from all elements in the figure except the highlighted data categories or points. An example of this strategy is provided in Figure 4-9.

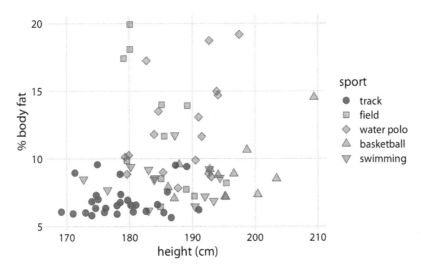

Figure 4-9. Track athletes are among the shortest and leanest of male professional ath-letes participating in popular sports. Data source: [Telford and Cunningham 1991].

Directory of Visualizations

This chapter provides a quick visual overview of the various plots and charts that are commonly used to visualize different types of data. It is meant both to serve as a table of contents, in case you are looking for a particular visualization whose name you may not know, and as a source of inspiration, if you need to find alternatives to the figures you routinely make.

Amounts

The most common approach to visualizing amounts (i.e., numerical values shown for some set of categories) is using bars, either vertically or horizontally arranged (Chapter 6). However, instead of using bars, we can also place dots at the location where the corresponding bar would end (Chapter 6).

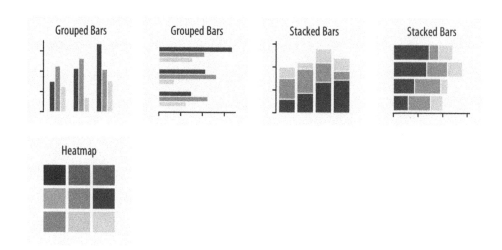

If there are two or more sets of categories for which we want to show amounts, we can group or stack the bars (Chapter 6). We can also map the categories onto the x and y axes and show amounts by color, via a heatmap (Chapter 6).

Distributions

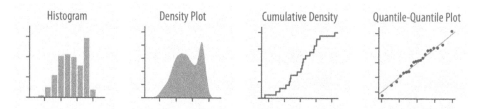

Histograms and density plots (Chapter 7) provide the most intuitive visualizations of a distribution, but both require arbitrary parameter choices and can be misleading. Cumulative densities and quantile-quantile (q-q) plots (Chapter 8) always represent the data faithfully but can be more difficult to interpret.

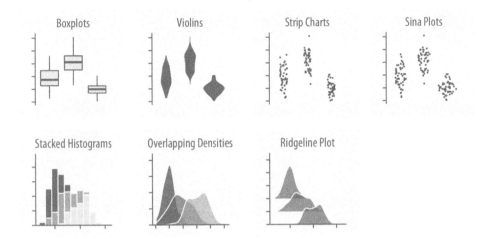

Boxplots, violin plots, strip charts, and sina plots are useful when we want to visualize many distributions at once and/or if we are primarily interested in overall shifts among the distributions (see "Visualizing Distributions Along the Vertical Axis" on page 81). Stacked histograms and overlapping densities allow a more in-depth comparison of a smaller number of distributions, though stacked histograms can be difficult to interpret and are best avoided (see "Visualizing Multiple Distributions at the Same Time" on page 64). Ridgeline plots can be a useful alternative to violin plots and are often useful when visualizing very large numbers of distributions or changes in distributions over time (see "Visualizing Distributions Along the Horizontal Axis" on page 88).

Proportions

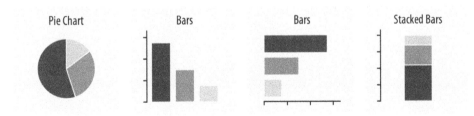

Proportions can be visualized as pie charts, side-by-side bars, or stacked bars (Chapter 10). As for amounts, when we visualize proportions with bars, the bars can be arranged either vertically or horizontally. Pie charts emphasize that the individual parts add up to a whole and highlight simple fractions. However, the individual pieces are more easily compared in side-by-side bars. Stacked bars look awkward for a single set of proportions, but can be useful when comparing multiple sets of proportions.

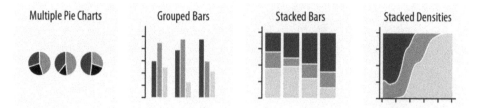

When visualizing multiple sets of proportions or changes in proportions across conditions, pie charts tend to be space-inefficient and often obscure relationships. Grouped bars work well as long as the number of conditions compared is moderate, and stacked bars can work for large numbers of conditions. Stacked densities (Chapter 10) are appropriate when the proportions change along a continuous variable.

When proportions are specified according to multiple grouping variables, mosaic plots, treemaps, or parallel sets are useful visualization approaches (Chapter 11). Mosaic plots assume that every level of one grouping variable can be combined with every level of another grouping variable, whereas treemaps do not make such an assumption. Treemaps work well even if the subdivisions of one group are entirely distinct from the subdivisions of another. Parallel sets work better than either mosaic plots or treemaps when there are more than two grouping variables.

x–y relationships

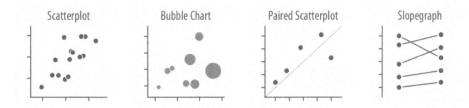

Scatterplots (Chapter 12) represent the archetypical visualization when we want to show one quantitative variable relative to another. If we have three quantitative variables, we can map one onto the dot size, creating a variant of the scatterplot called a bubble chart. For paired data, where the variables along the x and y axes are measured in the same units, it is generally helpful to add a line indicating $x = y$ (see "Paired Data" on page 127). Paired data can also be shown as a slopegraph of paired points connected by straight lines.

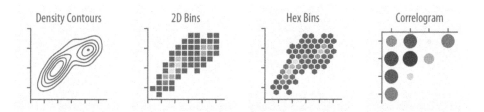

For large numbers of points, regular scatterplots can become uninformative due to overplotting. In this case, contour lines, 2D bins, or hex bins may provide an alternative (Chapter 18). When we want to visualize more than two quantities, on the other hand, we may choose to plot correlation coefficients in the form of a correlogram instead of the underlying raw data (see "Correlograms" on page 121).

When the x axis represents time or a strictly increasing quantity such as a treatment dose, we commonly draw line graphs (Chapter 13). If we have a temporal sequence of two response variables we can draw a connected scatterplot, where we first plot the two response variables in a scatterplot and then connect dots corresponding to adjacent time points (see "Time Series of Two or More Response Variables" on page 138). We can use smooth lines to represent trends in a larger dataset (Chapter 14).

Geospatial Data

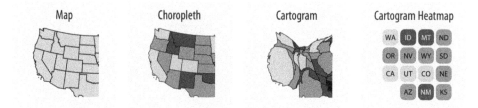

The primary mode of showing geospatial data is in the form of a map (Chapter 15). A map takes coordinates on the globe and projects them onto a flat surface, such that shapes and distances on the globe are approximately represented by shapes and distances in the 2D representation. In addition, we can show data values in different regions by coloring those regions in the map according to the data. Such a map is called a choropleth (see "Choropleth Mapping" on page 172). In some cases, it may be helpful to distort the different regions according to some other quantity (e.g., population number) or simplify each region into a square. Such visualizations are called cartograms (see "Cartograms" on page 176).

Uncertainty

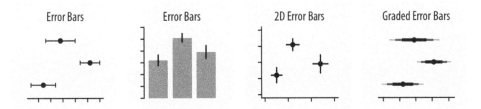

Error bars are meant to indicate the range of likely values for some estimate or measurement. They extend horizontally and/or vertically from some reference point representing the estimate or measurement (Chapter 16). Reference points can be shown in various ways, such as by dots or by bars. Graded error bars show multiple ranges at the same time, where each range corresponds to a different degree of confidence. They are in effect multiple error bars with different line thicknesses plotted on top of each other.

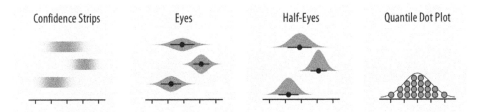

To achieve a more detailed visualization than is possible with error bars or graded error bars, we can visualize the actual confidence or posterior distributions (Chapter 16). Confidence strips provide a visual sense of uncertainty but are difficult to read accurately. Eyes and half-eyes combine error bars with approaches to visualize distributions (violins and ridgelines, respectively), and thus show both precise ranges for some confidence levels and the overall uncertainty distribution. A quantile dot plot can serve as an alternative visualization of an uncertainty distribution (see "Framing Probabilities as Frequencies" on page 181). Because it shows the distribution in discrete units, the quantile dot plot is not as precise but can be easier to read than the continuous distribution shown by a violin or ridgeline plot.

For smooth line graphs, the equivalent of an error bar is a confidence band (see "Visualizing the Uncertainty of Curve Fits" on page 197). It shows a range of values the line might pass through at a given confidence level. Like with error bars, we can draw graded confidence bands that show multiple confidence levels at once. We can also show individual fitted draws in lieu of or in addition to the confidence bands.

## CHAPTER 6

Visualizing Amounts

In many scenarios, we are interested in the magnitude of some set of numbers. For example, we might want to visualize the total sales volume of different brands of cars, or the total number of people living in different cities, or the age of Olympians performing different sports. In all these cases, we have a set of categories (e.g., brands of cars, cities, or sports) and a quantitative value for each category. I refer to these cases as visualizing amounts, because the main emphasis in these visualizations will be on the magnitude of the quantitative values. The standard visualization in this scenario is the bar plot, which has several variations, including simple bars as well as grouped and stacked bars. Alternatives to the bar plot are the dot plot and the heatmap.

Bar Plots

To motivate the concept of a bar plot, consider the total ticket sales for the most popular movies on a given weekend. Table 6-1 shows the top five highest-grossing films for the weekend before Christmas in 2017. *Star Wars: The Last Jedi* was by far the most popular movie on that weekend, outselling the fourth- and fifth-ranked movies, *The Greatest Showman* and *Ferdinand*, by almost a factor of 10.

Table 6-1. Highest-grossing movies for the weekend of December 22–24, 2017. Data source: Box Office Mojo (http://www.boxofficemojo.com). Used with permission.

Rank	Title	Weekend gross
1	*Star Wars: The Last Jedi*	$71,565,498
2	*Jumanji: Welcome to the Jungle*	$36,169,328
3	*Pitch Perfect 3*	$19,928,525
4	*The Greatest Showman*	$8,805,843
5	*Ferdinand*	$7,316,746

This kind of data is commonly visualized with vertical bars. For each movie, we draw a bar that starts at zero and extends all the way to the dollar value for that movie's weekend gross (Figure 6-1). This visualization is called a *bar plot* or *bar chart*.

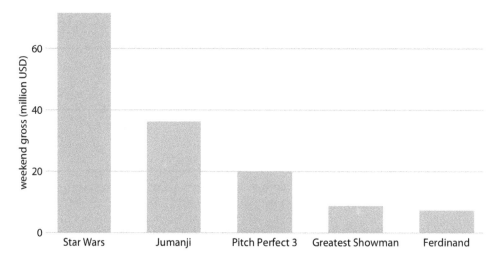

Figure 6-1. Highest-grossing movies for the weekend of December 22–24, 2017, displayed as a bar plot. Data source: Box Office Mojo (http://www.boxofficemojo.com). Used with permission.

One problem we commonly encounter with vertical bars is that the labels identifying each bar take up a lot of horizontal space. In fact, I had to make Figure 6-1 fairly wide and space out the bars so that I could place the movie titles underneath. To save horizontal space, we could place the bars closer together and rotate the labels (Figure 6-2). However, I am not a big proponent of rotated labels. I find the resulting plots awkward and difficult to read. And, in my experience, whenever the labels are too long to place horizontally, they also don't look good rotated.

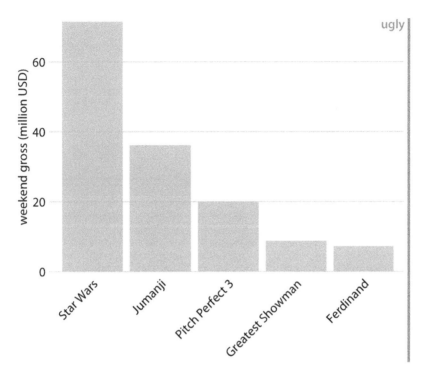

Figure 6-2. Highest-grossing movies for the weekend of December 22–24, 2017, displayed as a bar plot with rotated axis tick labels. Rotated axis tick labels tend to be difficult to read and require awkward space use underneath the plot. For these reasons, I generally consider plots with rotated tick labels to be ugly. Data source: Box Office Mojo (http:// www.boxofficemojo.com). Used with permission.

The better solution for long labels is usually to swap the *x* and *y* axes, so that the bars run horizontally (Figure 6-3). After swapping the axes, we obtain a compact figure in which all visual elements, including all text, are horizontally oriented. As a result, the figure is much easier to read than Figure 6-2 or even Figure 6-1.

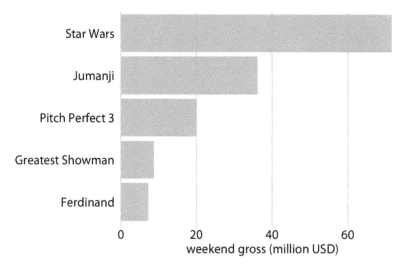

Figure 6-3. Highest-grossing movies for the weekend of December 22–24, 2017, displayed as a horizontal bar plot. Data source: Box Office Mojo (http://www.boxofficemojo.com). Used with permission.

Regardless of whether we place bars vertically or horizontally, we need to pay attention to the order in which the bars are arranged. I often see bar plots where the bars are arranged arbitrarily or by some criterion that is not meaningful in the context of the figure. Some plotting programs arrange bars by default in alphabetical order of the labels, and other similarly arbitrary arrangements are possible (Figure 6-4). In general, the resulting figures are more confusing and less intuitive than figures where bars are arranged in order of their size.

We should only rearrange bars, however, when there is no natural ordering to the categories the bars represent. Whenever there is a natural ordering (i.e., when our categorical variable is an ordered factor), we should retain that ordering in the visualization. For example, Figure 6-5 shows the median annual income in the US by age groups. In this case, the bars should be arranged in order of increasing age. Sorting by bar height while shuffling the age groups makes no sense (Figure 6-6).

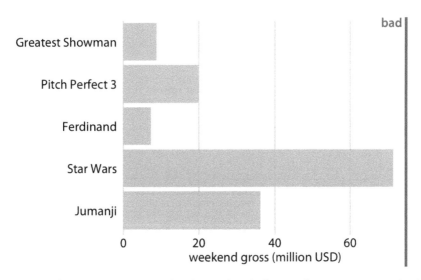

Figure 6-4. Highest-grossing movies for the weekend of December 22–24, 2017, displayed as a horizontal bar plot. Here, the bars have been placed in descending order of the lengths of the movie titles. This arrangement of bars is arbitrary, doesn't serve a meaningful purpose, and makes the resulting figure much less intuitive than Figure 6-3. Data source: Box Office Mojo (http://www.boxofficemojo.com). Used with permission.

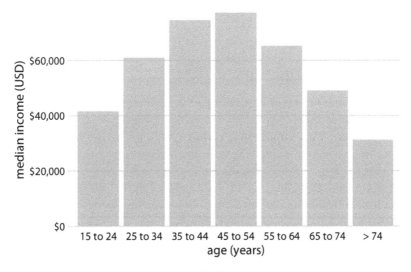

Figure 6-5. 2016 median US annual household income versus age group. The 45-to-54-year age group has the highest median income. Data source: US Census Bureau.

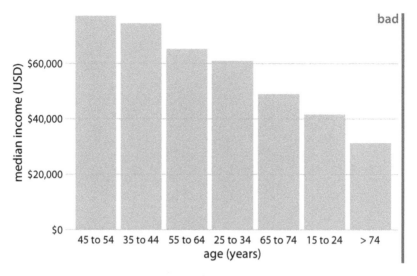

Figure 6-6. 2016 median US annual household income versus age group, sorted by income. While this order of bars looks visually appealing, the order of the age groups is now confusing. Data source: US Census Bureau.

Pay attention to the bar order. If the bars represent unordered categories, order them by ascending or descending data values.

Grouped and Stacked Bars

All the examples from the previous section showed how a quantitative amount varied with respect to one categorical variable. Frequently, however, we are interested in two categorical variables at the same time. For example, the US Census Bureau provides median income levels broken down by both age and race. We can visualize this dataset with a *grouped bar plot* (Figure 6-7). In a grouped bar plot, we draw a group of bars at each position along the x axis, determined by one categorical variable, and then we draw bars within each group according to the other categorical variable.

Grouped bar plots show a lot of information at once, and they can be confusing. In fact, even though I have not labeled Figure 6-7 as bad or ugly, I find it difficult to read. In particular, it is difficult to compare median incomes across age groups for a given racial group. So, this figure is only appropriate if we are primarily interested in the differences in income levels among racial groups, separately for specific age groups. If we care more about the overall pattern of income levels among racial groups, it may be preferable to show race along the *x* axis and show ages as distinct bars within each racial group (Figure 6-8).

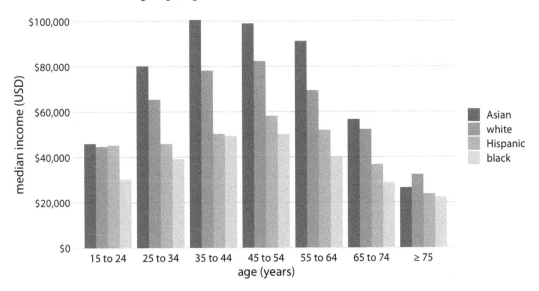

Figure 6-7. 2016 median US annual household income versus age group and race. Age groups are shown along the x *axis, and for each age group there are four bars, corresponding to the median income of Asian, white, Hispanic, and black people, respectively. Data source: US Census Bureau.*

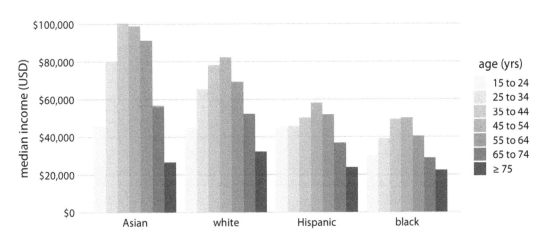

Figure 6-8. 2016 median US annual household income versus age group and race. In contrast to Figure 6-7, now race is shown along the x *axis, and for each race we show seven bars according to the seven age groups. Data source: US Census Bureau.*

Both Figures 6-7 and 6-8 encode one categorical variable by position along the *x* axis and the other by bar color. And in both cases, the encoding by position is easy to read while the encoding by bar color requires more mental effort, as we have to mentally match the colors of the bars against the colors in the legend. We can avoid this added mental effort by showing four separate regular bar plots rather than one grouped bar plot (Figure 6-9). Which of these various options we choose is ultimately a matter of taste. I would likely choose Figure 6-9, because it circumvents the need for different bar colors.

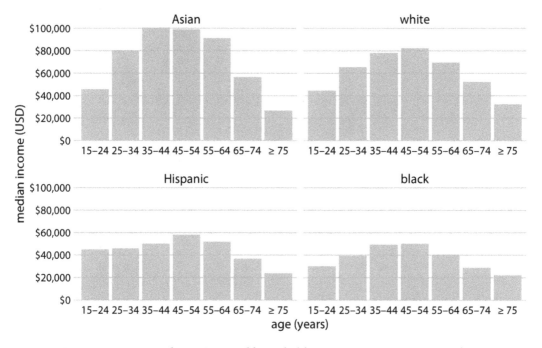

Figure 6-9. 2016 median US annual household income versus age group and race. Instead of displaying this data as a grouped bar plot, as in Figures 6-7 and 6-8, we now show the data as four separate regular bar plots. This choice has the advantage that we don't need to encode either categorical variable by bar color. Data source: US Census Bureau.

Instead of drawing groups of bars side-by-side, it is sometimes preferable to stack bars on top of each other. Stacking is useful when the sum of the amounts represented by the individual stacked bars is in itself a meaningful amount. So, while it would not make sense to stack the median income values of Figure 6-7 (the sum of two median income values is not a meaningful value), it might make sense to stack the weekend gross values of Figure 6-1 (the sum of the weekend gross values of two movies is the total gross for the two movies combined). Stacking is also appropriate when the individual bars represent counts. For example, in a dataset of people, we can either count men and women separately or we can count them together. If we stack a bar representing a count of women on top of a bar representing a count of men, then the combined bar height represents the total count of people regardless of gender.

I will demonstrate this principle using a dataset about the passengers of the transatlantic ocean liner *Titanic*, which sank on April 15, 1912. On board were approximately 1,300 passengers, not counting crew. The passengers were traveling in one of three classes (first, second, or third), and there were almost twice as many male as female passengers on the ship. To visualize the breakdown of passengers by class and gender, we can draw separate bars for each class and gender and stack the bars representing women on top of the bars representing men, separately for each class (Figure 6-10). The combined bars represent the total number of passengers in each class.

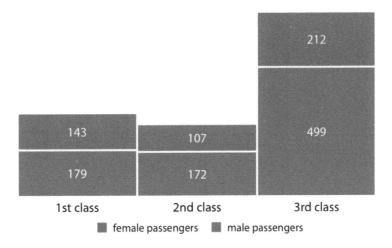

Figure 6-10. Numbers of female and male passengers on the Titanic *traveling in 1st, 2nd, and 3rd class. Data source: Encyclopedia Titanica.*

Figure 6-10 differs from the previous bar plots I have shown in that there is no explicit *y* axis. I have instead shown the actual numerical values that each bar represents. Whenever a plot is meant to display only a small number of different values, it makes sense to add the actual numbers to the plot. This substantially increases the amount of information conveyed by the plot without adding much visual noise, and it removes the need for an explicit *y* axis.

Dot Plots and Heatmaps

Bars are not the only option for visualizing amounts. One important limitation of bars is that they need to start at zero, so that the bar length is proportional to the amount shown. For some datasets, this can be impractical or may obscure key features. In this case, we can indicate amounts by placing dots at the appropriate locations along the *x* or *y* axis.

Figure 6-11 demonstrates this visualization approach for a dataset of life expectancies in 25 countries in the Americas. The citizens of these countries have life expectancies between 60 and 81 years, and each individual life expectancy value is shown with a blue dot at the appropriate location along the *x* axis. By limiting the axis range to the interval from 60 to 81 years, the figure highlights the key features of this dataset: Canada has the highest life expectancy among all listed countries, and Bolivia and Haiti have much lower life expectancies than all other countries. If we had used bars instead of dots (Figure 6-12), we'd have made a much less compelling figure. Because the bars are so long in this figure, and they all have nearly the same length, the eye is drawn to the middle of the bars rather than to their endpoints, and the figure fails to convey its message.

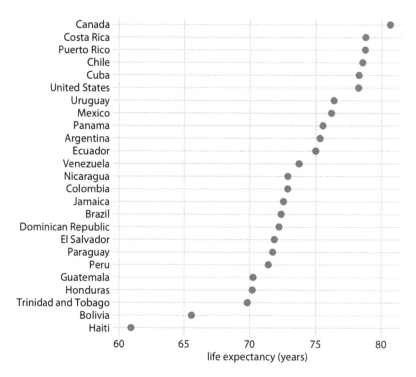

Figure 6-11. Life expectancies of countries in the Americas, for the year 2007. Data source: Gapminder.

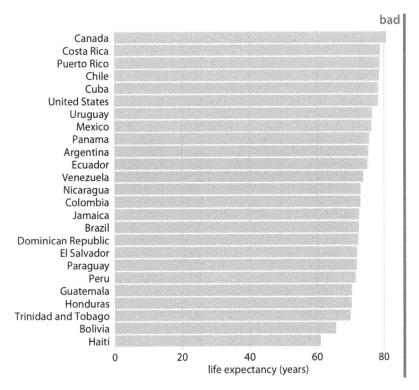

Figure 6-12. Life expectancies of countries in the Americas, for the year 2007, shown as bars. This dataset is not suitable for being visualized with bars. The bars are too long and they draw attention away from the key feature of the data, the differences in life expectancy among the different countries. Data source: Gapminder.

Regardless of whether we use bars or dots, however, we need to pay attention to the ordering of the data values. In Figures 6-11 and 6-12, the countries are ordered in descending order of life expectancy. If we instead ordered them alphabetically, we'd end up with a disordered cloud of points that is confusing and fails to convey a clear message (Figure 6-13).

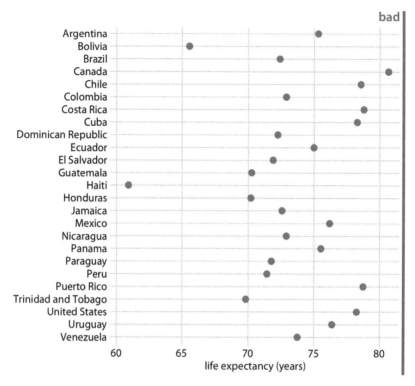

Figure 6-13. Life expectancies of countries in the Americas, for the year 2007. Here, the countries are ordered alphabetically, which causes the dots to form a disordered cloud of points. This makes the figure difficult to read, and therefore it deserves to be labeled as "bad." Data source: Gapminder.

All the examples so far have represented amounts by location along a position scale, either through the endpoint of a bar or the placement of a dot. For very large datasets, neither of these options may be appropriate, because the resulting figure would become too busy. We already saw in Figure 6-7 that just seven groups of four data values can result in a figure that is complex and not that easy to read. If we had 20 groups of 20 data values, a similar figure would likely be quite confusing.

As an alternative to mapping data values onto positions via bars or dots, we can map data values onto colors. Such a figure is called a *heatmap*. Figure 6-14 uses this approach to show the percentage of internet users over time in 20 countries and for 23 years, from 1994 to 2016. While this visualization makes it harder to determine the exact data values shown (e.g., what's the exact percentage of internet users in the United States in 2015?), it does an excellent job of highlighting broader trends. We can see in which countries internet use began early and in which it did not, and we can also see which countries have high internet penetration in the final year covered by the dataset (2016).

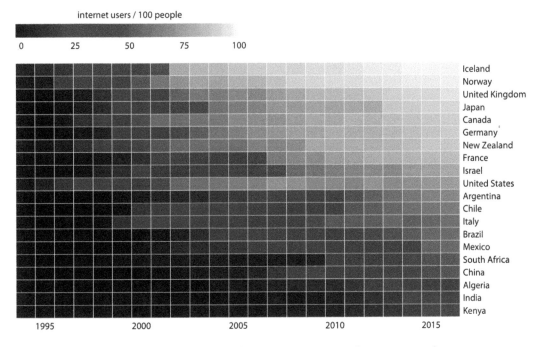

Figure 6-14. Internet adoption over time, for select countries. Color represents the percent of internet users for the respective country and year. Countries were ordered by percent internet users in 2016. Data source: World Bank.

As is the case with all other visualization approaches discussed in this chapter, we need to pay attention to the ordering of the categorical data values when making heatmaps. In Figure 6-14, countries are ordered by the percentage of internet users in 2016. This ordering places the United Kingdom, Japan, Canada, and Germany above the United States, because all these countries had higher internet penetration in 2016 than the United States, even though the United States saw significant internet use at an earlier time. Alternatively, we could order countries by how early they started to see significant internet usage. In Figure 6-15, countries are ordered by the year in which internet usage first rose to above 20%. In this figure, the United States falls into the third position from the top, and it stands out for having relatively low internet usage in 2016 compared to how early internet usage started there. A similar pattern can be seen for Italy. Israel and France, by contrast, started relatively late but gained ground rapidly.

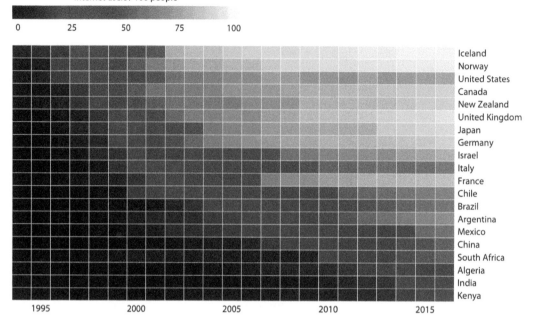

Figure 6-15. Internet adoption over time, for select countries. Countries were ordered by the year in which their internet usage first exceeded 20%. Data source: World Bank.

Both Figures 6-14 and 6-15 are valid representations of the data. Which one is preferred depends on the story we want to convey. If our story is about internet usage in 2016, then Figure 6-14 is probably the better choice. If, however, our story is about how early or late adoption of the internet relates to current-day usage, then Figure 6-15 is preferable.

## CHAPTER 7

Visualizing Distributions: Histograms and Density Plots

We frequently encounter the situation where we would like to understand how a particular variable is distributed in a dataset. To give a concrete example, we will consider the passengers of the *Titanic*, a dataset we encountered in Chapter 6. There were approximately 1,300 passengers on the *Titanic* (not counting crew), and we have reported ages for 756 of them. We might want to know how many passengers of what ages there were on the *Titanic*, i.e., how many children, young adults, middle-aged people, seniors, and so on. We call the relative proportions of different ages among the passengers the *age distribution* of the passengers.

Visualizing a Single Distribution

We can obtain a sense of the age distribution among the passengers by grouping all passengers into bins with comparable ages and then counting the number of passengers in each bin. This procedure results in a table such as Table 7-1.

Table 7-1. Numbers of passengers with known age on the Titanic.

Age range	Count	Age range	Count	Age range	Count
0–5	36	31–35	76	61–65	16
6–10	19	36–40	74	66–70	3
11–15	18	41–45	54	71–75	3
16–20	99	46–50	50		
21–25	139	51–55	26		
26–30	121	56–60	22		

We can visualize this table by drawing filled rectangles whose heights correspond to the counts and whose widths correspond to the width of the age bins (Figure 7-1). Such a visualization is called a *histogram*. (Note that all bins must have the same width for the visualization to be a valid histogram.)

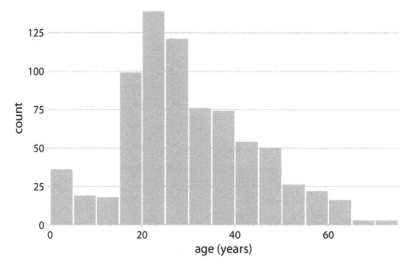

Figure 7-1. Histogram of the ages of Titanic *passengers. Data source: Encyclopedia Titanica.*

Because histograms are generated by binning the data, their exact visual appearance depends on the choice of the bin width. Most visualization programs that generate histograms will choose a bin width by default, but chances are that bin width is not the most appropriate one for any histogram you may want to make. It is therefore critical to always try different bin widths to verify that the resulting histogram reflects the underlying data accurately. In general, if the bin width is too small, then the histogram becomes overly peaky and visually busy and the main trends in the data may be obscured. On the other hand, if the bin width is too large, then smaller features in the distribution of the data, such as the dip around age 10 in this example, may disappear.

For the age distribution of *Titanic* passengers, we can see that a bin width of 1 year is too small and a bin width of 15 years is too large, whereas bin widths of between 3 to 5 years work fine (Figure 7-2).

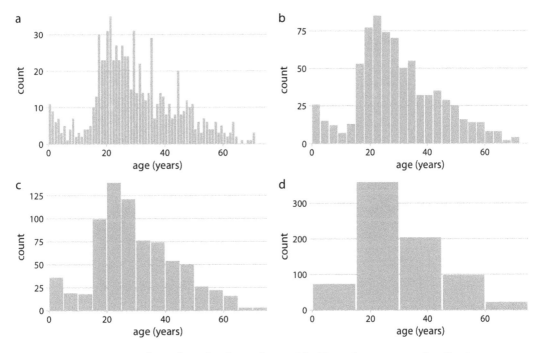

Figure 7-2. Histograms depend on the chosen bin width. Here, the same age distribution of Titanic *passengers is shown with four different bin widths: (a) 1 year; (b) 3 years; (c) 5 years; (d) 15 years. Data source: Encyclopedia Titanica.*

When making a histogram, always explore multiple bin widths.

Histograms have been a popular visualization option since at least the 18th century, in part because they are easily generated by hand. More recently, as extensive computing power has become available in everyday devices such as laptops and cell phones, we see them increasingly being replaced by *density plots*. In a density plot, we attempt to visualize the underlying probability distribution of the data by drawing an appropriate continuous curve (Figure 7-3). This curve needs to be estimated from the data, and the most commonly used method for this estimation procedure is called *kernel density estimation*. In kernel density estimation, we draw a continuous curve (the kernel) with a small width (controlled by a parameter called *bandwidth*) at the location of each data point, and then we add up all these curves to obtain the final density estimate. The most widely used kernel is a Gaussian kernel (i.e., a Gaussian bell curve), but there are many other choices.

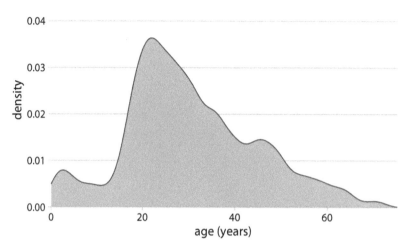

Figure 7-3. Kernel density estimate of the age distribution of passengers on the Titanic. *The height of the curve is scaled such that the area under the curve equals 1. The density estimate was performed with a Gaussian kernel and a bandwidth of 2. Data source: Encyclopedia Titanica.*

Just as is the case with histograms, the exact visual appearance of a density plot depends on the kernel and bandwidth choices (Figure 7-4). The bandwidth parameter behaves similarly to the bin width in histograms. If the bandwidth is too small, then the density estimate can become overly peaky and visually busy and the main trends in the data may be obscured. On the other hand, if the bandwidth is too large, then smaller features in the distribution of the data may disappear. In addition, the choice of the kernel affects the shape of the density curve. For example, a Gaussian kernel will have a tendency to produce density estimates that look Gaussian-like, with smooth features and tails. By contrast, a rectangular kernel can generate the appearance of steps in the density curve (Figure 7-4d). In general, the more data points there are in the dataset, the less the choice of the kernel matters. Therefore, density plots tend to be quite reliable and informative for large datasets but can be misleading for datasets of only a few points.

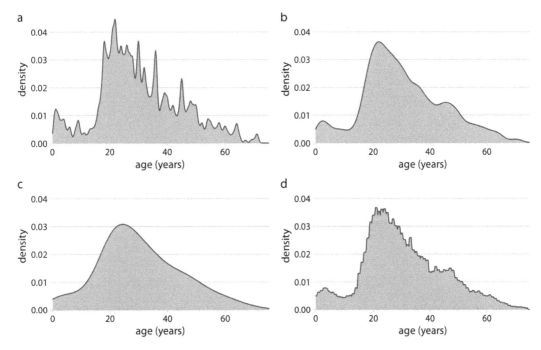

Figure 7-4. Kernel density estimates depend on the chosen kernel and bandwidth. Here, the same age distribution of Titanic *passengers is shown for four different combinations of these parameters: (a) Gaussian kernel, bandwidth = 0.5; (b) Gaussian kernel, bandwidth = 2; (c) Gaussian kernel, bandwidth = 5; (d) rectangular kernel, bandwidth = 2. Data source: Encyclopedia Titanica.*

Density curves are usually scaled such that the area under the curve equals 1. This convention can make the *y* axis scale confusing, because it depends on the units of the *x* axis. For example, in the case of the age distribution, the data range on the *x* axis goes from 0 to approximately 75. Therefore, we expect the mean height of the density curve to be 1/75 = 0.013. Indeed, when looking at the age density curves (e.g., Figure 7-4), we see that the *y* values range from 0 to approximately 0.04, with an average of somewhere close to 0.01.

Kernel density estimates have one pitfall that we need to be aware of: they have a tendency to produce the appearance of data where none exists, in particular in the tails. As a consequence, careless use of density estimates can easily lead to figures that make nonsensical statements. For example, if we don't pay attention, we might generate a visualization of an age distribution that includes negative ages (Figure 7-5).

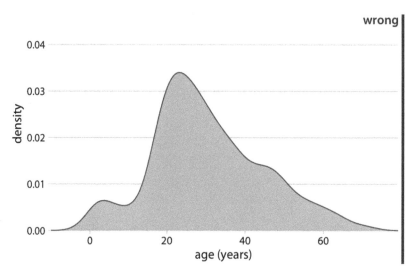

Figure 7-5. *Kernel density estimates can extend the tails of the distribution into areas where no data exists and no data is even possible. Here, the density estimate for ages of* Titanic *passengers has been allowed to extend into the negative age range. This is non-sensical and should be avoided. Data source: Encyclopedia Titanica.*

Always verify that your density estimate does not predict the existence of nonsensical data values.

So should you choose a histogram or a density plot to visualize a distribution? Heated discussions can be had on this topic. Some people are vehemently against density plots and believe that they are arbitrary and misleading. Others realize that histograms can be just as arbitrary and misleading. I think the choice is largely a matter of taste, but sometimes one or the other option may more accurately reflect the specific features of interest in the data at hand. There is also the possibility of using neither and instead choosing empirical cumulative density functions or q-q plots (Chapter 8). However, I believe that density estimates have an inherent advantage over histograms as soon as we want to visualize more than one distribution at a time.

Visualizing Multiple Distributions at the Same Time

In many scenarios we have multiple distributions we would like to visualize simultaneously. For example, let's say we'd like to see how the ages of *Titanic* passengers are distributed between men and women. Were male and female passengers generally of the same age, or was there an age difference between the genders? One commonly employed visualization strategy in this case is a *stacked histogram*, where we draw the histogram bars for women on top of the bars for men, in a different color (Figure 7-6).

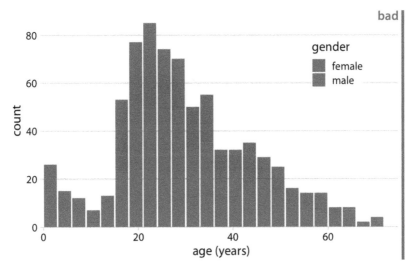

Figure 7-6. Histogram of the ages of Titanic *passengers stratified by gender. This figure has been labeled as "bad" because stacked histograms are easily confused with overlapping histograms (see Figure 7-7). In addition, the heights of the bars representing female passengers cannot easily be compared to each other. Data source: Encyclopedia Titanica.*

In my opinion, this type of visualization should be avoided. There are two key problems here. First, from just looking at the figure, it is never entirely clear where exactly the bars begin. Do they start where the color changes or are they meant to start at zero? In other words, are there about 25 females of age 18–20, or are there almost 80? (The former is the case.) Second, the bar heights for the female counts cannot be directly compared to each other, because the bars all start at a different height. For example, the men were on average older than the women, and this fact is not at all visible in Figure 7-6.

We could try to address these problems by having all bars start at zero and making the bars partially transparent (Figure 7-7).

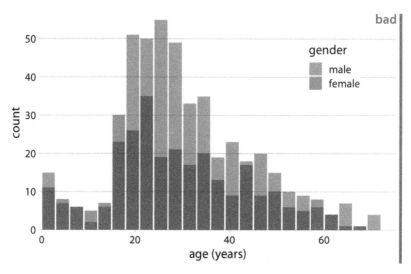

Figure 7-7. Age distributions of male and female Titanic *passengers, shown as two over-lapping histograms. This figure has been labeled as "bad" because there is no clear visual indication that all blue bars start at a count of 0. Data source: Encyclopedia Titanica.*

However, this approach generates new problems. Now it appears that there are actually three different groups, not just two, and we're still not entirely sure where each bar starts and ends. Overlapping histograms don't work well because a semi-transparent bar drawn on top of another tends to not look like a semitransparent bar but instead like a bar drawn in a different color.

Overlapping density plots don't typically have the problem that overlapping histograms have, because the continuous density lines help the eye keep the distributions separate. However, for this particular dataset, the age distributions for male and female passengers are nearly identical up to around age 17 and then diverge, so that the resulting visualization is still not ideal (Figure 7-8).

A solution that works well for this dataset is to show the age distributions of male and female passengers separately, each as a proportion of the overall age distribution (Figure 7-9). This visualization shows intuitively and clearly that there were many fewer women than men in the 20-to-50-year age range on the *Titanic*.

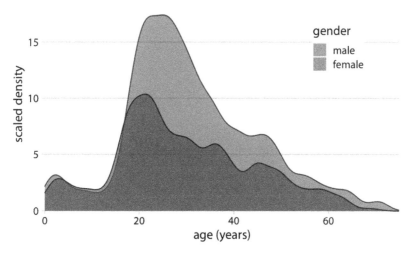

Figure 7-8. Density estimates of the ages of male and female Titanic *passengers. To highlight that there were more male than female passengers, the density curves were scaled such that the area under each curve corresponds to the total number of male and female passengers with known age (468 and 288, respectively). Data source: Encyclopedia Titanica.*

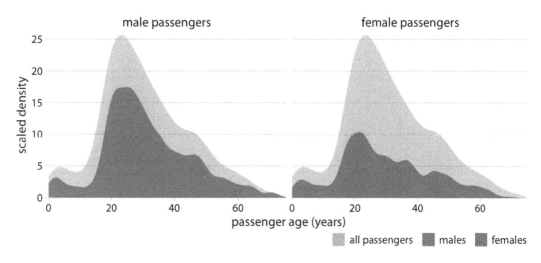

Figure 7-9. Age distributions of male and female Titanic *passengers, shown as proportions of the total number of passengers. The colored areas show the density estimates of the ages of male and female passengers, respectively, and the gray areas show the overall passenger age distribution. Data source: Encyclopedia Titanica.*

Finally, when we want to visualize exactly two distributions, we can also make two separate histograms, rotate them by 90 degrees, and have the bars in one histogram point in the opposite direction of the other. This trick is commonly employed when visualizing age distributions, and the resulting plot is usually called an *age pyramid* (Figure 7-10).

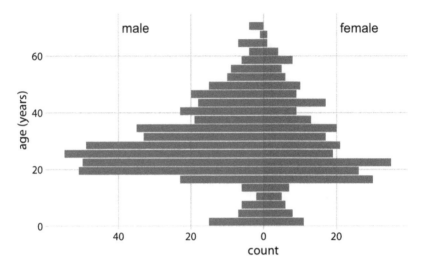

Figure 7-10. The age distributions of male and female Titanic *passengers visualized as an age pyramid. Data source: Encyclopedia Titanica.*

Importantly, this trick does not work when there are more than two distributions we want to visualize at the same time. For multiple distributions, histograms tend to become confusing, whereas density plots work well as long as the distributions are somewhat distinct and contiguous. For example, to visualize the distribution of butterfat percentage in the milk of cows from four different cattle breeds, density plots are fine (Figure 7-11).

 To visualize several distributions at once, kernel density plots will generally work better than histograms.

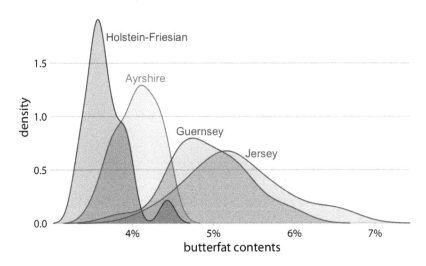

Figure 7-11. Density estimates of the butterfat percentage in the milk of four cattle breeds. Data source: Canadian Record of Performance for Purebred Dairy Cattle.

## CHAPTER 8

Visualizing Distributions: Empirical Cumulative Distribution Functions and Q-Q Plots

In Chapter 7, I described how we can visualize distributions with histograms or density plots. Both of these approaches are intuitive and visually appealing. However, as discussed in that chapter, they both share the limitation that the resulting figure depends to a substantial degree on parameters the user has to choose, such as the bin width for histograms and the bandwidth for density plots. As a result, both have to be considered as an interpretation of the data rather than a direct visualization of the data itself.

As an alternative to using histograms or density plots, we could simply show all the data points individually, as a point cloud. However, this approach becomes unwieldy for very large datasets, and in any case there is value in aggregate methods that highlight properties of the distribution rather than the individual data points. To solve this problem, statisticians have invented empirical cumulative distribution functions (ECDFs) and quantile-quantile (q-q) plots. These types of visualizations require no arbitrary parameter choices, and they show all of the data at once. Unfortunately, they are a little less intuitive than a histogram or a density plot is, and I don't see them used frequently outside of highly technical publications. They are quite popular among statisticians, though, and I think anybody interested in data visualization should be familiar with these techniques.

Empirical Cumulative Distribution Functions

To illustrate ECDFs, I will begin with a hypothetical example that is closely modeled after something I deal with a lot as a professor in the classroom: a dataset of student grades. Assume our hypothetical class has 50 students, and the students just completed an exam on which they could score between 0 and 100 points. How can we best visualize the class's performance, for example to determine appropriate grade boundaries?

We can plot the total number of students that have received at most a certain number of points versus all possible point scores. This plot will be an ascending function, starting at 0 for 0 points and ending at 50 for 100 points. A different way of thinking about this visualization is the following: we can rank all students by the number of points they obtained, in ascending order (so the student with the fewest points receives the lowest rank and the student with the most points the highest), and then plot the rank versus the actual points obtained. The result is an empirical cumulative distribution function, or simply *cumulative distribution*. Each dot represents one student, and the lines visualize the highest student rank observed for any possible point value (Figure 8-1).

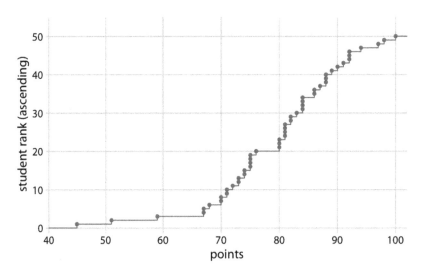

Figure 8-1. Empirical cumulative distribution function of student grades for a hypothetical class of 50 students.

You may wonder what happens if we rank the students the other way round, in descending order. This ranking simply flips the function on its head. The result is still an empirical cumulative distribution function, but the lines now represent the lowest student rank observed for any possible point value (Figure 8-2).

Ascending cumulative distribution functions are more widely known and more commonly used than descending ones, but both have important applications. Descending cumulative distribution functions are critical when we want to visualize highly skewed distributions, as discussed in the next section.

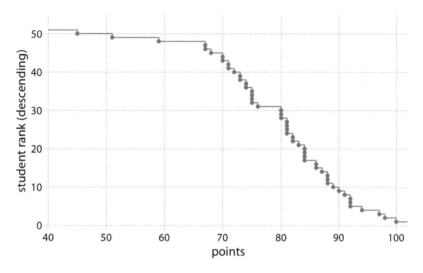

Figure 8-2. Distribution of student grades plotted as a descending ECDF.

In practical applications, it is quite common to draw the ECDF without highlighting the individual points and to normalize the ranks by the maximum rank, so that the *y* axis represents the cumulative frequency (Figure 8-3).

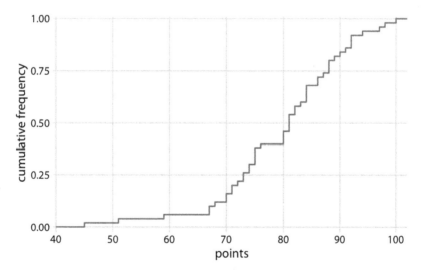

Figure 8-3. ECDF of student grades. The student ranks have been normalized to the total number of students, such that the y values plotted correspond to the fraction of students in the class with at most that many points.

We can directly read off key properties of the student grade distribution from this plot. For example, approximately a quarter of the students (25%) received less than 75 points. The median point value (corresponding to a cumulative frequency of 0.5) is 81. Approximately 20% of the students received 90 points or more.

I find ECDFs handy for assigning grade boundaries because they help me locate the exact cutoffs that minimize student unhappiness. For example, in this example, there's a fairly long horizontal line right below 80 points, followed by a steep rise right at 80. This feature is caused by three students receiving 80 points on their exam while the student with the next highest grade received only 76 points. In this scenario, I might decide that everybody with a point score of 80 or more receives a B and everybody with 79 or less receives a C. The three students with 80 points are happy that they just made a B, and the student with 76 realizes that they would have had to perform much better to not receive a C. If I were to set the cutoff at 77, the distribution of letter grades would be exactly the same, but I might find the student with 76 points visiting my office hoping to negotiate their grade. Likewise, if I had set the cutoff at 81, I would likely have had three students in my office trying to negotiate their grade.

Highly Skewed Distributions

Many empirical datasets display highly skewed distributions, in particular with heavy tails to the right, and these distributions can be challenging to visualize. Examples of such distributions include the number of people living in different cities or counties, the number of contacts in a social network, the frequency with which individual words appear in a book, the number of academic papers written by different authors, the net worth of individuals, and the number of interaction partners of individual proteins in protein–protein interaction networks [Clauset, Shalizi, and Newman 2009]. All these distributions have in common that their right tail decays slower than an exponential function. In practice, this means that very large values are not that rare, even if the mean of the distribution is small. An important class of such distributions are *power-law* distributions, where the likelihood of observing a value that is x times larger than some reference point declines as a power of x. To give a concrete example, consider net worth in the US, which is distributed according to a power law with exponent 2. At any given level of net worth (say, $1 million), people with half that net worth are four times as frequent, and people with twice that net worth are one-fourth as frequent. Importantly, the same relationship holds if we use $10,000 as reference point or if we use $100 million. For this reason, power-law distributions are also called *scale-free* distributions.

Here, I will visualize the number of people living in different US counties according to the 2010 US Census. This distribution has a very long tail to the right. Even though most counties have relatively small numbers of inhabitants (the median is 25,857), a few counties have extremely large numbers of inhabitants (e.g., Los Angeles County, with 9,818,605 inhabitants). If we try to visualize the distribution of population counts as either a density plot or an ECDF, we obtain figures that are essentially useless (Figure 8-4).

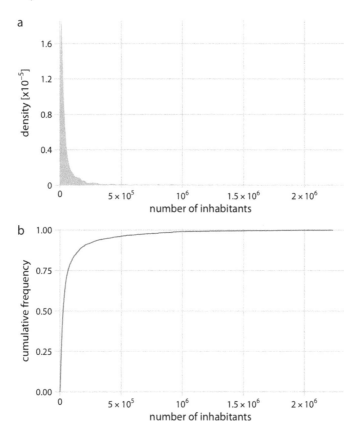

Figure 8-4. Distribution of the number of inhabitants in US counties. (a) Density plot. (b) Empirical cumulative distribution function. Data source: 2010 US Decennial Census.

The density plot (Figure 8-4a) shows a sharp peak right at 0, and virtually no details of the distribution are visible. Similarly, the ECDF (Figure 8-4b) shows a rapid rise near 0, and again no details of the distribution are visible. For this particular dataset, we can log-transform the data and visualize the distribution of the log-transformed values. This transformation works here because the distribution of population numbers in counties is not actually a power law, but instead is a nearly perfect log-normal distribution (see "Quantile-Quantile Plots" on page 78). Indeed, the density plot of the log-transformed values shows a nice bell curve and the corresponding ECDF shows a nice sigmoidal shape (Figure 8-5).

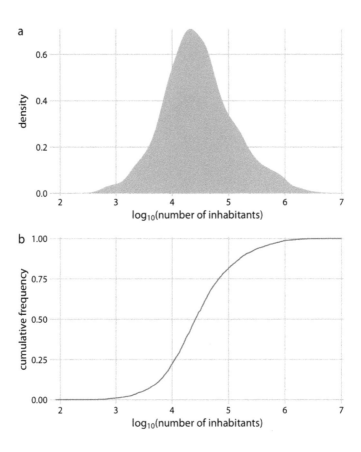

Figure 8-5. Distribution of the logarithm of the number of inhabitants in US counties. (a) Density plot. (b) Empirical cumulative distribution function. Data source: 2010 US Decennial Census.

To see that this distribution is not a power law, we plot it as a descending ECDF with logarithmic x and y axes. In this visualization, a power law appears as a perfect straight line. For the population counts in counties, the right tail forms almost but not quite a straight line on the descending log-log ECDF plot (Figure 8-6).

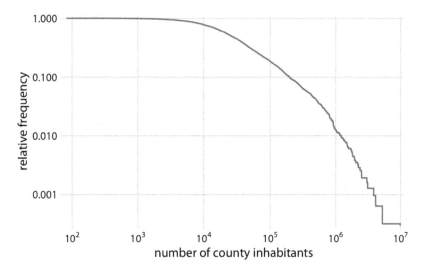

Figure 8-6. Relative frequency of counties with at least that many inhabitants versus the number of county inhabitants. Data source: 2010 US Decennial Census.

As a second example, I will use the distribution of word frequencies for all words that appear in the novel *Moby Dick*. This distribution follows a perfect power law. When plotted as a descending ECDF with logarithmic axes, we see a nearly perfect straight line (Figure 8-7).

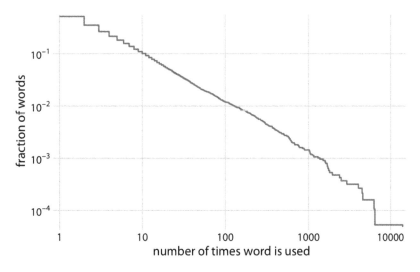

Figure 8-7. Distribution of word counts in the novel Moby Dick. *Shown is the relative frequency of words that occur at least that many times in the novel versus the number of times words are used. Data source: [Clauset, Shalizi, and Newman 2009].*

Quantile-Quantile Plots

Quantile-quantile (q-q) plots are useful visualizations when we want to determine to what extent the observed data points do or do not follow a given distribution. Just like ECDFs, q-q plots are also based on ranking the data and visualizing the relationship between ranks and actual values. However, in q-q plots we don't plot the ranks directly; rather, we use them to predict where a given data point would fall if the data were distributed according to a specified reference distribution. Most commonly, q-q plots are constructed using a normal distribution as the reference. To give a concrete example, assume the actual data values have a mean of 10 and a standard deviation of 3. Then, assuming a normal distribution, we would expect a data point ranked at the 50th percentile to lie at position 10 (the mean), a data point at the 84th percentile to lie at position 13 (one standard deviation above the mean), and a data point at the 2.3rd percentile to lie at position 4 (two standard deviations below the mean). We can carry out this calculation for all points in the dataset and then plot the observed values (i.e., values in the dataset) against the theoretical values (i.e., values expected given each data point's rank and the assumed reference distribution).

When we perform this procedure for the student grades distribution from the beginning of this chapter, we obtain Figure 8-8.

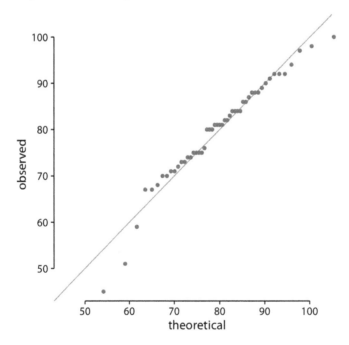

Figure 8-8. q-q plot of hypothetical student grades.

The solid line here is not a regression line but indicates the points where x equals y, i.e., where the observed values equal the theoretical ones. To the extent that points fall onto that line, the data follows the assumed distribution (here, normal). We see that the student grades follow mostly a normal distribution, with a few deviations at the bottom and at the top (a few students performed worse than expected on either end). The deviations from the distribution at the top end are caused by the maximum point value of 100 in the hypothetical exam; regardless of how good the best student is, they can at most obtain 100 points.

We can also use a q-q plot to test my assertion from earlier in this chapter that the population counts in US counties follow a log-normal distribution. If these counts are log-normally distributed, then their log-transformed values are normally distributed and hence should fall right onto the $x = y$ line. When making this plot, we see that the agreement between the observed and the theoretical values is exceptional (Figure 8-9). This demonstrates that the distribution of population counts among counties is indeed log-normal.

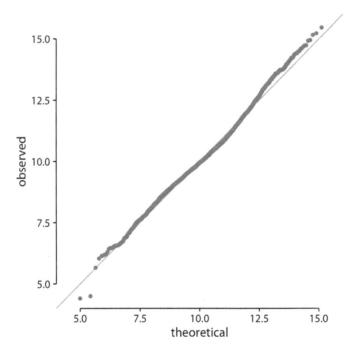

Figure 8-9. q-q plot of the logarithm of the number of inhabitants in US counties. Data source: 2010 US Decennial Census.

## CHAPTER 9

Visualizing Many Distributions at Once

There are many scenarios in which we want to visualize multiple distributions at the same time. For example, consider weather data. We may want to visualize how temperature varies across different months while also showing the distribution of observed temperatures within each month. This scenario requires showing a dozen temperature distributions at once, one for each month. None of the visualizations discussed in Chapters 7 or 8 work well in this case. Instead, viable approaches include boxplots, violin plots, and ridgeline plots.

Whenever we are dealing with many distributions, it is helpful to think in terms of the response variable and one or more grouping variables. The *response variable* is the variable whose distributions we want to show. The *grouping variables* define subsets of the data with distinct distributions of the response variable. For example, for temperature distributions across months, the response variable is the temperature and the grouping variable is the month. All techniques discussed in this chapter draw the response variable along one axis and the grouping variable(s) along the other. In the following sections, I will first describe approaches that show the response variable along the vertical axis, and then I will describe approaches that show the response variable along the horizontal axis. In all cases discussed, we could flip the axes and arrive at an alternative and viable visualization. I am showing here the canonical forms of the various visualizations.

Visualizing Distributions Along the Vertical Axis

The simplest approach to showing many distributions at once is to show their mean or median as points, with some indication of the variation around the mean or median shown by error bars. Figure 9-1 demonstrates this approach for the distributions of monthly temperatures in Lincoln, Nebraska, in 2016. I have labeled this figure as "bad" because there are multiple problems with this approach. First, by representing each distribution by only one point and two error bars, we are losing a lot of information about the data. Second, it is not immediately obvious what the points represent, even though most readers would likely guess that they represent either the mean or the median. Third, it is definitely not obvious what the error bars represent. Do they represent the standard deviation of the data, the standard error of the mean, a 95% confidence interval, or something else altogether? There is no commonly accepted standard. By reading the figure caption of Figure 9-1, we can see that they represent here twice the standard deviation of the daily mean temperatures, meant to indicate the range that contains approximately 95% of the data. However, error bars are more commonly employed to visualize the standard error (or twice the standard error for a 95% confidence interval), and it is easy for readers to confuse the standard error with the standard deviation. The standard error quantifies how accurate our estimate of the mean is, whereas the standard deviation estimates how much spread there is in the data around the mean. It is possible for a dataset to have both a very small standard error of the mean and a very large standard deviation. Fourth, symmetric error bars are misleading if there is any skew in the data, which is the case here and is almost always for real-world datasets.

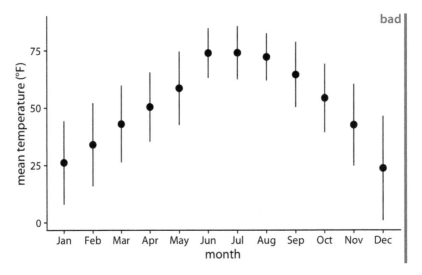

Figure 9-1. Mean daily temperatures in Lincoln, NE, in 2016. Points represent the average daily mean temperatures for each month, averaged over all days of the month, and error bars represent twice the standard deviation of the daily mean temperatures within each month. This figure has been labeled as "bad" because error bars are conventionally used to visualize the uncertainty of an estimate, not the variability in a population. Data source: Weather Underground.

We can address all four shortcomings of Figure 9-1 by using a traditional and commonly used method for visualizing distributions, the *boxplot*. A boxplot divides the data into quartiles and visualizes them in a standardized manner (Figure 9-2).

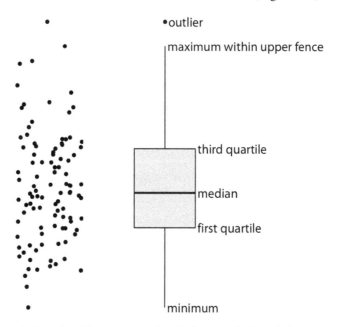

Figure 9-2. Anatomy of a boxplot. Shown are a cloud of points (left) and the corresponding boxplot (right).

Only the *y* values of the points are visualized in the boxplot in Figure 9-2. The line in the middle of the boxplot represents the median, and the box encloses the middle 50% of the data. The vertical lines extending upwards and downwards from the box are called *whiskers*. The top and bottom whiskers extend either to the maximum and minimum values of the data or to the maximum or minimum values that fall within 1.5 times the height of the box, whichever yields the shorter whisker. The distances of 1.5 times the height of the box in either direction are called the upper and lower *fences*. Individual data points that fall beyond the fences are referred to as outliers and are usually shown as individual dots.

Boxplots are simple yet informative, and they work well when plotted next to each other to visualize many distributions at once. For the Lincoln temperature data, using boxplots leads to Figure 9-3. In that figure, we can now see that temperature is highly skewed in December (most days are moderately cold and a few are extremely cold) and not very skewed at all in some other months, such as in July.

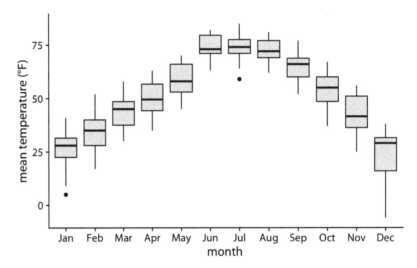

Figure 9-3. Mean daily temperatures in Lincoln, NE, visualized as boxplots. Data source: Weather Underground.

Boxplots were invented by the statistician John Tukey in the early 1970s, and they quickly gained popularity because they were highly informative while being easy to draw by hand, which is how most data visualizations were drawn at that time. However, with modern computing and visualization capabilities, we are not limited to what is easily drawn by hand. Therefore, more recently we see boxplots being replaced by *violin plots* (Figure 9-4). Violins can be used whenever one would otherwise use a boxplot, and they provide a much more nuanced picture of the data. In particular, violin plots will accurately represent bimodal data whereas a boxplot will not.

Only the *y* values of the points are visualized in the violin plot. The width of the violin at a given *y* value represents the point density at that *y* value. Technically, a violin plot is a density estimate rotated by 90 degrees and then mirrored (Chapter 7). Violins are therefore symmetric. Violins begin and end at the minimum and maximum data values, respectively. The thickest part of the violin corresponds to the highest point density in the dataset.

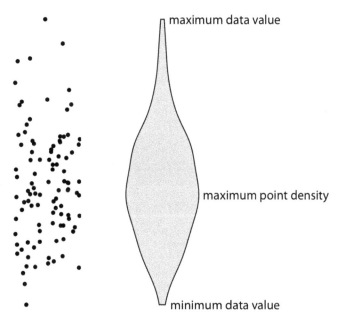

Figure 9-4. Anatomy of a violin plot. Shown are a cloud of points (left) and the corresponding violin plot (right).

Before using violins to visualize distributions, verify that you have sufficiently many data points in each group to justify showing the point densities as smooth lines.

When we visualize the Lincoln temperature data with violins, we obtain Figure 9-5. We can now see that some months do have moderately bimodal data. For example, the month of November seems to have had two temperature clusters, one around 50 degrees and one around 35 degrees Fahrenheit.

Because violin plots are derived from density estimates, they have similar shortcomings. In particular, they can generate the appearance that there is data where none exists, or that the dataset is very dense when actually it is quite sparse. We can try to circumvent these issues by simply plotting all the individual data points directly, as dots (Figure 9-6). Such a figure is called a *strip chart*. Strip charts are fine in principle, as long as we make sure that we don't plot too many points on top of each other. A simple solution to overplotting is to spread out the points somewhat along the *x* axis, by adding some random noise in the *x* dimension (Figure 9-7). This technique is called *jittering*.

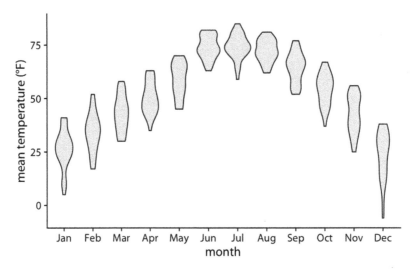

Figure 9-5. Mean daily temperatures in Lincoln, NE, visualized as violin plots. Data source: Weather Underground.

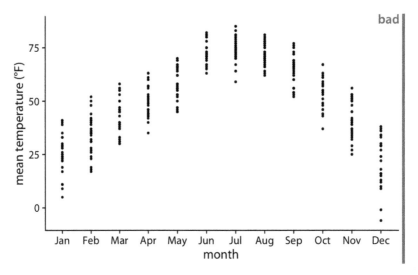

Figure 9-6. Mean daily temperatures in Lincoln, NE, visualized as strip charts. Each point represents the mean temperature for one day. This figure is labeled as "bad" because so many points are plotted on top of each other that it is not possible to ascertain which temperatures were the most common in each month. Data source: Weather Underground.

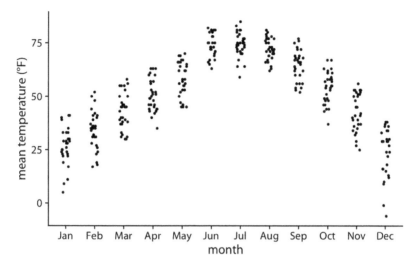

Figure 9-7. Mean daily temperatures in Lincoln, NE, visualized as strip charts. The points have been jittered along the x axis to better show the density of points at each temperature value. Data source: Weather Underground.

Whenever the dataset is too sparse to justify the violin visualization, plotting the raw data as individual points will be possible.

Finally, we can combine the best of both worlds by spreading out the dots in proportion to the point density at a given *y* coordinate. This method, called a *sina plot* [Sidiropoulos et al. 2018],[1] can be thought of as a hybrid between a violin plot and jittered points, and it shows each individual point while also visualizing the distributions. In Figure 9-8, I have drawn the sina plots on top of the violins to highlight the relationship between these two approaches.

---

1 The name *sina plot* is meant to honor Sina Hadi Sohi, a student at the University of Copenhagen, Denmark, who wrote the first version of the code that researchers at the university used to make such plots (Frederik O. Bagger, personal communication).

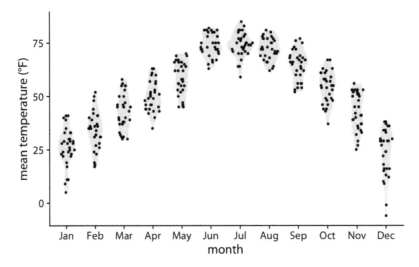

Figure 9-8. Mean daily temperatures in Lincoln, NE, visualized as sina plots (a combination of individual points and violins). The points have been jittered along the x axis in proportion to the point density at the respective temperature. Here, the sina plots are shown superimposed on violin plots. Data source: Weather Underground.

Visualizing Distributions Along the Horizontal Axis

In Chapter 7, we visualized distributions along the horizontal axis using histograms and density plots. Here, we will expand on this idea by staggering the distribution plots in the vertical direction. The resulting visualization is called a *ridgeline plot*, because these plots look like mountain ridgelines. Ridgeline plots tend to work particularly well if you want to show trends in distributions over time.

The standard ridgeline plot uses density estimates (Figure 9-9). It is quite closely related to the violin plot, but frequently evokes a more intuitive understanding of the data. For example, the two clusters of temperatures around 35 degrees and 50 degrees Fahrenheit in November are much more obvious in Figure 9-9 than in Figure 9-5.

Because the *x* axis shows the response variable and the *y* axis shows the grouping variable, there is no separate axis for the density estimates in a ridgeline plot. Density estimates are shown alongside the grouping variable. This is no different from the violin plot, where densities are also shown alongside the grouping variable, without a separate, explicit scale. In both cases, the purpose of the plot is not to show specific density values but instead to allow for easy comparison of density shapes and relative heights across groups.

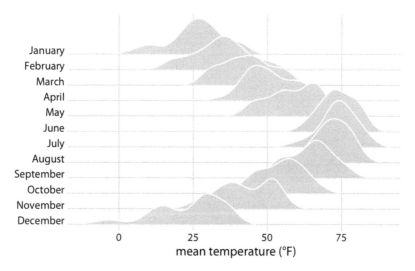

Figure 9-9. Temperatures in Lincoln, NE, in 2016, visualized as a ridgeline plot. For each month, we show the distribution of daily mean temperatures measured in Fahrenheit. Original figure concept: [Wehrwein 2017]. Data source: Weather Underground.

In principle, we can use histograms instead of density plots in a ridgeline visualization. However, the resulting figures often don't look very good (Figure 9-10). The problems are similar to those of stacked or overlapping histograms (see "Visualizing Multiple Distributions at the Same Time" on page 64). Because the vertical lines in these ridgeline histograms always appear at the exact same *x* values, the bars from different histograms align with each other in confusing ways. In my opinion, it is better to not draw such overlapping histograms.

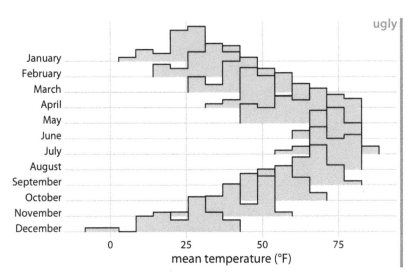

ugly

Figure 9-10. Temperatures in Lincoln, NE, in 2016, visualized as a ridgeline plot of histograms. The individual histograms don't separate well visually, and the overall figure is quite busy and confusing. Data source: Weather Underground.

Ridgeline plots scale to very large numbers of distributions. For example, Figure 9-11 shows the distributions of movie lengths from 1913 to 2005. This figure contains almost 100 distinct distributions and yet it is very easy to read. We can see that in the 1920s, movies came in many different lengths, but since about 1960 movie length has standardized to approximately 90 minutes.

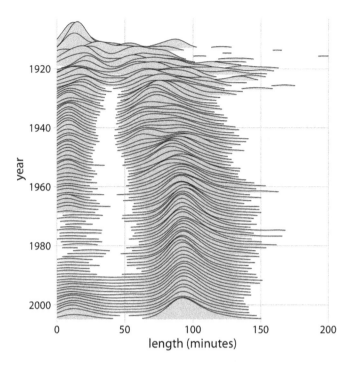

Figure 9-11. Evolution of movie lengths over time. Since the 1960s, the majority of all movies have been approximately 90 minutes long. Data source: Internet Movie Database (IMDB).

Ridgeline plots also work well if we want to compare two trends over time. This is a scenario that arises commonly if we want to analyze the voting patterns of the members of two different parties. We can make this comparison by staggering the distributions vertically by time and drawing two differently colored distributions at each time point, representing the two parties (Figure 9-12).

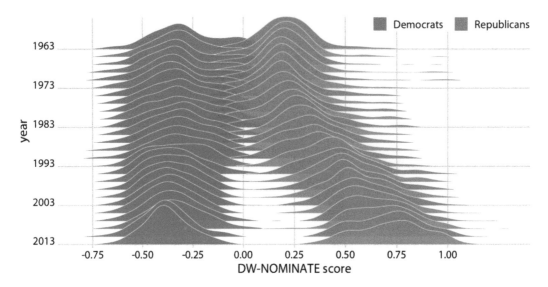

Figure 9-12. Voting patterns in the US House of Representatives have become increasingly polarized. DW-NOMINATE scores are frequently used to compare voting patterns of representatives between parties and over time. Here, score distributions are shown for each Congress from 1963 to 2013 separately for Democrats and Republicans. Each Congress is represented by its first year. Original figure concept: [McDonald 2017]. Data source: Keith Poole.

## CHAPTER 10

Visualizing Proportions

We often want to show how some group, entity, or amount breaks down into individual pieces that each represent a *proportion* of the whole. Common examples include the proportions of men and women in a group of people, the percentages of people voting for different political parties in an election, or the market shares of companies. The archetypal such visualization is the pie chart, omnipresent in any business presentation and much maligned among data scientists. As we will see, visualizing proportions can be challenging, in particular when the whole is broken into many different pieces or when we want to see changes in proportions over time or across conditions. There is no single ideal visualization that always works. To illustrate this issue, I discuss a few different scenarios that each call for a different type of visualization.

Remember, you always need to pick the visualization that best fits your specific dataset and that highlights the key data features you want to show.

A Case for Pie Charts

From 1961 to 1983, the German parliament (called the *Bundestag*) was composed of members of three different parties, CDU/CSU, SPD, and FDP. During most of this time, CDU/CSU and SPD had approximately comparable numbers of seats, while FDP typically held only a small fraction of seats. For example, in the eighth Bundestag, from 1976–1980, CDU/CSU held 243 seats, SPD 214, and FDP 39, for a total of 496. Such parliamentary data is most commonly visualized as a pie chart (Figure 10-1).

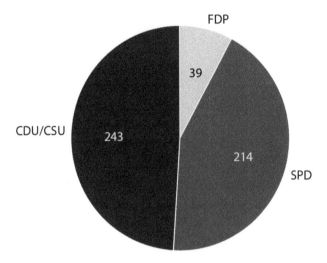

Figure 10-1. Party composition of the eighth German Bundestag, 1976–1980, visualized as a pie chart. This visualization highlights that the ruling coalition of SPD and FDP had a small majority over the opposition CDU/CSU. Data source: Wikipedia.

A pie chart breaks a circle into slices such that the area of each slice is proportional to the fraction of the total it represents. The same procedure can be performed on a rectangle, and the result is a stacked bar chart (Figure 10-2). Depending on whether we slice the bar vertically or horizontally, we obtain vertically stacked bars (Figure 10-2a) or horizontally stacked bars (Figure 10-2b).

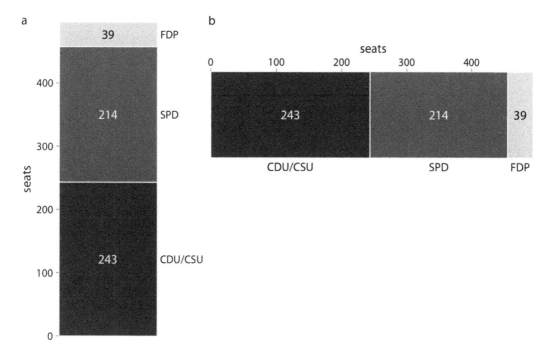

Figure 10-2. Party composition of the eighth German Bundestag, 1976–1980, visualized as stacked bars. (a) Bars stacked vertically. (b) Bars stacked horizontally. It is not immediately obvious that SPD and FDP jointly had more seats than CDU/CSU. Data source: Wikipedia.

We can also take the bars from Figure 10-2a and place them side-by-side rather than stacking them on top of each other. This visualization makes it easier to perform a direct comparison of the three groups, though it obscures other aspects of the data (Figure 10-3). Most importantly, in a side-by-side bar plot the relationship of each bar to the total is not visually obvious.

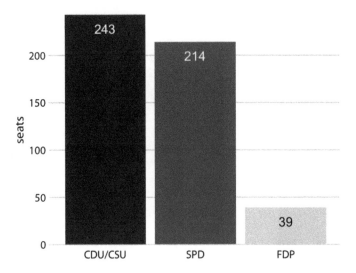

Figure 10-3. Party composition of the eighth German Bundestag, 1976–1980, visualized as side-by-side bars. As in Figure 10-2, it is not immediately obvious that SPD and FDP jointly had more seats than CDU/CSU. Data source: Wikipedia.

Many authors categorically reject pie charts and argue in favor of side-by-side or stacked bars. Others defend the use of pie charts in some applications. My own opinion is that none of these visualizations is consistently superior over any other. Depending on the features of the dataset and the specific story you want to tell, you may want to favor one or the other approach. In the case of the eighth German Bundestag, I think that a pie chart is the best option. It highlights that the ruling coalition of SPD and FDP jointly had a small majority over CDU/CSU (Figure 10-1). This fact is not visually obvious in any of the other plots (Figures 10-2 and 10-3).

In general, pie charts work well when the goal is to emphasize simple fractions, such as one-half, one-third, or one-quarter. They also work well when we have very small datasets. A single pie chart, as in Figure 10-1, looks just fine, but a single column of stacked bars, as in Figure 10-2a, looks awkward. Stacked bars, on the other hand, can work for side-by-side comparisons of multiple conditions or in a time series, and side-by-side bars are preferred when we want to directly compare the individual fractions to each other. A summary of the various pros and cons of pie charts, stacked bars, and side-by-side bars is provided in Table 10-1.

Table 10-1. *Pros and cons of common approaches to visualizing proportions: pie charts, stacked bars, and side-by-side bars.*

	Pie chart	Stacked bars	Side-by-side bars
Clearly visualizes the data as proportions of a whole	✓	✓	✗
Allows easy visual comparison of the relative proportions	✗	✗	✓
Visually emphasizes simple fractions, such as 1/2, 1/3, 1/4	✓	✗	✗
Looks visually appealing even for very small datasets	✓	✗	✓
Works well when the whole is broken into many pieces	✗	✗	✓
Works well for the visualization of many sets of proportions or time series of proportions	✗	✓	✗

A Case for Side-by-Side Bars

I will now demonstrate a case where pie charts fail. This example is modeled after a critique of pie charts originally posted on Wikipedia [Wikipedia 2007]. Consider the hypothetical scenario of five companies, A, B, C, D, and E, who all have roughly comparable market share of approximately 20%. Our hypothetical dataset lists the market share of each company for three consecutive years. When we visualize this dataset with pie charts, it is difficult to see specific trends (Figure 10-4). It appears that the market share of company A is growing and the one of company E is shrinking, but beyond this one observation we can't tell what's going on. In particular, it is unclear how exactly the market shares of the different companies compare within each year.

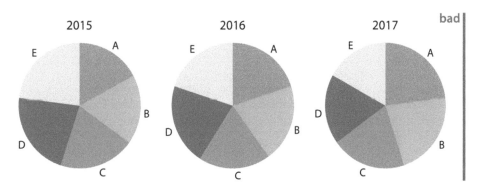

Figure 10-4. *Market share of five hypothetical companies, A–E, for the years 2015–2017, visualized as pie charts. This visualization has two major problems: (i) a comparison of relative market share within years is nearly impossible, and (ii) changes in market share across years are difficult to see.*

The picture becomes a little clearer when we switch to stacked bars (Figure 10-5). Now the trends of a growing market share for company A and a shrinking market share for company E are clearly visible. However, the relative market shares of the five companies within each year are still hard to compare. And it is difficult to compare the market shares of companies B, C, and D across years, because the bars are shifted relative to each other across years. This is a general problem of stacked-bar plots, and the main reason why I normally do not recommend this type of visualization.

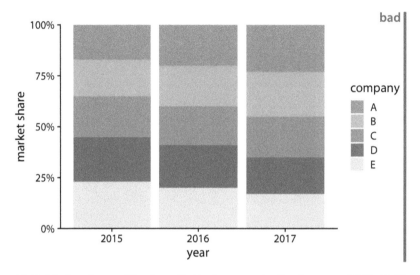

Figure 10-5. Market share of five hypothetical companies for the years 2015–2017, visualized as stacked bars. This visualization has two major problems: (i) a comparison of relative market shares within years is difficult, and (ii) changes in market share across years are difficult to see for the middle companies (B, C, and D) because the location of the bars changes across years.

For this hypothetical dataset, side-by-side bars are the best choice (Figure 10-6). This visualization highlights that both companies A and B have increased their market share from 2015 to 2017 while both companies D and E have reduced theirs. It also shows that market shares increase sequentially from company A to E in 2015 and similarly decrease in 2017.

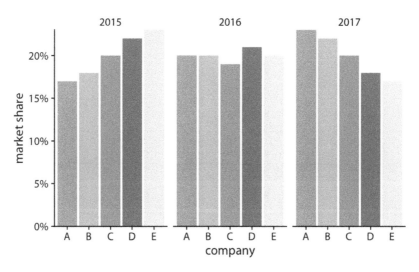

Figure 10-6. Market share of five hypothetical companies for the years 2015–2017, visualized as side-by-side bars.

A Case for Stacked Bars and Stacked Densities

In the previous section, I wrote that I don't normally recommend sequences of stacked bars, because the locations of the internal bars shift along the sequence. However, the problem of shifting internal bars disappears if there are only two bars in each stack, and in those cases the resulting visualization can be quite clear. As an example, consider the proportion of women in a country's national parliament. We will specifically look at the African country Rwanda, which as of 2016 tops the list of countries with the highest proportion of female parliament members. Rwanda has had a majority female parliament since 2008, and since 2013 nearly two-thirds of its members of parliament have been female. To visualize how the proportion of women in the Rwandan parliament has changed over time, we can draw a sequence of stacked bar graphs (Figure 10-7). This figure provides an immediate visual representation of the changing proportions over time. To help the reader see exactly when the majority turned female, I have added a dashed horizontal line at 50%. Without this line, it would be near impossible to determine whether from 2003 to 2007 the majority was male or female. I have not added similar lines at 25% and 75%, to avoid making the figure too cluttered.

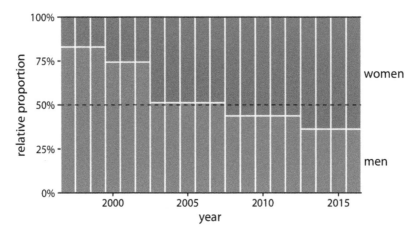

Figure 10-7. Change in the gender composition of the Rwandan parliament over time, 1997 to 2016. Data source: Inter-Parliamentary Union (IPU) (https://ipu.org).

If we want to visualize how proportions change in response to a continuous variable, we can switch from stacked bars to stacked densities. Stacked densities can be thought of as the limiting case of infinitely many, infinitely small stacked bars arranged side-by-side. The densities in stacked density plots are typically obtained from kernel density estimation, as described in Chapter 7, and I refer you to that chapter for a general discussion of the strengths and weaknesses of this method.

To give an example where stacked densities may be appropriate, consider the health status of people as a function of age. Age can be considered a continuous variable, and visualizing the data in this way works reasonably well (Figure 10-8). Even though we have four health categories here, and I'm generally not a fan of stacking multiple conditions, as discussed previously, I think in this case the figure is acceptable. We can see that overall health declines as people age, and we can also see that despite this trend, over half of the population remains in good or excellent health until very old age.

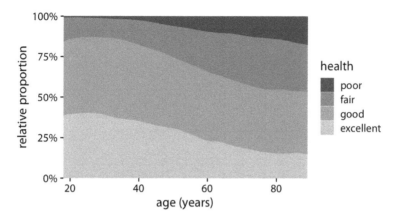

Figure 10-8. Health status by age. Data source: General Social Survey (GSS).

Nevertheless, this figure has a major limitation: by visualizing the proportions of the four health conditions as percentages of the total, the figure obscures that there are many more young people than old people in the dataset. Thus, even though the *percentage* of people reporting to be in good health remains approximately unchanged across ages spanning seven decades, the *absolute number* of people in good health declines as the total number of people at a given age declines. I will present a potential solution to this problem in the next section.

Visualizing Proportions Separately as Parts of the Total

Side-by-side bars have the problem that they don't visualize the size of the individual parts relative to the whole, and stacked bars have the problem that the different bars cannot be compared easily because they have different baselines. We can resolve these two issues by making a separate plot for each part and in each plot showing the respective part relative to the whole. For the health dataset of Figure 10-8, this procedure results in Figure 10-9. The overall age distribution in the dataset is shown as the shaded gray areas, and the age distributions for each health status are shown in blue. This figure highlights that in absolute terms, the number of people with excellent or good health declines past ages 30–40, while the number of people with fair health remains approximately constant across all ages.

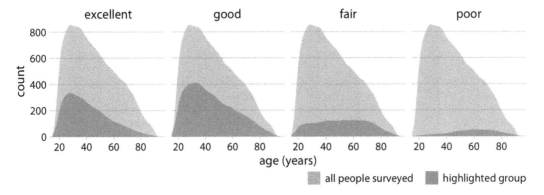

Figure 10-9. Health status by age, shown as proportion of the total number of people in the survey. The colored areas show the density estimates of the ages of people with the respective health status and the gray areas show the overall age distribution. Data source: GSS.

To provide a second example, let's consider a different variable from the same survey: marital status. Marital status changes much more drastically with age than does health status, and a stacked densities plot of marital status versus age is not very illuminating (Figure 10-10).

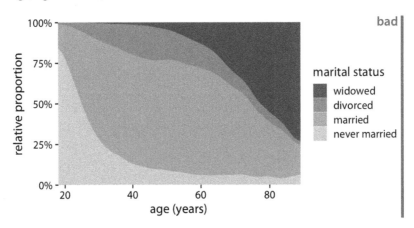

Figure 10-10. Marital status by age. To simplify the figure, I have removed a small number of cases that report as separated. I have labeled this figure as "bad" because the frequency of people who have never been married or are widowed changes so drastically with age that the age distributions of married and divorced people are highly distorted and difficult to interpret. Data source: GSS.

The same dataset visualized as partial densities is much clearer (Figure 10-11). In particular, we see that the proportion of married people peaks around the late 30s, the proportion of divorced people peaks around the early 40s, and the proportion of widowed people peaks around the mid 70s.

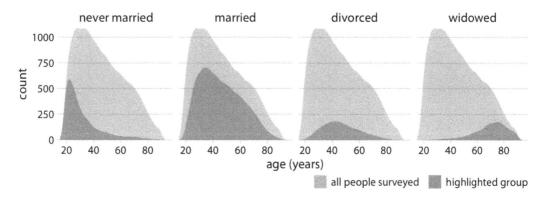

Figure 10-11. Marital status by age, shown as proportion of the total number of people in the survey. The colored areas show the density estimates of the ages of people with the respective marital status, and the gray areas show the overall age distribution. Data source: GSS.

However, one downside of Figure 10-11 is that this representation doesn't make it easy to determine relative proportions at any given point in time. For example, if we wanted to know at what age more than 50% of all people surveyed are married, we could not easily tell from Figure 10-11. To answer this question, we can use the same type of display but show relative proportions instead of absolute counts along the *y* axis (Figure 10-12). Now we see that married people are in the majority starting in the late 20s, and widowed people are in the majority starting in the mid 70s.

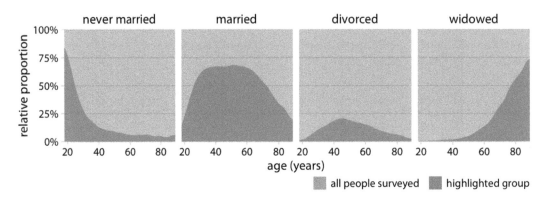

Figure 10-12. Marital status by age, shown as proportion of the total number of people in the survey. The areas colored in blue show the percent of people at the given age with the respective status, and the areas colored in gray show the percent of people with all other marital statuses. Data source: GSS.

## CHAPTER 11

Visualizing Nested Proportions

In the preceding chapter, I discussed scenarios where a dataset is broken into pieces defined by one categorical variable, such as political party, company, or health status. It is not uncommon, however, that we want to drill down further and break down a dataset by multiple categorical variables at once. For example, in the case of parliamentary seats, we could be interested in the proportions of seats by party and by the gender of the representatives. Similarly, in the case of people's health status, we could ask how health status further breaks down by marital status. I refer to these scenarios as *nested proportions*, because each additional categorical variable that we add creates a finer subdivision of the data nested within the previous proportions. There are several suitable approaches to visualize such nested proportions, including mosaic plots, treemaps, and parallel sets.

Nested Proportions Gone Wrong

I will begin by demonstrating two flawed approaches to visualizing nested proportions. While these approaches may seem nonsensical to any experienced data scientist, I have seen them in the wild and therefore think they warrant discussion. Throughout this chapter, I will work with a dataset of 106 bridges in Pittsburgh. This dataset contains various pieces of information about the bridges, such as the material from which they are constructed (steel, iron, or wood) and the year when they were erected. Based on the year of erection, bridges are grouped into distinct categories, such as crafts bridges that were erected before 1870 and modern bridges that were erected after 1940.

Let's assume we want to visualize both the fraction of bridges made from steel, iron, or wood and the fraction that are crafts or modern. We might be tempted to do so by drawing a combined pie chart (Figure 11-1). However, this visualization is not valid. All the slices in a pie chart must add up to 100%, and here the slices add up to 135%.

We reach a total percentage in excess of 100% because we are double-counting bridges. Every bridge in the dataset is made of steel, iron, or wood, so these three slices of the pie already represent 100% of the bridges. Every crafts or modern bridge is also a steel, iron, or wood bridge, and hence is counted twice in the pie chart.

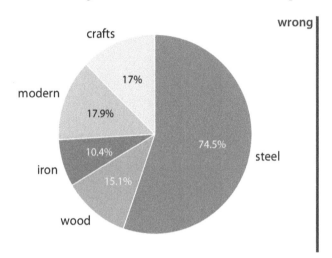

Figure 11-1. Breakdown of bridges in Pittsburgh by construction material (steel, wood, iron) and by date of construction (crafts, before 1870, and modern, after 1940), shown as a pie chart. Numbers represent the percentages of bridges of a given type among all bridges. This figure is invalid, because the percentages add up to more than 100%. There is overlap between construction material and date of construction. For example, all modern bridges are made of steel, and the majority of crafts bridges are made of wood. Data source: Yoram Reich and Steven J. Fenves, via the UCI Machine Learning Repository [Dua and Karra Taniskidou 2017].

Double-counting is not necessarily a problem if we choose a visualization that does not require the proportions to sum to 100%. As discussed in the preceding chapter, side-by-side bars meet this criterion. We can show the various proportions of bridges as bars in a single plot, and this plot is not technically wrong (Figure 11-2). Nevertheless, I have labeled it as "bad" because it does not immediately show that there is overlap among some of the categories shown. A casual observer might conclude from Figure 11-2 that there are five separate categories of bridges, and that, for example, modern bridges are neither made of steel nor of wood or iron.

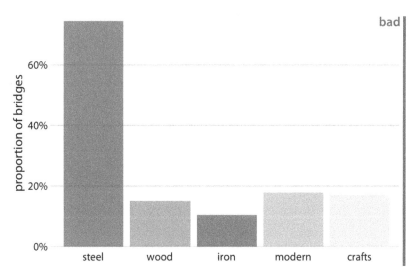

Figure 11-2. Breakdown of bridges in Pittsburgh by construction material (steel, wood, iron) and by date of construction (crafts, before 1870, and modern, after 1940), shown as a bar plot. Unlike Figure 11-1, this visualization is not technically wrong, since it doesn't imply that the bar heights need to add up to 100%. However, it also does not clearly indicate the overlap among different groups, and therefore I have labeled it "bad." Data source: Yoram Reich and Steven J. Fenves.

Mosaic Plots and Treemaps

Whenever we have categories that overlap, it is best to show explicitly how they relate to each other. This can be done with a *mosaic plot* (Figure 11-3). On first glance, a mosaic plot looks similar to a stacked bar plot (e.g., Figure 10-5). However, unlike in a stacked bar plot, in a mosaic plot both the heights and the widths of individual shaded areas vary. Note that in Figure 11-3, we see two additional construction eras, emerging (from 1870 to 1889) and mature (1890 to 1939). In combination with crafts and modern, these construction eras cover all bridges in the dataset, as do the three building materials. This is a critical condition for a mosaic plot: every categorical variable shown must cover all the observations in the dataset.

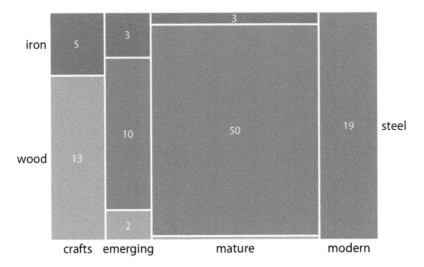

Figure 11-3. Breakdown of bridges in Pittsburgh by construction material (steel, wood, iron) and by era of construction (crafts, emerging, mature, modern), shown as a mosaic plot. The widths of each rectangle are proportional to the number of bridges constructed in that era, and the heights are proportional to the number of bridges constructed from that material. Numbers represent the counts of bridges within each category. Data source: Yoram Reich and Steven J. Fenves.

To draw a mosaic plot, we begin by placing one categorical variable along the *x* axis (here, era of bridge construction) and subdividing the *x* axis by the relative proportions that make up the categories. We then place the other categorical variable along the *y* axis (here, building material) and, within each category along the *x* axis, subdivide the *y* axis by the relative proportions that make up the categories of the *y* variable. The result is a set of rectangles whose areas are proportional to the number of cases representing each possible combination of the two categorical variables.

The bridges dataset can also be visualized in a related but distinct format called a *treemap*. In a treemap, just as is the case in a mosaic plot, we take an enclosing rectangle and subdivide it into smaller rectangles whose areas represent the proportions. However, the method of placing the smaller rectangles into the larger one is different compared to the mosaic plot. In a treemap, we recursively nest rectangles inside each other. For example, in the case of the Pittsburgh bridges, we can first subdivide the total area into three parts representing the three building materials, wood, iron, and steel. Then we can subdivide each of those areas further to represent the construction eras represented for each building material (Figure 11-4). In principle we could keep going, nesting ever more smaller subdivisions inside each other, though relatively quickly the result would become unwieldy or confusing.

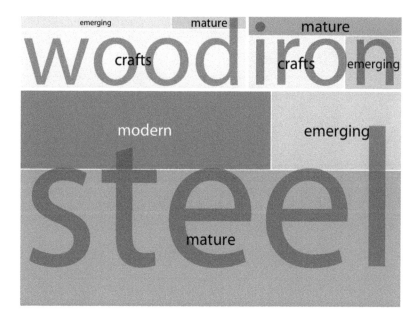

Figure 11-4. Breakdown of bridges in Pittsburgh by construction material (steel, wood, iron) and by era of construction (crafts, emerging, mature, modern), shown as a tree-map. The area of each rectangle is proportional to the number of bridges of that type. Data source: Yoram Reich and Steven J. Fenves.

While mosaic plots and treemaps are closely related, they have different points of emphasis and different application areas. Here, the mosaic plot (Figure 11-3) emphasizes the temporal evolution in building material use from the crafts era to the modern era, whereas the treemap (Figure 11-4) emphasizes the total number of steel, iron, and wood bridges.

More generally, mosaic plots assume that all of the proportions shown can be identified via combinations of two or more orthogonal categorical variables. For example, in Figure 11-3, every bridge can be described by a choice of building material (wood, iron, steel) and a choice of time period (crafts, emerging, mature, modern). Moreover, in principle every combination of these two variables is possible, even though in practice this need not be the case. (Here, there are no steel crafts bridges and no wood or iron modern bridges.) By contrast, such a requirement does not exist for treemaps. In fact, treemaps tend to work well when the proportions cannot meaningfully be described by combining multiple categorical variables. For example, we can separate the US into four regions (West, Northeast, Midwest, and South) and each region into distinct states, but the states in one region have no relationship to the states in another region (Figure 11-5).

Figure 11-5. States in the US visualized as a treemap. Each rectangle represents one state, and the area of each rectangle is proportional to the state's land surface area. The states are grouped into four regions, West, Northeast, Midwest, and South. The coloring is proportional to the number of inhabitants for each state, with darker colors representing larger numbers of inhabitants. Data source: 2010 US Decennial Census.

Both mosaic plots and treemaps are commonly used and can be illuminating, but they have similar limitations to stacked bars (Table 10-1); namely, a direct comparison among conditions can be difficult, because different rectangles do not necessarily share baselines that enable visual comparison. In mosaic plots or treemaps, this problem is exacerbated by the fact that the shapes of the different rectangles can vary. For example, there are the same number of iron bridges (three) among the emerging and mature bridges, but this is difficult to discern in the mosaic plot (Figure 11-3) because the two rectangles representing these two groups of three bridges have entirely different shapes. There isn't necessarily a solution to this problem—visualizing nested proportions can be tricky. Whenever possible, I recommend showing the actual counts or percentages on the plot, so readers can verify that their intuitive interpretation of the shaded areas is correct.

Nested Pies

At the beginning of this chapter, I visualized the bridges dataset with a flawed pie chart (Figure 11-1), and I then argued that a mosaic plot or a treemap is more appropriate. However, both of these latter plot types are closely related to pie charts, since they all use area to represent data values. The primary difference is the type of coordinate system: polar in the case of a pie chart versus Cartesian in the case of a mosaic plot or treemap. This close relationship between these different plots begs the question of whether some variant of a pie chart can be used to visualize this dataset.

There are two possibilities. First, we can draw a pie chart composed of an inner and an outer circle (Figure 11-6). The inner circle shows the breakdown of the data by one variable (here, building material), and the outer circle shows the breakdown of each slice of the inner circle by the second variable (here, era of bridge construction). This visualization is reasonable, but I have my reservations, and therefore I have labeled it "ugly." Most importantly, the two separate circles obscure the fact that each bridge in the dataset has both a building material and an era of construction. In effect, in Figure 11-6, we are still double-counting each bridge. If we add up all the numbers shown in the two circles we obtain 212, which is twice the number of bridges in the dataset.

Alternatively, we can first slice the pie into pieces representing the proportions according to one variable (e.g., material) and then subdivide these slices further according to the other variable (construction era) (Figure 11-7). In this way, in effect we are making a normal pie chart with a large number of small pie slices. However, we can then use coloring to indicate the nested nature of the pie. In Figure 11-7, green colors represent wood bridges, orange colors represent iron bridges, and blue colors represent steel bridges. The darkness of each color represents the construction era, with darker colors corresponding to more recently constructed bridges. By using a nested color scale in this way, we can visualize the breakdown of the data both by the primary variable (construction material) and by the secondary variable (construction era).

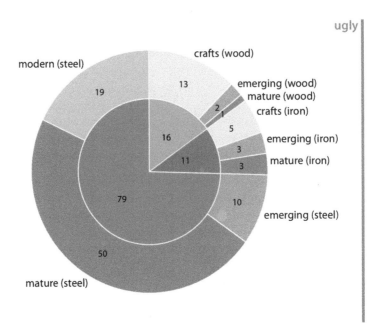

Figure 11-6. Breakdown of bridges in Pittsburgh by construction material (steel, wood, iron; inner circle) and by era of construction (crafts, emerging, mature, modern; outer circle). Numbers represent the counts of bridges within each category. Data source: Yoram Reich and Steven J. Fenves.

The pie chart of Figure 11-7 represents a reasonable visualization of the bridges dataset, but in a direct comparison to the equivalent treemap (Figure 11-4) I think the treemap is preferable, for two reasons. First, the rectangular shape of the treemap allows it to make better use of the available space. Figures 11-4 and 11-7 are of exactly equal size, but in Figure 11-7 much of the figure is wasted as whitespace. Figure 11-4, the treemap, has virtually no superfluous whitespace. This matters because it enables me to place the labels inside the shaded areas in the treemap. Inside labels always create a stronger visual unit with the data than outside labels and hence are preferred. Second, some of the pie slices in Figure 11-7 are very thin and thus hard to see. By contrast, every rectangle in Figure 11-4 is of a reasonable size.

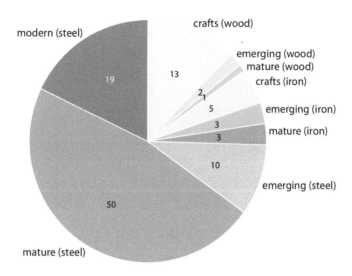

Figure 11-7. Breakdown of bridges in Pittsburgh by construction material (steel, wood, iron) and by era of construction (crafts, emerging, mature, modern). Numbers represent the counts of bridges within each category. Data source: Yoram Reich and Steven J. Fenves.

Parallel Sets

When we want to visualize proportions described by more than two categorical variables, mosaic plots, treemaps, and pie charts all can quickly become unwieldy. A viable alternative in this case can be a *parallel sets plot*. In a parallel sets plot, we show how the total dataset breaks down by each individual categorical variable, and then we draw shaded bands that show how the subgroups relate to each other. See Figure 11-8 for an example. In this figure, I have broken down the bridges dataset by construction material (iron, steel, wood), the length of each bridge (long, medium, short), the era during which each bridge was constructed (crafts, emerging, mature, modern), and the river each bridge spans (Allegheny, Monongahela, Ohio). The bands that connect the parallel sets are colored by construction material. This shows, for example, that wood bridges are mostly of medium length (with a few short bridges), were primarily erected during the crafts period (with a few bridges of medium length erected during the emerging and mature periods), and span primarily the Allegheny river (with a few crafts bridges spanning the Monongahela river). By contrast, iron bridges are all of medium length, were primarily erected during the crafts period, and span the Allegheny and Monongahela rivers in approximately equal proportions.

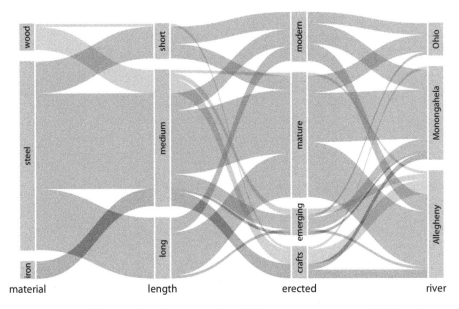

Figure 11-8. Breakdown of bridges in Pittsburgh by construction material, length, era of construction, and the river they span, shown as a parallel sets plot. The coloring of the bands highlights the construction material of the different bridges. Data source: Yoram Reich and Steven J. Fenves.

The same visualization looks quite different if we color by a different criterion, such as by river (Figure 11-9). This figure is visually busy, with many crisscrossing bands, but we do see that nearly any bridge of any type can be found to span each river.

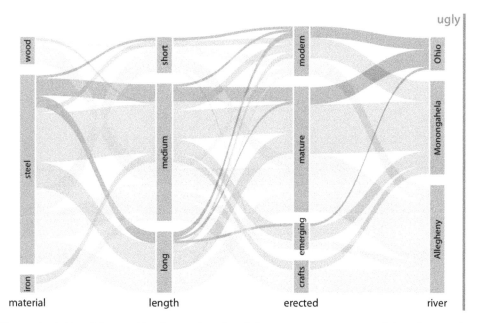

Figure 11-9. Breakdown of bridges in Pittsburgh by construction material, length, era of construction, and the river they span. This figure is similar to Figure 11-8, but now the coloring of the bands highlights the river spanned by the different bridges. This figure is labeled "ugly" because the arrangement of the colored bands in the middle of the figure is very busy, and also because the bands need to be read from right to left. Data source: Yoram Reich and Steven J. Fenves.

I have labeled Figure 11-9 as "ugly" because I think it is overly complex and confusing. First, since we are used to reading from left to right I think the sets that define the coloring should appear all the way to the left, not on the right. This will make it easier to see where the coloring originates and how it flows through the dataset. Second, it is a good idea to change the order of the sets such that the number of crisscrossing bands is minimized. Following these principles, I arrive at Figure 11-10, which I consider preferable to Figure 11-9.

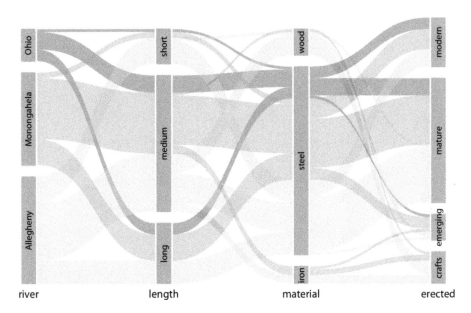

river   length   material   erected

Figure 11-10. Breakdown of bridges in Pittsburgh by river, era of construction, length, and construction material. This figure differs from Figure 11-9 only in the order of the parallel sets. The modified order results in a figure that is easier to read and less busy. Data source: Yoram Reich and Steven J. Fenves.

## CHAPTER 12

Visualizing Associations Among Two or More Quantitative Variables

Many datasets contain two or more quantitative variables, and we may be interested in how these variables relate to each other. For example, we may have a dataset of quantitative measurements of different animals, such as the animals' height, weight, length, and daily energy demands. To plot the relationship of just two such variables, such as the height and weight, we will normally use a scatterplot. If we want to show more than two variables at once, we may opt for a bubble chart, a scatterplot matrix, or a correlogram. Finally, for very high-dimensional datasets, it may be useful to perform dimension reduction, for example in the form of principal components analysis.

Scatterplots

I will demonstrate the basic scatterplot and several variations thereof using a dataset of measurements performed on 123 blue jay birds. The dataset contains information such as the head length (measured from the tip of the bill to the back of the head), the skull size (head length minus bill length), and the body mass of each bird. We expect that there are relationships between these variables. For example, birds with longer bills would be expected to have larger skull sizes, and birds with higher body mass should have larger bills and skulls than birds with lower body mass.

To explore these relationships, I begin with a plot of head length against body mass (Figure 12-1). In this plot, head length is shown along the y axis and body mass along the x axis, and each bird is represented by one dot. (Note the terminology: we say that we plot the variable shown along the y axis against the variable shown along the x axis.) The dots form a dispersed cloud (hence the term *scatterplot*), yet undoubtedly there is a trend for birds with higher body mass to have longer heads. The bird with the longest head falls close to the maximum body mass observed, and the bird with the shortest head falls close to the minimum body mass observed.

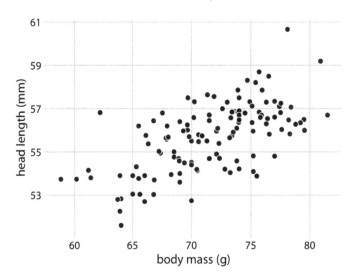

Figure 12-1. Head length (measured from the tip of the bill to the back of the head, in mm) versus body mass (in grams), for 123 blue jays. Each dot corresponds to one bird. There is a moderate tendency for heavier birds to have longer heads. Data source: Keith Tarvin, Oberlin College.

The blue jay dataset contains both male and female birds, and we may want to know whether the overall relationship between head length and body mass holds up separately for each sex. To address this question, we can color the points in the scatterplot by the sex of the bird (Figure 12-2). This figure reveals that the overall trend in head length and body mass is at least in part driven by the sex of the birds. At the same body mass, females tend to have shorter heads than males. At the same time, females tend to be lighter than males on average.

Because the head length is defined as the distance from the tip of the bill to the back of the head, a larger head length could imply a longer bill, a larger skull, or both. We can disentangle bill length and skull size by looking at another variable in the dataset, the skull size, which is similar to the head length but excludes the bill. As we are already using the *x* position for body mass, the *y* position for head length, and the dot color for bird sex, we need another aesthetic to which we can map skull size. One option is to use the size of the dots, resulting in a visualization called a *bubble chart* (Figure 12-3).

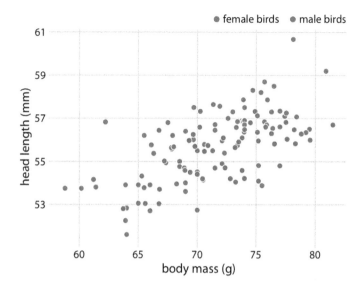

Figure 12-2. *Head length versus body mass for 123 blue jays. The birds' sex is indicated by color. At the same body mass, male birds tend to have longer heads (and specifically, longer bills) than female birds. Data source: Keith Tarvin, Oberlin College.*

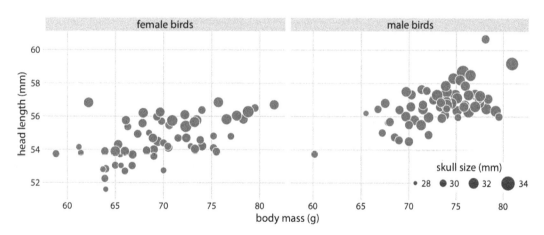

Figure 12-3. *Head length versus body mass for 123 blue jays. The birds' sex is indicated by color and the birds' skull size by symbol size. Head length measurements include the length of the bill while skull size measurements do not. Head length and skull size tend to be correlated, but there are some birds with unusually long or short bills given their skull size. Data source: Keith Tarvin, Oberlin College.*

Bubble charts have the disadvantage that they show the same types of variables—quantitative variables—with two different types of scales, position and size. This makes it difficult to visually ascertain the strengths of associations between the various variables. Moreover, differences between data values encoded as bubble size are harder to perceive than differences between data values encoded as position. Because even the largest bubbles need to be somewhat small compared to the total figure size, the size differences between the largest and the smallest bubbles are necessarily small. Consequently, smaller differences in data values will correspond to very small size differences that can be virtually impossible to see. In Figure 12-3, I used a size mapping that visually amplifies the difference between the smallest skulls (around 28 mm) and the largest skulls (around 34 mm), and yet it is difficult to determine what the relationship is between skull size and either body mass or head length.

As an alternative to a bubble chart, it may be preferable to show an all-against-all matrix of scatterplots, where each individual plot shows two data dimensions (Figure 12-4). This figure shows clearly that the relationship between skull size and body mass is comparable for female and male birds, except that the female birds tend to be somewhat smaller. However, the same is not true for the relationship between head length and body mass. There is a clear separation by sex. Male birds tend to have longer bills than female birds, all else being equal.

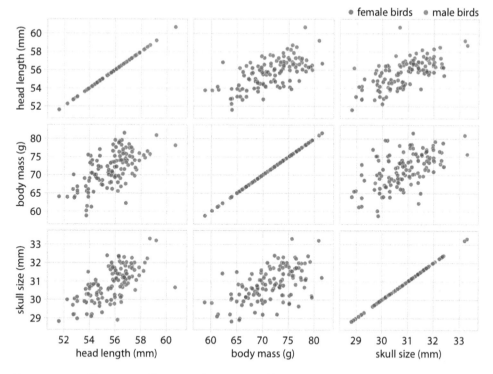

Figure 12-4. All-against-all scatterplot matrix of head length, body mass, and skull size, for 123 blue jays. This figure shows the exact same data as Figure 12-3. Because we are better at judging position than symbol size, correlations between skull size and the other two variables are easier to perceive in the pairwise scatterplots than in Figure 12-3. Data source: Keith Tarvin, Oberlin College.

Correlograms

When we have more than three to four quantitative variables, all-against-all scatterplot matrices quickly become unwieldy. In this case, it is more useful to quantify the amount of association between pairs of variables and visualize these quantities rather than the raw data. One common way to do this is to calculate *correlation coefficients*. The correlation coefficient r is a number between −1 and 1 that measures to what extent two variables covary. A value of $r = 0$ means there is no association whatsoever, and a value of either 1 or −1 indicates a perfect association. The sign of the correlation coefficient indicates whether the variables are *correlated* (larger values in one variable coincide with larger values in the other) or *anticorrelated* (larger values in one variable coincide with smaller values in the other). To provide visual examples of what different correlation strengths look like, in Figure 12-5 I show randomly generated sets of points that differ widely in the degree to which the *x* and *y* values are correlated.

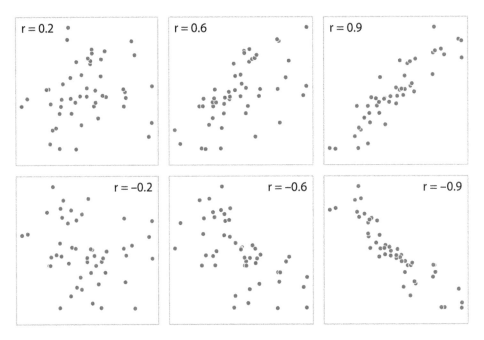

Figure 12-5. Examples of correlations of different magnitude and direction, with associated correlation coefficient r. In both rows, from left to right correlations go from weak to strong. In the top row the correlations are positive (larger values for one quantity are associated with larger values for the other) and in the bottom row they are negative (larger values for one quantity are associated with smaller values for the other). In all six panels, the sets of x and y values are identical, but the pairings between individual x and y values have been reshuffled to generate the specified correlation coefficients.

The correlation coefficient is defined as:

$$r = \frac{\Sigma_i (x_i - \bar{x})(y_i - \bar{y})}{\sqrt{\Sigma_i (x_i - \bar{x})^2} \sqrt{\Sigma_i (y_i - \bar{y})^2}}$$

where x_i and y_i are two sets of observations and $\bar{x}$ and $\bar{y}$ are the corresponding sample means. We can make a number of observations from this formula. First, the formula is symmetric in x_i and y_i, so the correlation of *x* with *y* is the same as the correlation of *y* with *x*. Second, the individual values x_i and y_i only enter the formula in the context of differences from the respective sample mean, so if we shift an entire dataset by a constant amount—for example, if we replace x_i with $x_i' = x_i + C$ for some constant

C—the correlation coefficient remains unchanged. Third, the correlation coefficient also remains unchanged if we rescale the data (e.g., $x_i' = Cx_i$), since the constant *C* will appear both in the numerator and the denominator of the formula and hence can be canceled.

Visualizations of correlation coefficients are called *correlograms*. To illustrate the use of a correlogram, we will consider a dataset of over 200 glass fragments obtained during forensic work. For each glass fragment, we have measurements about its composition, expressed as the percent in weight of various mineral oxides. There are seven different oxides for which we have measurements, yielding a total of 6 + 5 + 4 + 3 + 2 + 1 = 21 pairwise correlations. We can display these 21 correlations at once as a matrix of colored tiles, where each tile represents one correlation coefficient (Figure 12-6). This correlogram allows us to quickly grasp trends in the data, such as that magnesium is negatively correlated with nearly all other oxides, and that aluminum and barium have a strong positive correlation.

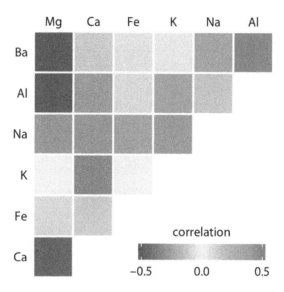

Figure 12-6. Correlations in mineral content for 214 samples of glass fragments obtained during forensic work. The dataset contains seven variables measuring the amounts of magnesium (Mg), calcium (Ca), iron (Fe), potassium (K), sodium (Na), aluminum (Al), and barium (Ba) found in each glass fragment. The colored tiles represent the correlations between pairs of these variables. Data source: B. German.

One weakness of the correlogram of Figure 12-6 is that low correlations—i.e., correlations with absolute value near zero—are not as visually suppressed as they should be. For example, magnesium (Mg) and potassium (K) are not at all correlated, but Figure 12-6 doesn't immediately show this. To overcome this limitation, we can display the correlations as colored circles and scale the circle size with the absolute value of the correlation coefficient (Figure 12-7). In this way, low correlations are suppressed and high correlations stand out better.

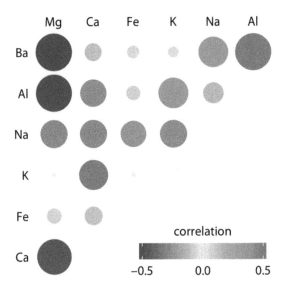

Figure 12-7. Correlations in mineral content for forensic glass samples. The color scale is identical to Figure 12-6. However, now the magnitude of each correlation is also encoded in the size of the colored circles. This choice visually deemphasizes cases with correlations near zero. Data source: B. German.

All correlograms have one important drawback: they are fairly abstract. While they show us important patterns in the data, they also hide the underlying data points and may cause us to draw incorrect conclusions. It is always better to visualize the raw data rather than abstract derived quantities that have been calculated from it. Fortunately, we can frequently find a middle ground between showing important patterns and showing the raw data by applying techniques of dimension reduction.

Dimension Reduction

Dimension reduction relies on the key insight that most high-dimensional datasets consist of multiple correlated variables that convey overlapping information. Such datasets can be reduced to a smaller number of key dimensions without loss of much critical information. As a simple, intuitive example, consider a dataset of multiple physical traits of people, including quantities such as each person's height and weight, the lengths of their arms and legs, the circumferences of their waist, hips, and chest, etc. We can understand intuitively that all these quantities will relate first and foremost to the overall size of each person. All else being equal, a larger person will be taller, weigh more, have longer arms and legs, and have larger waist, hip, and chest circumferences. The next important dimension is going to be the person's sex. Male and female measurements are substantially different for persons of comparable size. For example, a woman will tend to have higher hip circumference than a man, all else being equal.

There are many techniques for dimension reduction. I will discuss only one technique here, the most widely used one, called *principal components analysis* (PCA). PCA introduces a new set of variables, called principal components (PCs), by linear combination of the original variables in the data, standardized to zero mean and unit variance (see Figure 12-8 for a toy example in two dimensions). The PCs are chosen such that they are uncorrelated, and they are ordered such that the first component captures the largest possible amount of variation in the data and subsequent components capture increasingly less. Usually, key features in the data can be seen from only the first two or three PCs.

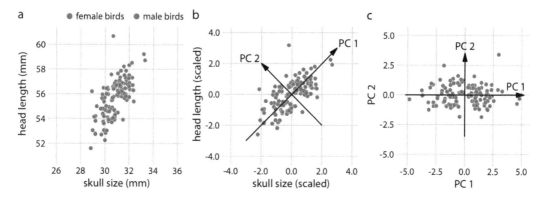

Figure 12-8. Example principal components analysis in two dimensions. (a) The original data. As example data, I am using the head length and skull size measurements from the blue jays dataset. Female and male birds are distinguished by color, but this distinction has no effect on the PCA. (b) As the first step in PCA, we scale the original data values to zero mean and unit variance. We then define new variables (the principal components) along the directions of maximum variation in the data. (c) Finally, we project the data into the new coordinates. Mathematically, this projection is equivalent to a rotation of the data points around the origin. In the 2D example shown here, the data points are rotated clockwise by 45 degrees. Data source: Keith Tarvin, Oberlin College.

When we perform PCA, we are generally interested in two pieces of information: the composition of the PCs and the locations of the individual data points in the principal components space. Let's look at these two pieces in a PCA of the forensic glass dataset.

First, we look at the component composition (Figure 12-9). Here, we only consider the first two components, PC 1 and PC 2. Because the PCs are linear combinations of the original variables (after standardization), we can represent the original variables as arrows indicating to what extent they contribute to the PCs. Here, we see that barium and sodium contribute primarily to PC 1 and not to PC 2, calcium and potassium contribute primarily to PC 2 and not to PC 1, and the other variables contribute in varying amounts to both components. The arrows are of varying lengths because there are more than two PCs. For example, the arrow for iron is particularly short because it contributes primarily to higher-order PCs (not shown).

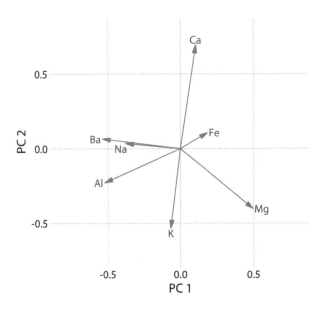

Figure 12-9. Composition of the first two components in a principal components analysis of the forensic glass dataset. Component one (PC 1) measures primarily the amount of aluminum, barium, sodium, and magnesium in a glass fragment, whereas component two (PC 2) measures primarily the amount of calcium and potassium, and to some extent the amount of aluminum and magnesium. Data source: B. German.

Next, we project the original data into the principal components space (Figure 12-10). We see a defined clustering of distinct types of glass fragments in this plot. Fragments from both headlamps and windows fall into clearly delineated regions in the PC plot, with few outliers. Fragments from tableware and from containers are a little more spread out, but nevertheless clearly distinct from both headlamp and window fragments. By comparing Figure 12-10 with Figure 12-9, we can conclude that window samples tend to have higher than average magnesium content and lower than average barium, aluminum, and sodium content, whereas the opposite is true for headlamp samples.

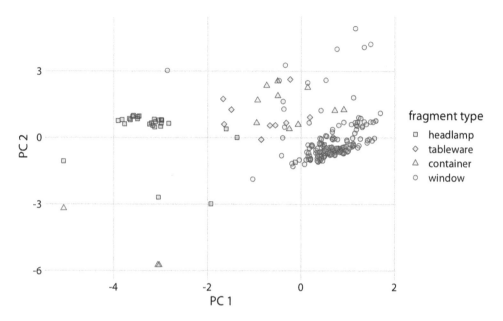

Figure 12-10. Composition of individual glass fragments visualized in the principal components space defined in Figure 12-9. We see that the different types of glass samples cluster at characteristic values of PCs 1 and 2. In particular, headlamps are characterized by a negative PC 1 value whereas windows tend to have a positive PC 1 value. Tableware and containers have PC 1 values close to zero and tend to have positive PC 2 values. However, there are a few exceptions where container fragments have both a negative PC 1 value and a negative PC 2 value. These are fragments whose composition drastically differs from all other fragments analyzed. Data source: B. German.

Paired Data

A special case of multivariate quantitative data is *paired data*: data where there are two or more measurements of the same quantity under slightly different conditions. Examples include two comparable measurements on each subject (e.g., the length of the right and the left arm of a person), repeat measurements on the same subject at different time points (e.g., a person's weight at two different times during the year), or measurements on two closely related subjects (e.g., the heights of two identical twins). For paired data, it is reasonable to assume that the two measurements belonging to each pair are more similar to each other than to the measurements belonging to other pairs. Two twins will be approximately of the same height but will differ in height from other twins. Therefore, for paired data, we need to choose visualizations that highlight any differences between the paired measurements.

An excellent choice in this case is a simple scatterplot on top of a diagonal line marking $x = y$. In such a plot, if the only difference between the two measurements of each pair is random noise, then all points in the sample will be scattered symmetrically around this line. Any systematic differences between the paired measurements, by contrast, will be visible in a systematic shift of the data points up or down relative to the diagonal. As an example, consider the carbon dioxide (CO_2) emissions per person, measured for 166 countries both in 1970 and in 2010 (Figure 12-11). This example highlights two common features of paired data. First, most points are relatively close to the diagonal line. Even though CO_2 emissions vary over nearly four orders of magnitude among countries, they are fairly consistent within each country over a 40-year time span. Second, the points are systematically shifted upwards relative to the diagonal line. The majority of countries have seen an increase in CO_2 emissions over the 40 years considered.

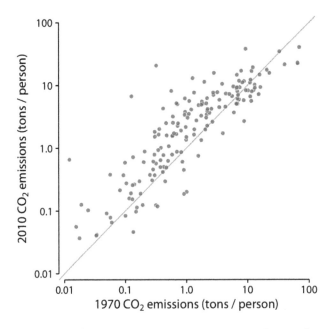

Figure 12-11. Carbon dioxide emissions per person in 1970 and 2010, for 166 countries. Each dot represents one country. The diagonal line represents identical CO_2 emissions in 1970 and 2010. The points are systematically shifted upwards relative to the diagonal line: in the majority of countries, emissions were higher in 2010 than in 1970. Data source: Carbon Dioxide Information Analysis Center.

Scatterplots such as Figure 12-11 work well when we have a large number of data points and/or are interested in a systematic deviation of the entire dataset from the null expectation. By contrast, if we have only a small number of observations and are primarily interested in the identity of each individual case, a *slopegraph* may be a better choice. In a slopegraph, we draw individual measurements as dots arranged into two columns and indicate pairings by connecting the paired dots with a line. The slope of each line highlights the magnitude and direction of change. Figure 12-12 uses this approach to show the 10 countries with the largest difference in CO_2 emissions per person from 2000 to 2010.

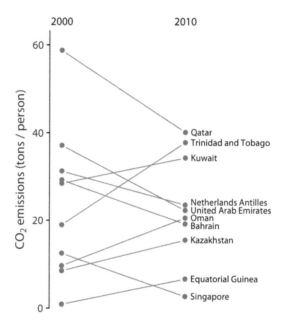

Figure 12-12. Carbon dioxide emissions per person in 2000 and 2010, for the 10 countries with the largest difference between these 2 years. Data source: Carbon Dioxide Information Analysis Center.

Slopegraphs have one important advantage over scatterplots: they can be used to compare more than two measurements at a time. For example, we can modify Figure 12-12 to show CO_2 emissions at three time points, here the years 2000, 2005, and 2010 (Figure 12-13). This choice highlights countries with a large change in emissions over the entire decade as well as countries such as Qatar or Trinidad and Tobago for which there is a large difference in the trend seen for the first five-year interval and the second one.

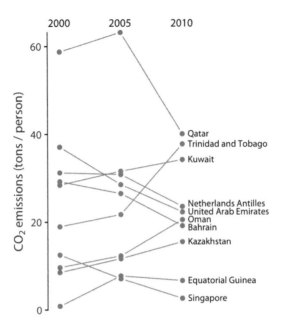

Figure 12-13. CO₂ emissions per person in 2000, 2005, and 2010, for the 10 countries with the largest difference between the years 2000 and 2010. Data source: Carbon Dioxide Information Analysis Center.

## CHAPTER 13

Visualizing Time Series and Other Functions of an Independent Variable

The preceding chapter discussed scatterplots, where we plot one quantitative variable against another. A special case arises when one of the two variables can be thought of as time, because time imposes additional structure on the data. Now the data points have an inherent order; we can arrange the points in order of increasing time and define a predecessor and successor for each data point. We frequently want to visualize this temporal order, and we do so with line graphs. Line graphs are not limited to time series, however. They are appropriate whenever one variable imposes an ordering on the data. This scenario arises also, for example, in a controlled experiment where a treatment variable is purposefully set to a range of different values. If we have multiple variables that depend on time, we can either draw separate line plots or we can draw a regular scatterplot and then draw lines to connect the neighboring points in time.

Individual Time Series

As a first demonstration of a time series, we will consider the pattern of monthly preprint submissions in biology. Preprints are scientific articles that researchers post online before formal peer review and publication in a scientific journal. The preprint server bioRxiv, which was founded in November 2013 specifically for researchers working in the biological sciences, has seen substantial growth in monthly submissions since. We can visualize this growth by making a form of scatterplot (Chapter 12) where we draw dots representing the number of submissions in each month (Figure 13-1).

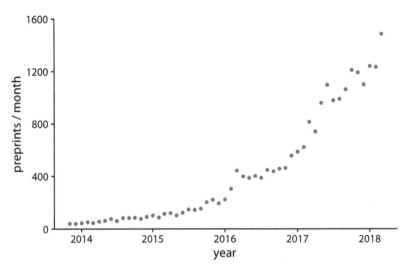

Figure 13-1. Monthly submissions to the preprint server bioRxiv, from its inception in November 2013 until April 2018. Each dot represents the number of submissions in one month. There has been a steady increase in submission volume throughout the entire 4.5-year period. Data source: Jordan Anaya, http://www.prepubmed.org.

There is an important difference, however, between Figure 13-1 and the scatterplots discussed in Chapter 12. In Figure 13-1, the dots are spaced evenly along the *x* axis, and there is a defined order among them. Each dot has exactly one left and one right neighbor (except the leftmost and rightmost points, which have only one neighbor each). We can visually emphasize this order by connecting neighboring points with lines (Figure 13-2). Such a plot is called a *line graph*.

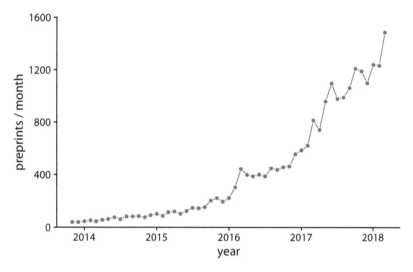

Figure 13-2. Monthly submissions to the preprint server bioRxiv, shown as dots connected by lines. The lines do not represent data and are only meant as a guide to the eye. By connecting the individual dots with lines, we emphasize that there is an order between the dots: each dot has exactly one neighbor that comes before it and one that comes after. Data source: Jordan Anaya, http://www.prepubmed.org.

Some people object to drawing lines between points because the lines do not represent observed data. In particular, if there are only a few observations spaced far apart, had observations been made at intermediate times they would probably not have fallen exactly onto the lines shown. Thus, in a sense, the lines correspond to made-up data. Yet they may help with perception when the points are spaced far apart or are unevenly spaced. We can somewhat resolve this dilemma by pointing it out in the figure caption, for example by writing "lines are meant as a guide to the eye" (see caption of Figure 13-2).

Using lines to represent time series is generally accepted practice, however, and frequently the dots are omitted altogether (Figure 13-3). Without dots, the figure places more emphasis on the overall trend in the data and less on individual observations. A figure without dots is also visually less busy. In general, the denser the time series, the less important it is to show individual observations with dots. For the preprint dataset shown here, I think omitting the dots is fine.

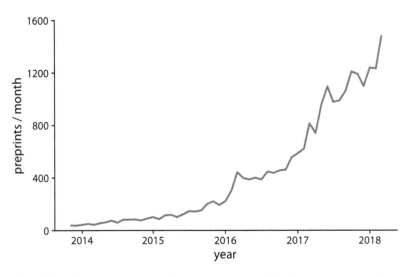

Figure 13-3. Monthly submissions to the preprint server bioRxiv, shown as a line graph without dots. Omitting the dots emphasizes the overall temporal trend while deemphasizing individual observations at specific time points. It is particularly useful when the time points are spaced very densely. Data source: Jordan Anaya, http://www.prepubmed.org.

We can also fill the area under the curve with a solid color (Figure 13-4). This choice further emphasizes the overarching trend in the data, because it visually separates the area above the curve from the area below. However, this visualization is only valid if the y axis starts at zero, so that the height of the shaded area at each time point represents the data value at that time point.

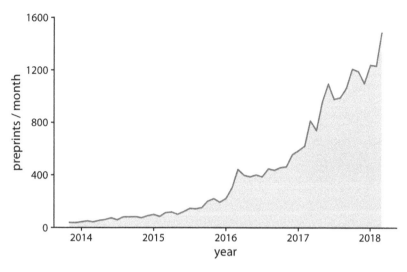

Figure 13-4. Monthly submissions to the preprint server bioRxiv, shown as a line graph with filled area underneath. By filling the area under the curve, we put even more emphasis on the overarching temporal trend than if we just draw a line (Figure 13-3). Data source: Jordan Anaya, http://www.prepubmed.org.

Multiple Time Series and Dose–Response Curves

We often have multiple time courses that we want to show at once. In this case, we have to be more careful in how we plot the data, because the figure can become confusing or difficult to read. For example, if we want to show the monthly submissions to multiple preprint servers, a scatterplot is not a good idea, because the individual time courses run into each other (Figure 13-5). Connecting the dots with lines alleviates this issue (Figure 13-6).

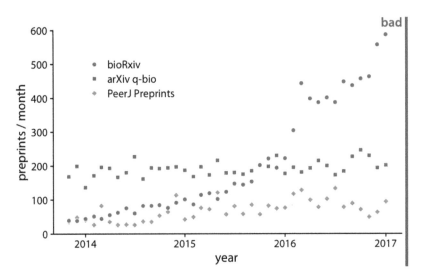

Figure 13-5. Monthly submissions to three preprint servers covering biomedical research: bioRxiv, the q-bio section of arXiv, and PeerJ Preprints. Each dot represents the number of submissions in one month to the respective preprint server. This figure is labeled "bad" because the three time courses visually interfere with each other and are difficult to read. Data source: Jordan Anaya, http://www.prepubmed.org.

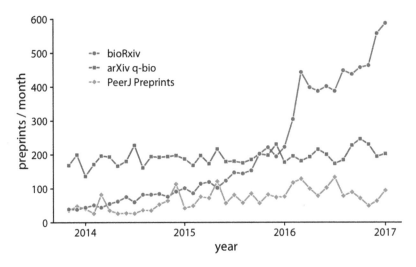

Figure 13-6. Monthly submissions to three preprint servers covering biomedical research. By connecting the dots in Figure 13-5 with lines, we help the viewer follow each individual time course. Data source: Jordan Anaya, http://www.prepubmed.org.

Figure 13-6 represents an acceptable visualization of the preprints dataset. However, the separate legend creates unnecessary cognitive load. We can reduce this cognitive load by labeling the lines directly (Figure 13-7). I have also eliminated the individual dots in this figure, for a result that is much more streamlined and easy to read than the original starting point, Figure 13-5.

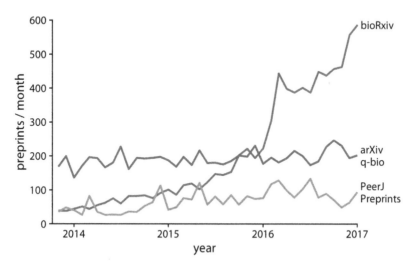

Figure 13-7. Monthly submissions to three preprint servers covering biomedical research. Directly labeling the lines instead of providing a legend reduces the cognitive load required to read the figure, and eliminating the legend removes the need for points of different shapes. This enables us to streamline Figure 13-6 further by eliminating the dots. Data source: Jordan Anaya, http://www.prepubmed.org.

Line graphs are not limited to time series. They are appropriate whenever the data points have a natural order that is reflected in the variable shown along the x axis, so that neighboring points can be connected with a line. This situation arises, for example, in dose–response curves, where we measure how changing some numerical parameter in an experiment (the dose) affects an outcome of interest (the response). Figure 13-8 shows a classic experiment of this type, measuring oat yield in response to increasing amounts of fertilization. The line graph visualization highlights how the dose–response curves have a similar shape for the three oat varieties considered but differ in the starting point in the absence of fertilization (i.e., some varieties have naturally higher yield than others).

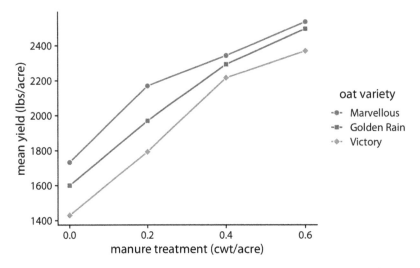

Figure 13-8. Dose–response curve showing the mean yield of oat varieties after fertilization with manure. The manure serves as a source of nitrogen, and oat yields generally increase as more nitrogen is available, regardless of variety. Here, manure application is measured in cwt (hundredweight) per acre. The hundredweight is an old imperial unit equal to 112 lbs or 50.8 kg. Data source: [Yates 1935].

Time Series of Two or More Response Variables

In the preceding examples we dealt with time courses of only a single response variable (e.g., preprint submissions per month or oat yield). It is not unusual, however, to have more than one response variable. Such situations arise commonly in macroeconomics. For example, we may be interested in the change in house prices from the previous 12 months as it relates to the unemployment rate. We may expect that house prices rise when the unemployment rate is low, and vice versa.

With the tools from the preceding sections, we can visualize such data as two separate line graphs stacked on top of each other (Figure 13-9). This plot directly shows the two variables of interest, and it is straightforward to interpret. However, because the two variables are shown as separate line graphs, drawing comparisons between them can be cumbersome. If we want to identify temporal regions when both variables move in the same or in opposite directions, we need to switch back and forth between the two graphs and compare the relative slopes of the two curves.

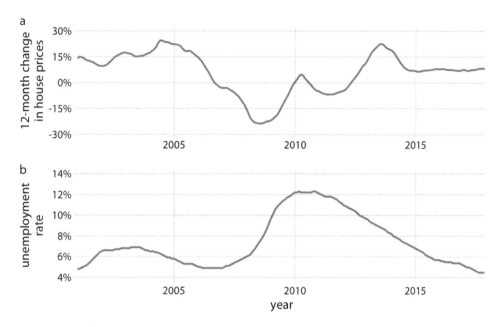

Figure 13-9. Twelve-month change in house prices (a) and unemployment rate (b) over time, from January 2001 through December 2017. Data sources: Freddie Mac House Prices Index, US Bureau of Labor Statistics.

As an alternative to showing two separate line graphs, we can plot the two variables against each other, drawing a path that leads from the earliest time point to the latest (Figure 13-10). Such a visualization is called a *connected scatterplot*, because we are technically making a scatterplot of the two variables against each other and then are connecting neighboring points. Physicists and engineers often call this a *phase portrait*, because in their disciplines it is commonly used to represent movement in phase space. We have previously encountered connected scatterplots in Chapter 3, where I plotted the daily temperature normals in Houston, TX, versus those in San Diego, CA (Figure 3-3).

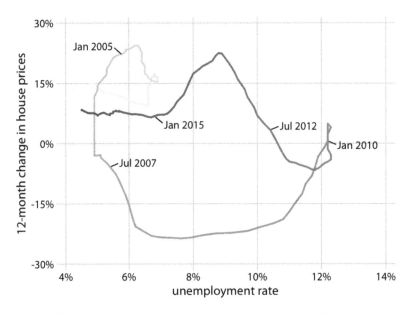

Figure 13-10. Twelve-month change in house prices versus unemployment rate, from January 2001 through December 2017, shown as a connected scatterplot. Darker shades represent more recent months. The anticorrelation seen in Figure 13-9 between the change in house prices and the unemployment rate causes the connected scatterplot to form two counterclockwise circles. Original figure concept: Len Kiefer. Data sources: Freddie Mac House Price Index, US Bureau of Labor Statistics.

In a connected scatterplot, lines going in the direction from the lower left to the upper right represent correlated movement between the two variables (as one variable grows, so does the other), and lines going in the perpendicular direction, from the upper left to the lower right, represent anticorrelated movement (as one variable grows, the other shrinks). If the two variables have a somewhat cyclic relationship, we will see circles or spirals in the connected scatterplot. In Figure 13-10, we see one small circle from 2001 through 2005 and one large circle for the remainder of the time course.

When drawing a connected scatterplot, it is important that we indicate both the direction and the temporal scale of the data. Without such hints, the plot can turn into a meaningless scribble (Figure 13-11). In Figure 13-10 I used a gradual darkening of the color to indicate direction; alternatively, one could draw arrows along the path.

Is it better to use a connected scatterplot or two separate line graphs? Separate line graphs tend to be easier to read, but once people are used to connected scatterplots they may be able to extract certain patterns (such as cyclical behavior with some irregularity) that can be difficult to spot in line graphs. In fact, to me the cyclical relationship between change in house prices and unemployment rate is hard to spot in Figure 13-9, but the counterclockwise spiral in Figure 13-10 reveals it. Research reports that readers are more likely to confuse order and direction in a connected scatterplot than in line graphs, and less likely to report correlation [Haroz, Kosara, and Franconeri 2016]. On the flip side, connected scatterplots seem to result in higher engagement, and thus such plots may be effective tools to draw readers into a story.

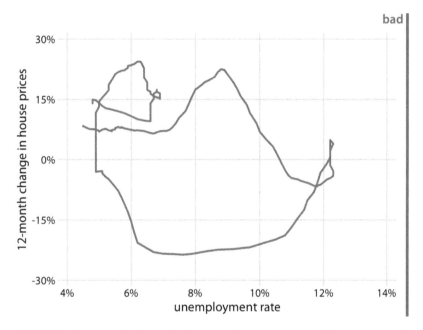

Figure 13-11. Twelve-month change in house prices versus unemployment rate, from January 2001 through December 2017. This figure is labeled "bad" because without the date markers and color shading of Figure 13-10, we can see neither the direction nor the speed of change in the data. Data sources: Freddie Mac House Prices Index, US Bureau of Labor Statistics.

Even though connected scatterplots can show only two variables at a time, we can also use them to visualize higher-dimensional datasets. The trick is to apply dimension reduction first (see Chapter 12). We can then draw a connected scatterplot in the dimension-reduced space. As an example of this approach, we will visualize a database of monthly observations of over 100 macroeconomic indicators, provided by the Federal Reserve Bank of St. Louis. We perform a principal components analysis (PCA) of all indicators and then draw a connected scatterplot of PC 2 versus PC 1 (Figure 13-12a) and versus PC 3 (Figure 13-12b).

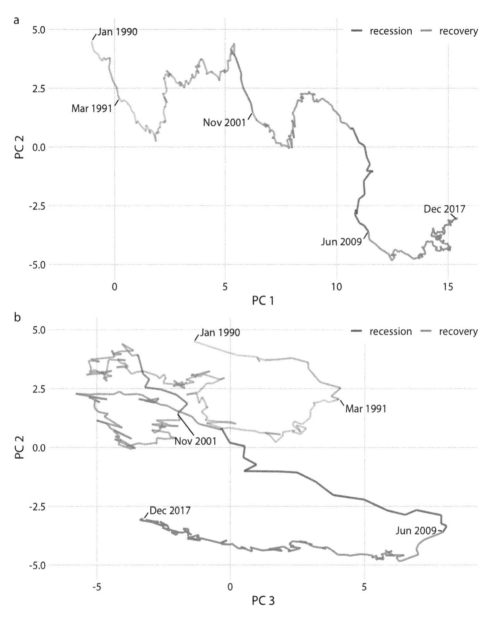

Figure 13-12. Visualizing a high-dimensional time series as a connected scatterplot in principal components space. The path indicates the joint movement of over 100 macro-economic indicators from January 1990 to December 2017. Times of recession and recovery are indicated via color, and the endpoints of the three recessions (March 1991, November 2001, and June 2009) are also labeled. (a) PC 2 versus PC 1. (b) PC 2 versus PC 3. Data source: M. W. McCracken, St. Louis Fed.

Notably, Figure 13-12a looks almost like a regular line plot, with time running from left to right. This pattern is caused by a common feature of PCA: the first component often measures the overall size of the system. Here, PC 1 approximately measures the overall size of the economy, which rarely decreases over time.

By coloring the connected scatterplot by times of recession and recovery, we can see that recessions are associated with a drop in PC 2 whereas recoveries do not correspond to a specific feature in either PC 1 or PC 2 (Figure 13-12a). The recoveries do, however, seem to correspond to a drop in PC 3 (Figure 13-12b). Moreover, in the PC 2 versus PC 3 plot, we see that the line follows the shape of a clockwise spiral. This pattern emphasizes the cyclical nature of the economy, with recessions following recoveries and vice versa.

## CHAPTER 14

Visualizing Trends

When making scatterplots (Chapter 12) or time series (Chapter 13), we are often more interested in the overarching trend of the data than in the specific detail of where each individual data point lies. By drawing the trend on top of or instead of the actual data points, usually in the form of a straight or curved line, we can create a visualization that helps the reader immediately see key features of the data. There are two fundamental approaches to determining a trend: we can either smooth the data by some method, such as a moving average, or we can fit a curve with a defined functional form and then draw the fitted curve. Once we have identified a trend in a dataset, it may also be useful to look specifically at deviations from the trend or to separate the data into multiple components, including the underlying trend, any existing cyclical components, and episodic components or random noise.

Smoothing

Let us consider a time series of the Dow Jones Industrial Average (Dow Jones for short), a stock market index representing the price of 30 large, publicly owned US companies. Specifically, we will look at the year 2009, right after the 2008 crash (Figure 14-1). During the tail end of the crash, in the first 3 months of the year 2009, the market lost over 2,400 points (~27%). Then it slowly recovered for the remainder of the year. How can we visualize these longer-term trends while deemphasizing the less important short-term fluctuations?

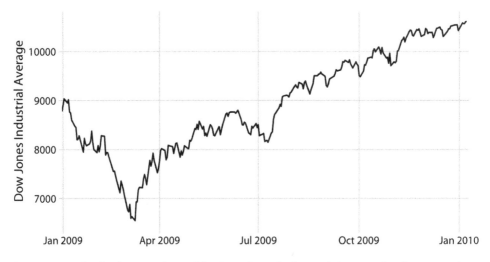

Figure 14-1. Daily closing values of the Dow Jones Industrial Average for the year 2009. Data source: Yahoo! Finance.

In statistical terms, we are looking for a way to *smooth* the stock market time series. The act of smoothing produces a function that captures key patterns in the data while removing irrelevant minor detail or noise. Financial analysts usually smooth stock market data by calculating *moving averages*. To generate a moving average, we take a time window, say the first 20 days in the time series, calculate the average price over these 20 days, then move the time window by one day, so it now spans the 2nd to 21st days. We then calculate the average over these 20 days, move the time window again, and so on. The result is a new time series consisting of a sequence of averaged prices.

To plot this sequence of moving averages, we need to decide which specific time point to associate with the average for each time window. Financial analysts often plot each average at the end of its respective time window. This choice results in curves that lag the original data (Figure 14-2a), with more severe lags corresponding to larger averaging time windows. Statisticians, on the other hand, plot the average at the center of the time window, which results in a curve that overlays perfectly on the original data (Figure 14-2b).

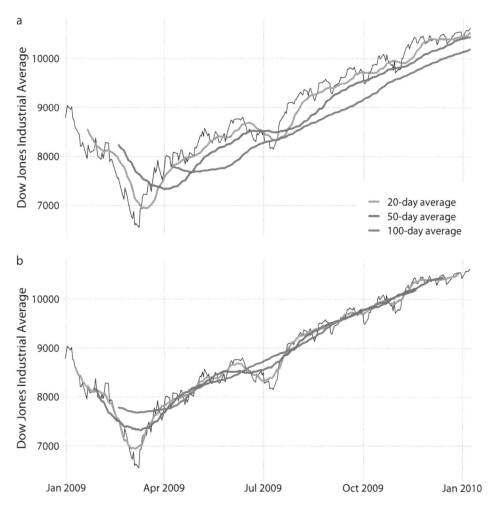

a

b

Figure 14-2. Daily closing values of the Dow Jones Industrial Average for the year 2009, shown together with their 20-day, 50-day, and 100-day moving averages. (a) The moving averages are plotted at the ends of the moving time windows. (b) The moving averages are plotted in the centers of the moving time windows. Data source: Yahoo! Finance.

Regardless of whether we plot the smoothed time series with or without lag, we can see that the length of the time window over which we average sets the scale of the fluctuations that remain visible in the smoothed curve. The 20-day moving average removes small, short-term spikes but otherwise follows the daily data closely. The 100-day moving average, on the other hand, removes even fairly substantial drops or spikes that play out over a time span of multiple weeks. For example, the massive drop to below 7,000 points in the first quarter of 2009 is not visible in the 100-day moving average, which replaces it with a gentle curve that doesn't dip much below

8,000 points (Figure 14-2). Similarly, the drop around July 2009 is completely invisible in the 100-day moving average.

The moving average is the most simplistic approach to smoothing, and it has some obvious limitations. First, it results in a smoothed curve that is shorter than the original curve (Figure 14-2). Parts are missing at either the beginning or the end or both. And the more the time series is smoothed (i.e., the larger the averaging window), the shorter the smoothed curve. Second, even with a large averaging window, a moving average is not necessarily that smooth. It may exhibit small bumps and wiggles even though larger-scale smoothing has been achieved (Figure 14-2). These wiggles are caused by individual data points that enter or exit the averaging window. Since all data points in the window are weighted equally, individual data points at the window boundaries can have a visible impact on the average.

Statisticians have developed numerous approaches to smoothing that alleviate the downsides of moving averages. These approaches are much more complex and computationally costly, but they are readily available in modern statistical computing environments. One widely used method is *locally estimated scatterplot smoothing* (LOESS) [Cleveland 1979], which fits low-degree polynomials to subsets of the data. Importantly, the points in the center of each subset are weighted more heavily than points at the boundaries, and this weighting scheme yields a much smoother result than we get from a weighted average. The LOESS curve shown in Figure 14-3 looks similar to the 100-day average in Figure 14-2, but this similarity should not be overinterpreted. The smoothness of a LOESS curve can be tuned by adjusting a parameter, and different parameter choices would have produced LOESS curves looking more like the 20-day or 50-day average.

Importantly, LOESS is not limited to time series. It can be applied to arbitrary scatterplots, as is apparent from its name, *locally estimated scatterplot smoothing*. For example, we can use LOESS to look for trends in the relationship between a car's fuel-tank capacity and its price (Figure 14-4). The LOESS line shows that tank capacity grows approximately linearly with price for cheap cars (below $20,000) but levels off for more expensive cars. Above a price of approximately $20,000, buying a more expensive car will not get you one with a larger fuel tank.

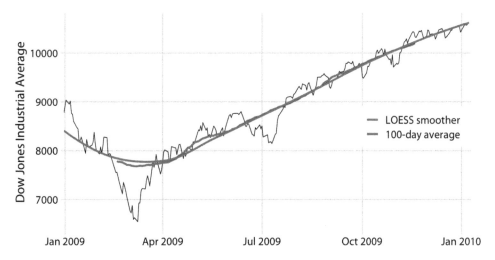

Figure 14-3. Comparison of LOESS fit to 100-day moving average for the Dow Jones data of Figure 14-2. The overall trend shown by the LOESS smooth is nearly identical to the 100-day moving average, but the LOESS curve is much smoother and it extends to the entire range of the data. Data source: Yahoo! Finance.

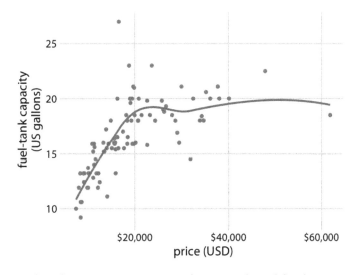

Figure 14-4. Fuel-tank capacity versus price of 93 cars released for the 1993 model year. Each dot corresponds to one car. The solid line represents a LOESS smooth of the data. We see that fuel-tank capacity increases approximately linearly with price, up to a price of approximately $20,000, and then it levels off. Data source: Robin H. Lock, St. Lawrence University.

LOESS is a very popular smoothing approach because it tends to produce results that look right to the human eye. However, it requires the fitting of many separate regression models. This makes it slow for large datasets, even on modern computing equipment.

As a faster alternative to LOESS, we can use spline models. A *spline* is a piecewise polynomial function that is highly flexible yet always looks smooth. When working with splines, we will encounter the term *knot*. The knots in a spline are the endpoints of the individual spline segments. If we fit a spline with k segments, we need to specify $k + 1$ knots. While spline fitting is computationally efficient, in particular if the number of knots is not too large, splines have their own downsides. Most importantly, there is a bewildering array of different types of splines, including cubic splines, B-splines, thin-plate splines, Gaussian process splines, and many others, and which one to pick may not be obvious. The specific choice of the type of spline and number of knots used can result in widely different smoothing functions for the same data (Figure 14-5).

Most data visualization software will provide smoothing features, likely implemented as either a type of local regression (such as LOESS) or a type of spline. The smoothing method may be referred to as a *generalized additive model* (GAM), which is a superset of all these types of smoothers. It is important to be aware that the output of the smoothing feature is dependent on the specific GAM model that is fit. Unless you try out a number of different choices you may never realize to what extent the results you see depend on the specific default choices made by your statistical software.

 Be careful when interpreting the results from a smoothing function. The same dataset can be smoothed in many different ways.

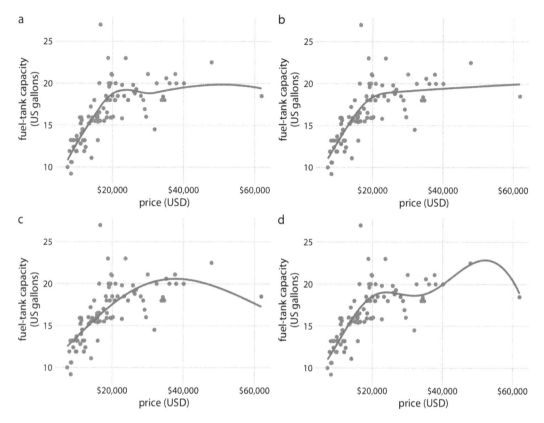

Figure 14-5. Different smoothing models display widely different behaviors, in particular near the boundaries of the data. (a) LOESS smoother, as in Figure 14-4. (b) Cubic regression splines with 5 knots. (c) Thin-plate regression spline with 3 knots. (d) Gaussian process spline with 6 knots. Data source: Robin H. Lock, St. Lawrence University.

Showing Trends with a Defined Functional Form

As we can see in Figure 14-5, the behavior of general-purpose smoothers can be somewhat unpredictable for any given dataset. These smoothers also do not provide parameter estimates that have a meaningful interpretation. Therefore, whenever possible, it is preferable to fit a curve with a specific functional form that is appropriate for the data and that uses parameters with clear meaning.

For the fuel-tank data, we need a curve that initially rises linearly but then levels off at a constant value. The function $y = A - B\exp(-mx)$ may fit that bill. Here, A, B, and m are the constants we adjust to fit the curve to the data. The function is approximately linear for small x, with $y \approx A - B + Bmx$; it approaches a constant value for large x, $y \approx A$, and it is strictly increasing for all values of x. Figure 14-6 shows that this equation fits the data at least as well as any of the smoothers we considered previously (Figure 14-5).

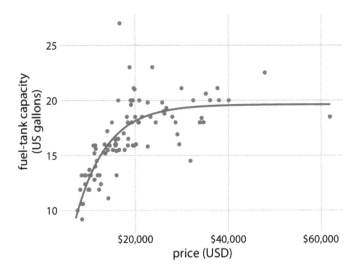

Figure 14-6. Fuel-tank data represented with an explicit analytical model. The solid line corresponds to a least-squares fit of the formula y = A – B *exp(–mx) to the data. Fitted parameters are A = 19.6, B = 29.2, m = 0.00015. Data source: Robin H. Lock, St. Lawrence University.*

A functional form that is applicable in many different contexts is the simple straight line, $y = A + mx$. Approximately linear relationships between two variables are surprisingly common in real-world datasets. For example, in Chapter 12, I discussed the relationship between head length and body mass in blue jays. This relationship is approximately linear, for both female and male birds, and drawing linear trend lines on top of the points in a scatterplot helps the reader perceive the trends (Figure 14-7).

When the data displays a nonlinear relationship, we need to guess what an appropriate functional form might be. In this case, we can assess the accuracy of our guess by transforming the axes in such a way that a linear relationship emerges. To demonstrate this principle, let's return to the monthly submissions to the preprint server bioRxiv, discussed in Chapter 12. If the increase in submissions in each month is proportional to the number of submissions in the previous month—i.e., if submissions grow by a fixed percentage each month—then the resulting curve is exponential. This assumption seems to be met for the bioRxiv data, because a curve with exponential form, $y = A \exp(mx)$, fits the bioRxiv submission data well (Figure 14-8).

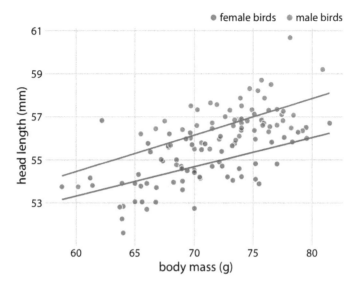

Figure 14-7. Head length versus body mass for 123 blue jays. The birds' sex is indicated by color. This figure is equivalent to Figure 12-2, except that now we have drawn linear trend lines on top of the individual data points. Data source: Keith Tarvin, Oberlin College.

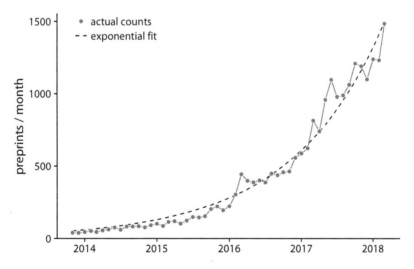

Figure 14-8. Monthly submissions to the preprint server bioRxiv. The solid blue line represents the actual monthly preprint counts and the dashed black line represents an exponential fit to the data, y = 60 exp[0.77(x – 2014)]. Data source: Jordan Anaya, http://www.prepubmed.org/.

If the original curve is exponential, $y = A\exp(mx)$, then a log-transformation of the y values will turn it into a linear relationship, $\log(y) = \log(A) + mx$. Therefore, plotting the data with log-transformed y values (or equivalently, with a logarithmic y axis) and looking for a linear relationship is a good way of determining whether a dataset exhibits exponential growth. For the bioRxiv submission numbers, we indeed obtain a linear relationship when using a logarithmic y axis (Figure 14-9).

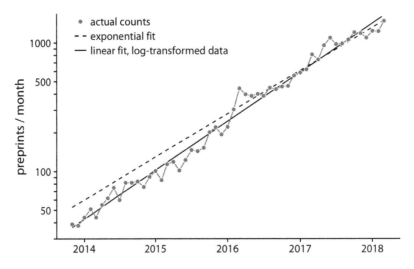

Figure 14-9. Monthly submissions to the preprint server bioRxiv, shown on a log scale. The solid blue line represents the actual monthly preprint counts, the dashed black line represents the exponential fit from Figure 14-8, and the solid black line represents a linear fit to log-transformed data, corresponding to $y = 43\exp[0.88(x - 2014)]$. Data source: Jordan Anaya, http://www.prepubmed.org/.

In Figure 14-9, in addition to the actual submission counts, I am also showing the exponential fit from Figure 14-8 and a linear fit to the log-transformed data. These two fits are similar but not identical. In particular, the slope of the dashed line seems somewhat off. The line systematically falls above the individual data points for half the time series. This is a common problem with exponential fits: the square deviations from the data points to the fitted curve are so much larger for the largest data values than for the smallest data values that the deviations of the smallest data values contribute little to the overall sum of squares that the fit minimizes. As a result, the fitted line systematically overshoots or undershoots the smallest data values. For this reason, I generally advise to avoid exponential fits and instead use linear fits on log-transformed data.

It is usually better to fit a straight line to transformed data than to fit a nonlinear curve to untransformed data.

A plot such as Figure 14-9 is commonly referred to as *log–linear*, since the *y* axis is logarithmic and the *x* axis is linear. Other plots we may encounter include *log–log*, where both the *y* and the *x* axis are logarithmic, and *linear–log*, where *y* is linear and *x* is logarithmic. In a log–log plot, power laws of the form $y \sim x^{\alpha}$ appear as straight lines (see Figure 8-7 for an example), and in a linear–log plot, logarithmic relationships of the form $y \sim \log(x)$ appear as straight lines. Other functional forms can be turned into linear relationships with more specialized coordinate transformations, but these three (log–linear, log–log, linear–log) cover a wide range of real-world applications.

Detrending and Time-Series Decomposition

For any time series with a prominent long-term trend, it may be useful to remove this trend to specifically highlight any notable deviations. This technique is called *detrending*, and I will demonstrate it here with house prices. In the US, the mortgage lender Freddie Mac publishes a monthly index called the *Freddie Mac House Price Index* that tracks the change in housing prices over time. The index attempts to capture the state of the entire house market in a given region, such that an increase in the index by, for example, 10% can be interpreted as an average house price increase of 10% in the respective market. The index is arbitrarily set to a value of 100 in December 2000.

Over long periods of time, house prices tend to display consistent annual growth, approximately in line with inflation. However, overlaid on top of this trend are housing bubbles that lead to severe boom and bust cycles. Figure 14-10 shows the actual house price index and its long-term trend for four select US states. We see that between 1980 and 2017, California underwent two bubbles, one in 1990 and one in the mid-2000s. During the same period, Nevada experienced only one bubble, in the mid-2000s, and house prices in Texas and West Virginia closely followed their long-term trends the entire time. Because house prices tend to grow in percent increments, i.e., exponentially, I have chosen a logarithmic *y* axis in Figure 14-10. The straight lines correspond to a 4.7% annual price increase in California and a 2.8% annual price increase each in Nevada, Texas, and West Virginia.

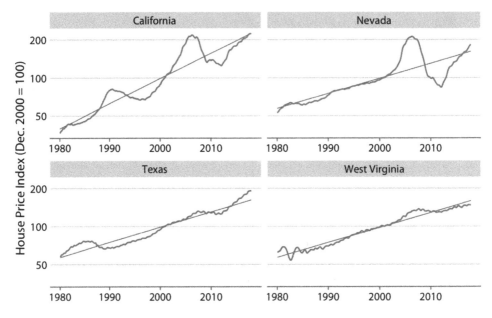

Figure 14-10. Freddie Mac House Price Index from 1980 through 2017, for four selected states (California, Nevada, Texas, and West Virginia). The House Price Index is a unit-less number that tracks relative house prices in the chosen geographic region over time. The index is scaled arbitrarily such that it equals 100 in December of the year 2000. The blue lines show the monthly fluctuations in the index and the straight gray lines show the long-term price trends in the respective states. Note that the y axes are logarithmic, so that the straight gray lines represent consistent exponential growth. Data source: Freddie Mac House Prices Index.

We *detrend* housing prices by dividing the actual price index at each time point by the respective value in the long-term trend. Visually, this division will look like we are subtracting the gray lines from the blue lines in Figure 14-10, because a division of the untransformed values is equivalent to a subtraction of the log-transformed values. The resulting detrended house prices show the housing bubbles more clearly (Figure 14-11), as the detrending emphasizes the unexpected movements in a time series. For example, in the original time series, the decline in home prices in California from 1990 to about 1998 looks modest (Figure 14-10). However, during that same time period, on the basis of the long-term trend we would have expected prices to rise. Relative to the expected rise the drop in prices was substantial, amounting to 25% at the lowest point (Figure 14-11).

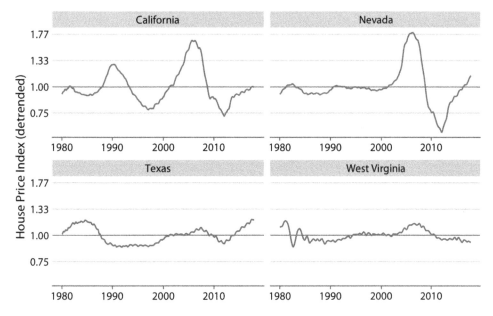

Figure 14-11. Detrended version of the Freddie Mac House Price Index shown in Figure 14-10. The detrended index was calculated by dividing the actual index (blue lines in Figure 14-10) by the expected value based on the long-term trend (straight gray lines in Figure 14-10). This visualization shows that California experienced two housing bubbles, around 1990 and in the mid-2000s, identifiable from a rapid rise and subsequent decline in the actual housing prices relative to what would have been expected from the long-term trend. Similarly, Nevada experienced one housing bubble, in the mid-2000s, and neither Texas nor West Virginia experienced much of a bubble at all. Data source: Freddie Mac House Prices Index.

Beyond simple detrending, we can also separate a time series into multiple distinct components, such that their sum recovers the original time series. In general, in addition to a long-term trend, there are three distinct components that may shape a time series. First, there is random noise, which causes small, erratic movements up and down. This noise is visible in all the time series shown in this chapter, but maybe the most in Figure 14-9. Second, there can be unique external events that leave their mark in the time series, such as the distinct housing bubbles seen in Figure 14-10. Third, there can be cyclical variations. For example, outside temperatures show daily cyclical variations. The highest temperatures are reached in the early afternoon and the lowest temperatures in the early morning. Outside temperatures also show yearly cyclical variations. They tend to rise in the spring, reach their maximum in the summer, and then decline in the fall and reach their minimum in the winter (Figure 3-2).

To demonstrate the concept of distinct time-series components, I will here decompose the Keeling curve, which shows changes in CO_2 abundance over time (Figure 14-12). Since 1958, CO_2 abundance has been continuously monitored at the Mauna Loa Observatory in Hawaii, initially under the direction of Charles Keeling.

CO_2 is measured in parts per million (ppm). We see a long-term increase in CO_2 abundance that is slightly faster than linear, from below 325 ppm in the 1960s to above 400 in the second decade of the 21st century (Figure 14-12). CO_2 abundance also fluctuates annually, following a consistent up-and-down pattern overlaid on top of the overall increase. The annual fluctuations are driven by plant growth in the northern hemisphere. Plants consume CO_2 during photosynthesis. Because most of the globe's land masses are located in the northern hemisphere, and plant growth is most active in the spring and summer, we see an annual global decline in atmospheric CO_2 that coincides with the summer months in the northern hemisphere.

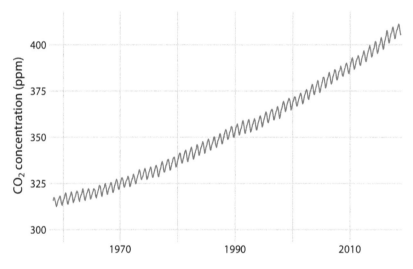

Figure 14-12. The Keeling curve. The Keeling curve shows the change of CO_2 abundance in the atmosphere over time. Shown here are monthly average CO_2 readings, expressed in parts per million (ppm). The CO_2 readings fluctuate annually with the seasons but show a consistent long-term trend of increase. Data source: Dr. Pieter Tans, NOAA/ ESRL, and Dr. Ralph Keeling, Scripps Institution of Oceanography.

We can decompose the Keeling curve into its long-term trend, seasonal fluctuations, and remainder (Figure 14-13). The specific method I am using here is called *seasonal decomposition of time series by LOESS* (STL) [Cleveland et al. 1990], but there are many other methods that achieve similar goals.

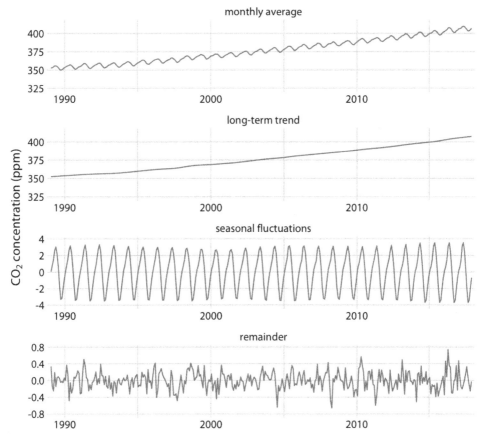

Figure 14-13. Time-series decomposition of the Keeling curve, showing the monthly average (as in Figure 14-12), the long-term trend, seasonal fluctuations, and the remainder. The remainder is the difference between the actual readings and the sum of the long-term trend and the seasonal fluctuations, and it represents random noise. I have zoomed into the most recent 30 years of data to emphasize the shape of the annual fluctuations. Data source: Dr. Pieter Tans, NOAA/ESRL, and Dr. Ralph Keeling, Scripps Institution of Oceanography.

The decomposition shows that over the last three decades, CO_2 abundance has increased by over 50 ppm. By comparison, seasonal fluctuations amount to less than 8 ppm (they never cause an increase or a decrease of more than 4 ppm relative to the long-term trend), and the remainder amounts to less than 1.6 ppm (Figure 14-13). The remainder is the difference between the actual readings and the sum of the long-term trend and the seasonal fluctuations, and here it corresponds to random noise in the monthly CO_2 readings. More generally, however, the remainder could also capture unique external events. For example, if a massive volcano eruption released substantial amounts of CO_2, such an event might be visible as a sudden spike in the remainder. Figure 14-13 shows that no such unique external events have had a major effect on the Keeling curve in recent decades.

## CHAPTER 15

Visualizing Geospatial Data

Many datasets contain information linked to locations in the physical world. For example, in an ecological study, a dataset may list where specific plants or animals have been found. Similarly, in a socioeconomic or political context, a dataset may contain information about where people with specific attributes (such as income, age, or educational attainment) live, or where man-made objects (e.g., bridges, roads, buildings) have been constructed. In all these cases, it can be helpful to visualize the data in their proper geospatial context, i.e., to show the data on a realistic map or alternatively as a map-like diagram.

Maps tend to be intuitive to readers, but they can be challenging to design. We need to think about concepts such as map projections and whether for our specific application the accurate representation of angles or areas is more critical. A common mapping technique, the *choropleth map,* consists of representing data values as differently colored spatial areas. Choropleth maps can at times be very useful and at other times quite misleading. As an alternative, we can construct map-like diagrams called *cartograms,* which may purposefully distort map areas or represent them in stylized form, for example as equal-sized squares.

Projections

The earth is approximately a sphere (Figure 15-1), and more precisely an oblate spheroid that is slightly flattened along its axis of rotation. The two locations where the axis of rotation intersects with the spheroid are called the *poles* (north and south). We separate the spheroid into two hemispheres, the northern and the southern hemisphere, by drawing a line equidistant to both poles around the spheroid. This line is called the *equator.* To uniquely specify a location on the earth, we need three pieces of information: where we are located along the direction of the equator (the *longitude*), how close we are to either pole when moving perpendicular to the equator (the *latitude*), and how far we are from the earth's center (the *altitude*). Longitude, latitude, and altitude are specified relative to a reference system called the *datum*. The datum specifies properties such as the shape and size of the earth, as well as the location of zero longitude, latitude, and altitude. One widely used datum is the World Geodetic System (WGS) 84, which is used by the Global Positioning System (GPS).

Figure 15-1. Orthographic projection of the world, showing Europe and Northern Africa as they would be visible from space. The lines emanating from the north pole and running south are called meridians, and the lines running orthogonal to the meridians are called parallels. All meridians have the same length, but parallels become shorter the closer we are to either pole.

While altitude is an important quantity in many geospatial applications, when visualizing geospatial data in the form of maps we are primarily concerned with the other two dimensions, longitude and latitude. Both longitude and latitude are angles, expressed in degrees. Degrees longitude measure how far east or west a location lies. Lines of equal longitude are referred to as *meridians*, and all meridians terminate at the two poles (Figure 15-1). The prime meridian, corresponding to 0° longitude, runs through the village of Greenwich in the United Kingdom. The meridian opposite to the prime meridian lies at 180° longitude (also referred to as 180°E), which is equivalent to −180° longitude (also referred to as 180°W), near the international date line. Degrees latitude measure how far north or south a location lies. The equator corresponds to 0° latitude, the north pole corresponds to 90° latitude (also referred to as 90°N), and the south pole corresponds to −90° latitude (also referred to as 90°S). Lines of equal latitude are referred to as *parallels*, since they run parallel to the equator. All meridians have the same length, corresponding to half of a great circle around the globe, whereas the length of parallels depends on their latitude (Figure 15-1). The longest parallel is the equator, at 0° latitude, and the shortest parallels lie at the north and south poles, 90°N and 90°S, and have length zero.

The challenge in map making is that we need to take the spherical surface of the earth and flatten it out so we can display it on a map. This process, called *projection,* necessarily introduces distortions, because a curved surface cannot be projected exactly onto a flat surface. Specifically, the projection can preserve either angles or areas but not both. A projection that does the former is called *conformal* and a projection that does the latter is called *equal-area*. Other projections may preserve neither angles nor areas but instead preserve other quantities of interest, such as distances to some reference point or line. Finally, some projections attempt to strike a compromise between preserving angles and areas. These compromise projections are frequently used to display the entire world in an aesthetically pleasing manner, and they accept some amount of both angular and area distortion (Figure 3-11). To systematize and keep track of different ways of projecting parts or all of the earth for specific maps, various standards bodies and organizations, such as the European Petroleum Survey Group (EPSG) and the Environmental Systems Research Institute (ESRI), maintain registries of projections. For example, EPSG:4326 represents unprojected longitude and latitude values in the WGS 84 coordinate system used by GPS. Several websites provide convenient access to these registered projections, including *http://spatialreference.org/* and *https://epsg.io/*.

One of the earliest map projections in use, the Mercator projection, was developed in the 16th century for nautical navigation. It is a conformal projection that accurately represents shapes but introduces severe area distortions near the poles (Figure 15-2). The Mercator projection maps the globe onto a cylinder and then unrolls the cylinder to arrive at a rectangular map. Meridians in this projection are evenly spaced vertical lines, whereas parallels are horizontal lines whose spacing increases the further we move away from the equator. The spacing between parallels increases in proportion to the extent to which they have to be stretched closer to the poles to keep the meridians perfectly vertical.

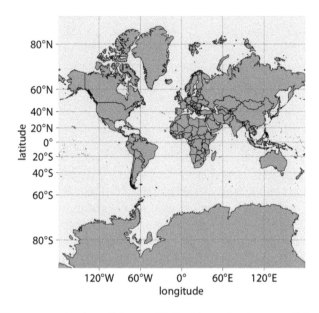

Figure 15-2. Mercator projection of the world. In this projection, parallels are straight horizontal lines and meridians are straight vertical lines. It is a conformal projection preserving local angles, but it introduces severe distortions in areas near the poles. For example, Greenland appears to be bigger than Africa in this projection, when in reality Africa is 14 times bigger than Greenland (see Figures 15-1 and 15-3).

Because of the severe area distortions it produces, the Mercator projection has fallen out of favor for maps of the entire world. However, variants of this projection continue to live on. For example, the transverse Mercator projection is routinely used for large-scale maps that show moderately small areas (spanning less than a few degrees in longitude) at large magnification. Another variant, the web Mercator projection, was introduced by Google for Google Maps and is used by several online mapping applications.

A whole-world projection that is perfectly area-preserving is the Goode homolosine (Figure 15-3). It is usually shown in its interrupted form, which has one cut in the northern hemisphere and three cuts in the southern hemisphere, carefully chosen so they don't interrupt major land masses (Figure 15-3). The cuts allow the projection to both preserve areas and approximately preserve angles, at the cost of noncontiguous oceans, a cut through the middle of Greenland, and several cuts through Antarctica. While the interrupted Goode homolosine has an unusual aesthetic and a strange name, it is a good choice for mapping applications that require accurate reproduction of areas on a global scale.

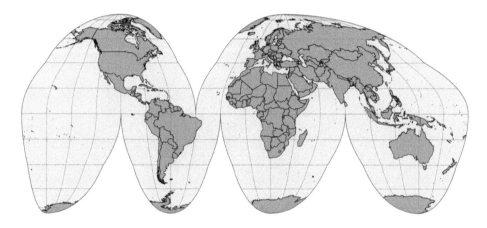

Figure 15-3. Interrupted Goode homolosine projection of the world. This projection accurately preserves areas while minimizing angular distortions, at the cost of showing oceans and some land masses (Greenland, Antarctica) in a noncontiguous way.

Shape or area distortions due to map projections are particularly prominent when we're attempting to make a map of the whole world, but they can cause trouble even at the scale of individual continents or countries. As an example, consider the United States, which consists of the *lower 48* (which are 48 contiguous states), Alaska, and Hawaii (Figure 15-4). While the lower 48 alone are reasonably easy to project onto a map, Alaska and Hawaii are so distant from the lower 48 that projecting all 50 states onto one map becomes awkward.

Figure 15-4. Relative locations of Alaska, Hawaii, and the lower 48 states shown on a globe.

Figure 15-5 shows a map of all 50 states made using an equal-area Albers projection. This projection provides a reasonable representation of the relative shapes, areas, and locations of the 50 states, but we notice some issues. First, Alaska seems weirdly stretched out compared to how it looks, for example, in Figures 15-2 or 15-4. Second, the map is dominated by ocean/empty space. It would be preferable to zoom in further, so that the lower 48 states take up a larger proportion of the map area.

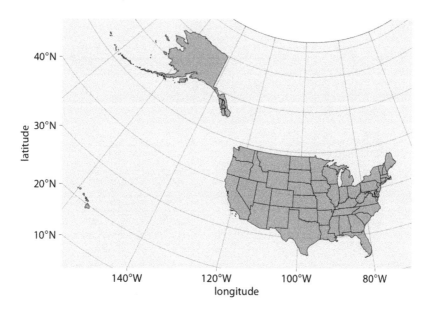

Figure 15-5. Map of the United States of America, using an area-preserving Albers projection (ESRI:102003, commonly used to project the lower 48 states). Alaska and Hawaii are shown in their true locations.

To address the problem of uninteresting empty space, it is common practice to project Alaska and Hawaii separately (to minimize shape distortions) and then move them so they are shown underneath the lower 48 (Figure 15-6). You may notice in Figure 15-6 that Alaska looks much smaller relative to the lower 48 than it does in Figure 15-5. The reason for this discrepancy is that Alaska has not only been moved, it also has been scaled so it looks comparable in size to typical midwestern or western states. This scaling, while common practice, is misleading, and therefore I have labeled the figure as "bad."

bad

Figure 15-6. Visualization of the United States, with the states of Alaska and Hawaii moved to lie underneath the lower 48 states. Alaska also has been scaled so its linear extent is only 35% of the state's true size. (In other words, the state's area has been reduced to approximately 12% of its true size.) Such a scaling is frequently applied to Alaska, to make it visually appear to be of similar size as typical midwestern or western states. However, the scaling is misleading, and therefore the figure has been labeled as "bad."

Instead of both moving and scaling Alaska, we could just move it without changing its scale (Figure 15-7). This visualization reveals that Alaska is the largest state, over twice the size of Texas. We are not used to seeing the US shown in this way, but in my mind it is a much more reasonable representation of the 50 states than is Figure 15-6.

Figure 15-7. Visualization of the United States, with the states of Alaska and Hawaii moved to lie underneath the lower 48 states.

Layers

To visualize geospatial data in the proper context, we usually create maps consisting of multiple layers showing different types of information. To demonstrate this concept, I will visualize the locations of wind turbines in the San Francisco Bay area. In the Bay Area, wind turbines are clustered in two locations. One location, which I will refer to as the Shiloh Wind Farm, lies near Rio Vista and the other lies east of Hayward near Tracy (Figure 15-8).

Figure 15-8 consists of four separate layers. At the bottom, we have the terrain layer, which shows hills, valleys, and water. The next layer shows the road network. On top of the road layer, I have placed a layer indicating the locations of individual wind turbines. This layer also contains the two rectangles highlighting the majority of the wind turbines. Finally, the top layer adds the locations and names of cities. These four layers are shown separately in Figure 15-9. For any given map we want to make, we may want to add or remove some of these layers. For example, if we wanted to draw a map of voting districts, we might consider terrain information to be irrelevant and distracting. Alternatively, if we wanted to draw a map of exposed or covered roof areas to assess potential for solar power generation, we might want to replace terrain information with satellite imagery that shows individual roofs and actual vegetation. You can interactively try these different types of layers in most online map applications, such as Google Maps. I would like to emphasize that regardless of which layers you decide to keep or remove, it is generally recommended to add a scale bar and a north arrow. The scale bar helps readers understand the size of the spatial features shown in the map, while the north arrow clarifies the map's orientation.

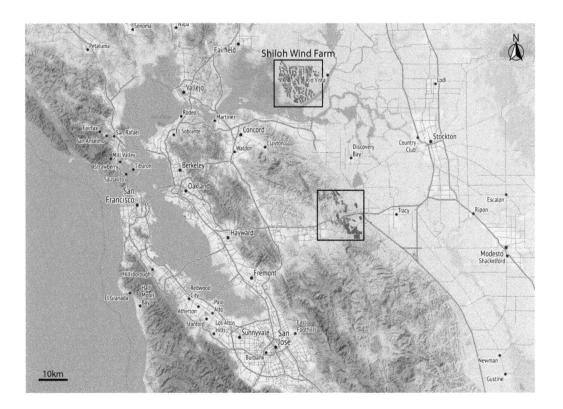

Figure 15-8. Wind turbines in the San Francisco Bay Area. Individual wind turbines are shown as purple-colored dots. Two regions with a high concentration of wind turbines are highlighted with black rectangles. I refer to the wind turbines near Rio Vista collectively as the Shiloh Wind Farm. Map tiles by Stamen Design, under CC BY 3.0. Map data by OpenStreetMap, under ODbL. Wind turbine data source: US Wind Turbine Database.

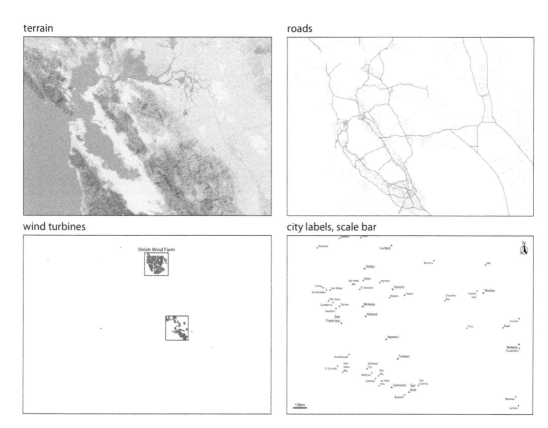

Figure 15-9. The individual layers of Figure 15-8. From bottom to top, the figure consists of a terrain layer, a roads layer, a layer showing the wind turbines, and a layer labeling cities and adding a scale bar and north arrow. Map tiles by Stamen Design, under CC BY 3.0. Map data by OpenStreetMap, under ODbL. Wind turbine data source: US Wind Turbine Database.

All the concepts discussed in Chapter 2 of mapping data onto aesthetics carry over to maps. We can place data points into their geographic context and show other data dimensions via aesthetics such as color or shape. For example, Figure 15-10 provides a zoomed-in view of the rectangle labeled "Shiloh Wind Farm" in Figure 15-8. Individual wind turbines are shown as dots, with the color representing when a specific turbine was built and the shape representing the project to which the wind turbine belongs. A map such as this one can provide a quick overview of how an area was developed. For example, here we see that EDF Renewables is a relatively small project built before 2000, High Winds is a moderately sized project built between 2000 and 2004, and Shiloh and Solano are the largest two projects in the area, both built over an extended period of time.

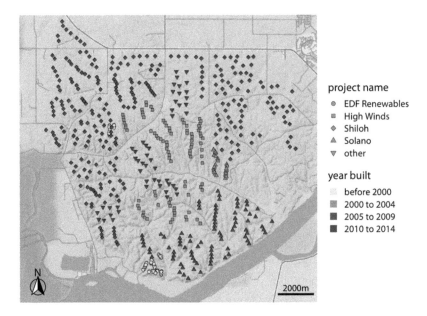

project name
⊙ EDF Renewables
▣ High Winds
◆ Shiloh
▲ Solano
▽ other

year built
before 2000
2000 to 2004
2005 to 2009
2010 to 2014

Figure 15-10. Locations of individual wind turbines in the Shiloh Wind Farm. Each dot highlights the location of one wind turbine. The map area corresponds to the top rectangle in Figure 15-8. Dots are colored by when the wind turbine was built, and the dot's shape represents the project to which an individual wind turbine belongs. Map tiles by Stamen Design, under CC BY 3.0. Map data by OpenStreetMap, under ODbL. Wind turbine data source: US Wind Turbine Database.

Choropleth Mapping

We frequently want to show how some quantity varies across locations. We can do so by coloring individual regions in a map according to the data dimension we want to display. Such maps are called *choropleth maps*.

As a simple example, consider the population density (persons per square kilometer) across the United States. We take the population number for each county in the US, divide it by the county's surface area, and then draw a map where the color of each county corresponds to the ratio between population number and area (Figure 15-11). We can see that the major cities on the East and West Coast are the most populated areas of the US, the Great Plains and western states have low population densities, and the state of Alaska is the least populated of all.

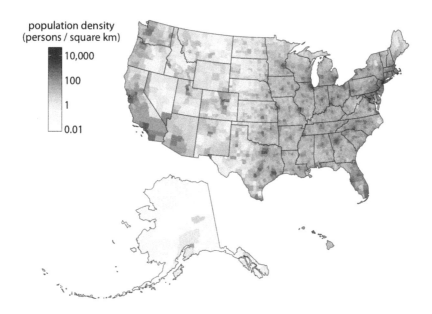

Figure 15-11. Population density in every US county, shown as a choropleth map. Population density is reported as persons per square kilometer. Data source: 2015 Five-Year American Community Survey.

Figure 15-11 uses light colors to represent low population densities and dark colors to represent high densities, so that high-density metropolitan areas stand out as dark colors on a background of light colors. We tend to associate darker colors with higher intensities when the background color of the figure is light. However, we can also pick a color scale where high values light up on a dark background (Figure 15-12). As long as the lighter colors fall into the red-yellow spectrum, so that they appear to be glowing, they can be perceived as representing higher intensities. As a general principle, when figures are meant to be printed on white paper, light-colored background areas (as in Figure 15-11) will typically work better. For online viewing or on a dark background, dark-colored background areas (as in Figure 15-12) may be preferable.

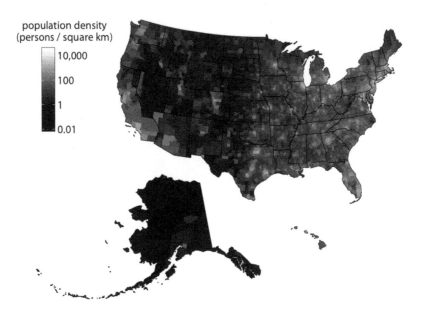

population density
(persons / square km)

10,000

100

1

0.01

Figure 15-12. Population density in every US county, shown as a choropleth map. This map is identical to Figure 15-11 except that now the color scale uses light colors for high population densities and dark colors for low population densities. Data source: 2015 Five-Year American Community Survey.

Choropleths work best when the coloring represents a density (i.e., some quantity divided by surface area, as in Figures 15-11 and 15-12). We perceive larger areas as corresponding to larger amounts than smaller areas (see also Chapter 17), and shading by density corrects for this effect. However, in practice, we often see choropleths colored according to some quantity that is not a density. For example, in Figure 4-4 I showed a choropleth of median annual income in Texas counties. Such choropleth maps can be appropriate when they are prepared with caution. There are two conditions under which we can color-map quantities that are not densities. First, if all the individual areas we color have approximately the same size and shape, then we don't have to worry about some areas drawing disproportionate attention solely due to their size. Second, if the individual areas we color are relatively small compared to the overall size of the map and if the quantity that color represents changes on a scale larger than the individual colored areas, then again we don't have to worry about some areas drawing disproportionate attention solely due to their size. Both of these conditions are approximately met in Figure 4-4.

It is also important to consider the effect of continuous versus discrete color scales in choropleth mapping. While continuous color scales tend to look visually appealing (e.g., Figures 15-11 and 15-12), they can be difficult to read. We are not very good at recognizing a specific color value and matching it against a continuous scale. There-fore, it is often appropriate to bin the data values into discrete groups that are represented with distinct colors. On the order of four to six bins is a good choice. The binning sacrifices some information, but on the flip side the binned colors can be uniquely recognized. As an example, Figure 15-13 expands the map of median income in Texas counties (Figure 4-4) to all counties in the US, and it uses a color scale consisting of five distinct income bins.

Figure 15-13. Median income in every US county, shown as a choropleth map. The median income values have been binned into five distinct groups, because binned color scales are generally easier to read than continuous color scales. Data source: 2015 Five-Year American Community Survey.

Even though counties are not quite as equal-sized and even-shaped across the entire US as they are just within Texas, I think Figure 15-13 still works as a choropleth map. No individual county overly dominates the map. However, things look different when we draw a comparable map at the state level (Figure 15-14). Then Alaska dominates the choropleth and, because of its size, suggests that median incomes above $70,000 are common. Yet Alaska is very sparsely populated (see Figures 15-11 and 15-12), and thus the income levels in Alaska apply only to a small portion of the US population. The vast majority of US counties, which are nearly all more populous than counties in Alaska, have a median income of below $60,000.

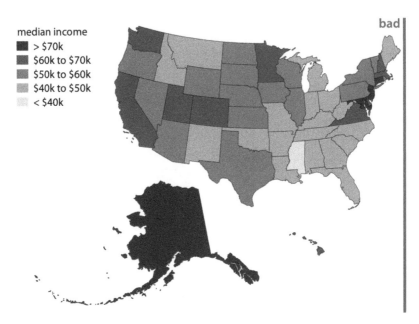

median income
> $70k
$60k to $70k
$50k to $60k
$40k to $50k
< $40k

bad

Figure 15-14. Median income in every US state, shown as a choropleth map. This map is visually dominated by the state of Alaska, which has a high median income but very low population density. At the same time, the densely populated high-income states on the East Coast do not appear very prominent on this map. In aggregate, this map provides a poor visualization of the income distribution in the US, and therefore I have labeled it as "bad." Data source: 2015 Five-Year American Community Survey.

Cartograms

Not every map-like visualization has to be geographically accurate to be useful. For example, the problem with Figure 15-14 is that some states take up a comparatively large area but are sparsely populated, while others take up a small area yet have a large number of inhabitants. What if we deformed the states so their size was proportional to their number of inhabitants? Such a modified map is called a *cartogram*, and Figure 15-15 shows what it can look like for the median income dataset. We can still recognize individual states, yet we also see how the adjustment for population numbers has introduced important modifications. The East Coast states, Florida, and California have grown a lot in size, whereas the other western states and Alaska have collapsed.

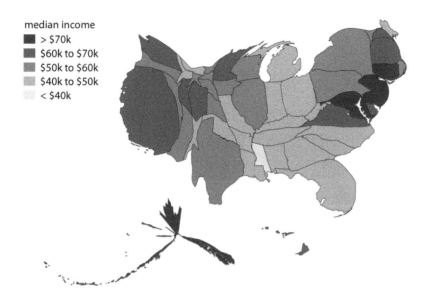

Figure 15-15. Median income in every US state, shown as a cartogram. The shapes of individual states have been modified such that their area is proportional to their number of inhabitants. Data source: 2015 Five-Year American Community Survey.

As an alternative to a cartogram with distorted shapes, we can also draw a much simpler *cartogram heatmap*, where each state is represented by a colored square (Figure 15-16). While this representation does not correct for the population number in each state, and thus underrepresents more populous states and overrepresents less populous states, at least it treats all states equally and doesn't weight them arbitrarily by their shape or size.

Finally, we can draw more complex cartograms by placing individual plots at the location of each state. For example, if we want to visualize the evolution of the unemployment rate over time for each state, it can help to draw an individual graph for each state and then arrange the graphs based on the approximate relative positions of the states to each other (Figure 15-17). For somebody who is familiar with the geography of the United States, this arrangement may make it easier to find the graphs for specific states than arranging them, for example, in alphabetical order. Furthermore, one would expect neighboring states to display similar patterns, and Figure 15-17 shows that this is indeed the case.

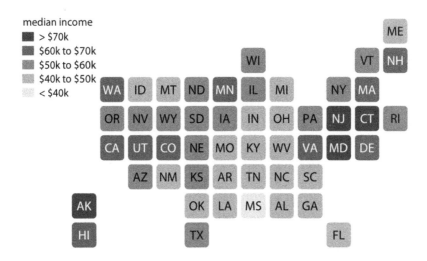

Figure 15-16. Median income in every US state, shown as a cartogram heatmap. Each state is represented by an equally sized square, and the squares are arranged according to the approximate position of each state relative to the other states. This representation gives the same visual weight to each state. Data source: 2015 Five-Year American Community Survey.

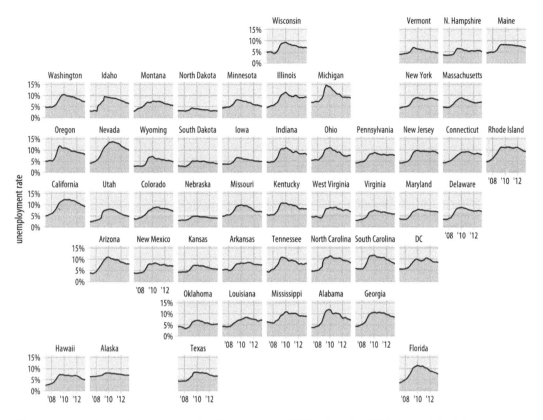

Figure 15-17. Unemployment rate leading up to and following the 2008 financial crisis, by state. Each panel shows the unemployment rate for one state, including the District of Columbia (DC), from January 2007 through May 2013. Vertical grid lines mark January of 2008, 2010, and 2012. States that are geographically close tend to show similar trends in the unemployment rate. Data source: US Bureau of Labor Statistics.

## CHAPTER 16

Visualizing Uncertainty

One of the most challenging aspects of data visualization is the visualization of uncertainty. When we see a data point drawn in a specific location, we tend to interpret it as a precise representation of the true data value. It is difficult to conceive that a data point could actually lie somewhere it hasn't been drawn. Yet this scenario is ubiquitous in data visualization. Nearly every dataset we work with has some uncertainty, and whether and how we choose to represent this uncertainty can make a major difference in how accurately our audience perceives the meaning of the data.

Two commonly used approaches to indicate uncertainty are error bars and confidence bands. These approaches were developed in the context of scientific publications, and they require some amount of expert knowledge to be interpreted correctly, yet they are precise and space-efficient. By using error bars, for example, we can show the uncertainties of many different parameter estimates in a single graph. For a lay audience, however, visualization strategies that create a strong intuitive impression of the uncertainty will be preferable, even if they come at the cost of either reduced visualization accuracy or less data-dense displays. Options here include frequency framing, where we explicitly draw different possible scenarios in approximate proportions, or animations that cycle through different possible scenarios.

Framing Probabilities as Frequencies

Before we can discuss how to visualize uncertainty, we need to define what it actually is. We can intuitively grasp the concept of uncertainty most easily in the context of future events. If I am going to flip a coin, I don't know ahead of time what the outcome will be. The eventual outcome is uncertain. I can also be uncertain about events in the past, however. If yesterday I looked out of my kitchen window exactly twice, once at 8 a.m. and once at 4 p.m., and I saw a red car parked across the street at 8 a.m. but not at 4 p.m., then I can conclude the car left at some point during the 8-hour window, but I don't know exactly when. It could have been 8:01 a.m., 9:30 a.m., 2 p.m., or any other time during those eight hours.

Mathematically, we deal with uncertainty by employing the concept of probability. A precise definition of probability is complicated and far beyond the scope of this book. Yet we can successfully reason about probabilities without understanding all the mathematical intricacies. For many problems of practical relevance it is sufficient to think about relative frequencies. Assume you perform some sort of random trial, such as a coin flip or rolling a die, and look for a particular outcome (e.g., heads or rolling a six). You can call this outcome *success*, and any other outcome *failure*. Then, the probability of success is approximately given by the fraction of times you'd see that outcome if you repeated the random trial over and over again. For instance, if a particular outcome occurs with a probability of 10%, then we expect that among many repeated trials that outcome will be seen in approximately 1 out of 10 cases.

Visualizing a single probability is difficult. How would you visualize the chance of winning in the lottery, or the chance of rolling a six with a fair die? In both cases, the probability is a single number. We could treat that number as an amount and display it using any of the techniques discussed in Chapter 6, such as a bar graph or a dot plot, but the result would not be very useful. Most people lack an intuitive understanding of how a probability value translates into experienced reality. Showing the probability value as a bar or as a dot placed on a line does not help with this problem.

We can make the concept of probability tangible by creating a graph that emphasizes both the frequency aspect and the unpredictability of a random trial, for example by drawing squares of different colors in a random arrangement. In Figure 16-1, I use this technique to visualize three different probabilities, a 1% chance of success, a 10% chance of success, and a 40% chance of success. To read this figure, imagine you are given the task of picking a dark square by choosing a square before you can see which of the squares will be dark and which ones will be light. (If you will, you can think of picking a square with your eyes closed.) Intuitively, you will probably understand that you would be unlikely to select the one dark square in the 1% chance case. Similarly, it would still be fairly unlikely for you to select a dark square in the 10% chance case. However, in the 40% chance case the odds don't look so bad. This style of visualization, where we show specific potential outcomes, is called a *discrete outcome visualization*, and the act of visualizing a probability as a frequency is called *frequency framing*. We are framing the probabilistic nature of a result in terms of easily understood frequencies of outcomes.

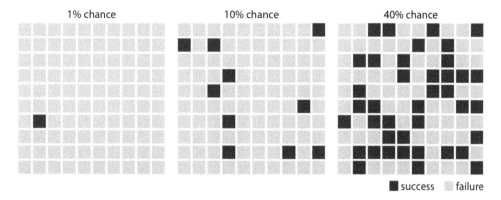

Figure 16-1. Visualizing probability as frequency. There are 100 squares in each grid, and each square represents either success of failure in some random trial. A 1% chance of success corresponds to 1 dark and 99 light squares, a 10% chance of success corresponds to 10 dark and 90 light squares, and a 40% chance of success corresponds to 40 dark and 60 light squares. By randomly placing the dark squares among the light squares, we can create a visual impression of randomness that emphasizes the uncertainty of the outcome of a single trial.

If we are only interested in two discrete outcomes, success or failure, then a visualization such as Figure 16-1 works fine. However, often we are dealing with more complex scenarios where the outcome of a random trial is a numeric variable. One common scenario is that of election predictions, where we are interested not only in who will win but also by how much. Let's consider a hypothetical example of an upcoming election with two parties, the yellow party and the blue party. Assume you hear on the radio that the blue party is predicted to have a 1 percentage point advantage over the yellow party, with a margin of error of 1.76 percentage points. What does this information tell you about the likely outcome of the election? It is human nature to hear "the blue party will win," but reality is more complicated. First, and most importantly, there are a range of different possible outcomes. The blue party could end up winning with a lead of two percentage points, or the yellow party could end up winning with a lead of half a percentage point. The range of possible outcomes with their associated likelihoods is called a *probability distribution*, and we can draw it as a smooth curve that rises and then falls over the range of possible outcomes (Figure 16-2). The higher the curve for a specific outcome, the more likely that outcome is. Probability distributions are closely related to the histograms and kernel densities discussed in Chapter 7, and you may want to re-read that chapter to refresh your memory.

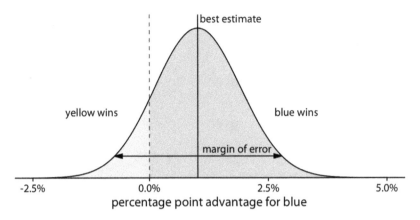

Figure 16-2. Hypothetical prediction of an election outcome. The blue party is predicted to win over the yellow party by approximately 1 percentage point (labeled "best estimate"), but that prediction has a margin of error (here drawn so it covers 95% of the likely outcomes, 1.76 percentage points in either direction from the best estimate). The area shaded in blue, corresponding to 87.1% of the total, represents all outcomes under which blue would win. Likewise, the area shaded in yellow, corresponding to 12.9% of the total, represents all outcomes under which yellow would win. In this example, blue has an 87% chance of winning the election.

By doing some math, we can calculate that for our made-up example, the chance of the yellow party winning is 12.9%. So, the chance of yellow winning is a tad better than the 10% chance scenario shown in Figure 16-1. If you favor the blue party, you may not be overly worried, but the yellow party has enough of a chance of winning that it might just be successful. If you compare Figure 16-2 to Figure 16-1, you may find that Figure 16-1 creates a much better sense of the uncertainty in outcome, even though the shaded areas in Figure 16-2 accurately represent the probabilities of blue or yellow winning. This is the power of a discrete outcome visualization. Research in human perception shows that we are much better at perceiving, counting, and judging the relative frequencies of discrete objects—as long as their total number is not too large—than we are at judging the relative sizes of different areas.

We can combine the discrete outcome nature of Figure 16-1 with a continuous distribution as in Figure 16-2 by drawing a *quantile dot plot* [Kay et al. 2016]. In the quantile dot plot, we subdivide the total area under the curve into evenly sized units and draw each unit as a circle. We then stack the circles such that their arrangement approximately represents the original distribution curve (Figure 16-3).

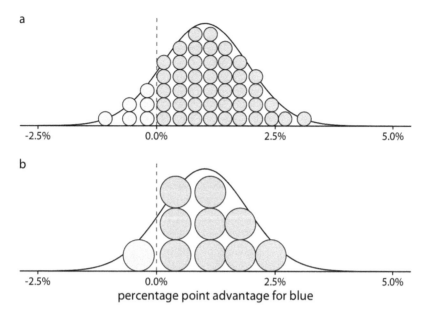

a

-2.5%   0.0%   2.5%   5.0%

b

-2.5%   0.0%   2.5%   5.0%

percentage point advantage for blue

Figure 16-3. Quantile dot plot representations of the election outcome distribution of Figure 16-2. (a) The smooth distribution is approximated with 50 dots representing a 2% chance each. The 6 yellow dots thus correspond to a 12% chance, reasonably close to the true value of 12.9%. (b) The smooth distribution is approximated with 10 dots representing a 10% chance each. The 1 yellow dot thus corresponds to a 10% chance, still close to the true value. Quantile dot plots with a smaller number of dots tend to be easier to read, so in this example, the 10-dot version might be preferable to the 50-dot version.

As a general principle, quantile dot plots should use a small to moderate number of dots. If there are too many dots, then we tend to perceive them as a continuum rather than as individual, discrete units. This negates the advantages of the discrete plots. Figure 16 3 shows variants with 50 dots (Figure 16-3a) and with 10 dots (Figure 16-3b). While the version with 50 dots more accurately captures the true probability distribution, the number of dots is too large to easily discriminate individual ones. The version with 10 dots more immediately conveys the relative chances of blue or yellow winning. One objection to the 10-dot version might be that it is not very precise. We are underrepresenting the chance of yellow winning by 2.9 percentage points. However, it is often worthwhile to trade some mathematical precision for more accurate human perception of the resulting visualization, in particular when communicating to a lay audience. A visualization that is mathematically correct but not properly perceived is not that useful in practice.

Visualizing the Uncertainty of Point Estimates

In Figure 16-2, I showed a "best estimate" and a "margin of error," but I didn't explain what exactly these quantities are or how they might be obtained. To understand them better, we need to take a quick detour into basic concepts of statistical sampling. In statistics, our overarching goal is to learn something about the world by looking at a small portion of it. To continue with the election example, assume there are many different electoral districts and the citizens of each district are going to vote for either the blue or the yellow party. We might want to predict how each district is going to vote, as well as the overall vote average across districts (the *mean*). To make a prediction before the election, we cannot poll each individual citizen in each district about how they are going to vote. Instead, we have to poll a subset of citizens in a subset of districts and use that data to arrive at a best guess. In statistical language, the total set of possible votes of all citizens in all districts is called the *population,* and the subset of citizens and/or districts we poll is the *sample.* The population represents the underlying true state of the world and the sample is our window into that world.

We are normally interested in specific quantities that summarize important properties of the population. In the election example, these could be the mean vote outcome across districts or the standard deviation among district outcomes. Quantities that describe the population are called *parameters,* and they are generally not knowable. However, we can use a sample to make a guess about the true parameter values, and statisticians refer to such guesses as *estimates.* The sample mean (or average) is an estimate for the population mean, which is a parameter. The estimates of individual parameter values are also called *point estimates,* since each can be represented by a point on a line.

Figure 16-4 shows how these key concepts are related to each other. The variable of interest (e.g., vote outcome in each district) has some distribution in the population, with a population mean and a population standard deviation. A sample will consist of a set of specific observations. The number of individual observations in the sample is called the *sample size.* From the sample we can calculate a sample mean and a sample standard deviation, and these will generally differ from the population mean and standard deviation. Finally, we can define a *sampling distribution,* which is the distribution of estimates we would obtain if we repeated the sampling process many times. The width of the sampling distribution is called the *standard error,* and it tells us how precise our estimates are. In other words, the standard error provides a measure of the uncertainty associated with our parameter estimate. As a general rule, the larger the sample size, the smaller the standard error and thus the less uncertain the estimate.

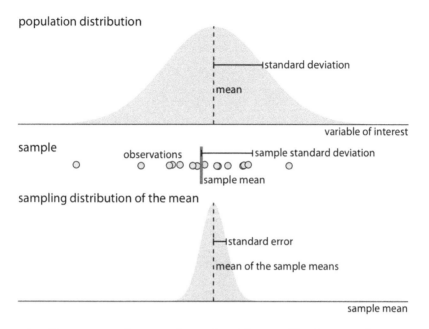

Figure 16-4. Key concepts of statistical sampling. The variable of interest that we are studying has some true distribution in the population, with a true population mean and standard deviation. Any finite sample of that variable will have a sample mean and standard deviation that differ from the population parameters. If we sampled repeatedly and calculated a mean each time, then the resulting means would be distributed according to the sampling distribution of the mean. The standard error provides information about the width of the sampling distribution, which informs us about how precisely we are estimating the parameter of interest (here, the population mean).

It is critical that we don't confuse the standard deviation and the standard error. The standard deviation is a property of the population. It tells us how much spread there is among individual observations we could make. For example, if we consider the population of voting districts, the standard deviation tells us how districts are different from one another. By contrast, the standard error tells us how precisely we have determined a parameter estimate. If we wanted to estimate the mean voting outcome over all districts, the standard error would tell us how accurate our estimate for the mean is.

All statisticians use samples to calculate parameter estimates and their uncertainties. However, they are divided in how they approach these calculations, into Bayesians and frequentists. Bayesians assume that they have some prior knowledge about the world, and they use the sample to update this knowledge. By contrast, frequentists attempt to make precise statements about the world without having any prior knowledge in hand. Fortunately, when it comes to visualizing uncertainty, Bayesians and frequentists can generally employ the same types of strategies. Here, I will first discuss the frequentist approach and then describe a few specific issues unique to the Bayesian context.

Frequentists most commonly visualize uncertainty with error bars. While error bars can be useful as a visualization of uncertainty, they are not without problems, as I already alluded to in Chapter 9 (see Figure 9-1). It is easy for readers to be confused about what an error bar represents. To highlight this problem, in Figure 16-5 I show five different uses of error bars for the same dataset. The dataset contains expert ratings of chocolate bars, rated on a scale from 1 to 5, for chocolate bars manufactured in a number of different countries. For Figure 16-5 I have extracted all ratings for chocolate bars manufactured in Canada. Underneath the sample, which is shown as a strip chart of jittered dots, we see the sample mean plus/minus the standard deviation of the sample, the sample mean plus/minus the standard error, and 80%, 95%, and 99% confidence intervals. All five error bars are derived from the variation in the sample, and they are all mathematically related, but they have different meanings. They are also visually quite distinct.

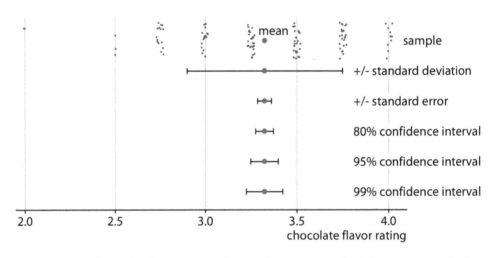

Figure 16-5. Relationship between sample, sample mean, standard deviation, standard error, and confidence intervals, in an example of chocolate bar ratings. The observations (shown as jittered green dots) that make up the sample represent expert ratings of 125 chocolate bars from manufacturers in Canada, rated on a scale from 1 (unpleasant) to 5 (elite). The large orange dot represents the mean of the ratings. Error bars indicate, from top to bottom, twice the standard deviation, twice the standard error (standard deviation of the mean), and 80%, 95%, and 99% confidence intervals of the mean. Data source: Brady Brelinski, Manhattan Chocolate Society.

Whenever you visualize uncertainty with error bars, you must specify what quantity and/or confidence level the error bars represent.

The standard error is approximately given by the sample standard deviation divided by the square root of the sample size, and confidence intervals are calculated by multiplying the standard error with small, constant values. For example, a 95% confidence interval extends approximately two times the standard error in either direction from the mean. Therefore, larger samples tend to have narrower standard errors and confidence intervals, even if their standard deviation is the same. We can see this effect when we compare ratings for chocolate bars from Canada to ones from Switzerland (Figure 16-6). The mean rating and sample standard deviation are comparable between Canadian and Swiss chocolate bars, but we have ratings for 125 Canadian bars and only 38 Swiss bars, and consequently the confidence intervals around the mean are much wider in the case of Swiss bars.

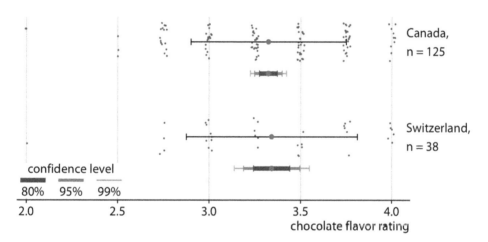

Figure 16-6. Confidence intervals widen with smaller sample size. Chocolate bars from Canada and Switzerland have comparable mean ratings and comparable standard deviations (indicated with simple black error bars). However, over three times as many Canadian bars were rated as Swiss bars, and therefore the confidence intervals (indicated with error bars of different colors and thickness drawn on top of one another) are substantially wider for the mean of the Swiss ratings than for the mean of the Canadian ratings. Data source: Brady Brelinski, Manhattan Chocolate Society.

In Figure 16-6, I am showing three different confidence intervals at the same time, using darker colors and thicker lines for the intervals representing lower confidence levels. I refer to these visualizations as *graded error bars*. The grading helps the reader perceive that there is a range of different possibilities. If I showed simple error bars (without grading) to a group of people, chances are at least some of them would perceive the error bars deterministically, for example as representing the minimum and maximum of the data. Alternatively, they might think the error bars delineate the range of possible parameter estimates—i.e., that the estimate could never fall outside the error bars. These types of misperceptions are called *deterministic construal errors*. The more we can minimize the risk of deterministic construal error, the better our visualization of uncertainty.

Error bars are convenient because they allow us to show many estimates with their uncertainties all at once. Therefore, they are commonly used in scientific publications, where the primary goal is usually to convey a large amount of information to an expert audience. As an example of this type of application, Figure 16-7 shows mean chocolate ratings and associated confidence intervals for chocolate bars manufactured in six different countries.

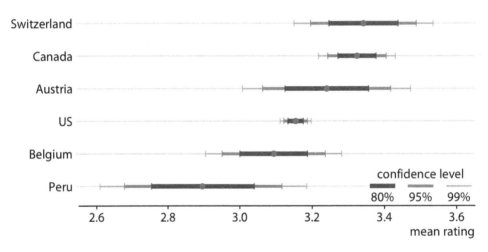

Figure 16-7. Mean chocolate flavor ratings and associated confidence intervals for chocolate bars from manufacturers in six different countries. Data source: Brady Brelinski, Manhattan Chocolate Society.

When looking at Figure 16-7, you may wonder what it tells us about the differences in mean ratings. The mean ratings of Canadian, Swiss, and Austrian bars are higher than the mean rating of US bars, but given the uncertainty in these mean ratings, are the differences in means *significant*? The word "significant" here is a technical term used by statisticians. We call a difference significant if with some level of confidence we can reject the assumption that the observed difference was caused by random sampling. Since only a finite number of Canadian and US bars were rated, the raters could have accidentally considered more of the better Canadian bars and fewer of the better US bars, and this random chance might look like a systematic rating advantage of Canadian over US bars.

Assessing significance from Figure 16-7 is difficult, because both the mean Canadian rating and the mean US rating have uncertainty. Both uncertainties matter to the question whether the means are different. Statistics textbooks and online tutorials sometimes publish rules of thumb of how to judge significance from the extent to which error bars do or don't overlap. However, these rules of thumb are not reliable and should be avoided. The correct way to assess whether there are differences in mean rating is to calculate confidence intervals for the differences. If those confidence intervals exclude zero, then we know the difference is significant at the respective confidence level. For the chocolate ratings dataset, we see that only bars from Canada are significantly higher-rated than bars from the US (Figure 16-8). For bars from Switzerland, the 95% confidence interval on the difference just barely includes the value zero. Thus, the difference between the mean ratings of US and Swiss chocolate bars is barely not significant at the 5% level. Finally, there is no evidence at all that Austrian bars have systematically higher mean ratings than US bars.

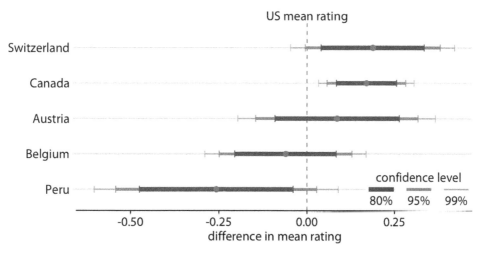

Figure 16-8. Mean chocolate flavor ratings for manufacturers from five different countries, relative to the mean rating of US chocolate bars. Canadian chocolate bars are rated significantly higher than US bars. For the other four countries there is no significant difference in mean rating compared to the US at the 95% confidence level. Confidence levels have been adjusted for multiple comparisons using Dunnett's method. Data source: Brady Brelinski, Manhattan Chocolate Society.

In the preceding figures, I have used two different types of error bars, graded and simple. More variations are possible. For example, we can draw error bars with or without a cap at the end (Figure 16-9a,c versus Figure 16-9b,d). There are advantages and disadvantages to all these choices. Graded error bars highlight the existence of different ranges corresponding to different confidence levels. However, the flip side of this additional information is added visual noise. Depending on how complex and information-dense a figure is otherwise, simple error bars may be preferable to graded ones. Whether to draw error bars with or without cap is primarily a question of personal taste. A cap highlights where exactly an error bar ends (Figure 16-9a,c), whereas an error bar without a cap puts equal emphasis on the entire range of the interval (Figure 16-9b,d). Also, again, caps add visual noise, so in a figure with many error bars omitting caps may be preferable.

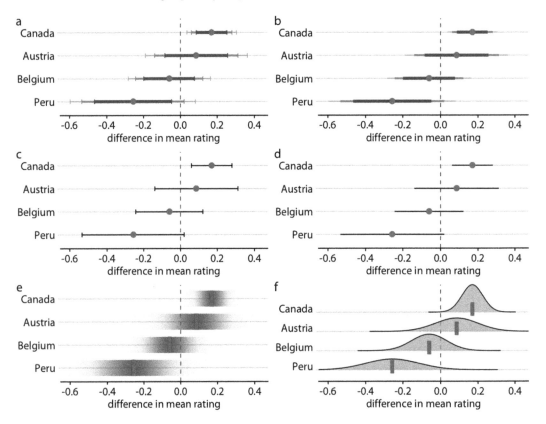

Figure 16-9. Mean chocolate flavor ratings for manufacturers from four different countries, relative to the mean rating of US chocolate bars. Each panel uses a different approach to visualizing the same uncertainty information: (a) graded error bars with caps; (b) graded error bars without caps; (c) single-interval error bars with caps; (d) single-interval error bars without caps; (e) confidence strips; (f) confidence distributions. Data source: Brady Brelinski, Manhattan Chocolate Society.

As an alternative to error bars, we could draw confidence strips that gradually fade into nothing (Figure 16-9e). Confidence strips better convey how probable different values are, but they are difficult to read. We would have to visually integrate the different shadings of color to determine where a specific confidence level ends. From Figure 16-9e we might conclude that the mean rating for Peruvian chocolate bars is significantly lower than that of US chocolate bars, and yet this is not the case. Similar problems arise when we show explicit confidence distributions (Figure 16-9f). It is difficult to visually integrate the area under the curve and to determine where exactly a given confidence level is reached. This issue can be somewhat alleviated, however, by drawing quantile dot plots as in Figure 16-3.

For simple 2D figures, error bars have one important advantage over more complex displays of uncertainty: they can be combined with many other types of plots. For nearly any visualization we may have, we can add some indication of uncertainty by adding error bars. For example, we can show amounts with uncertainty by drawing a bar plot with error bars (Figure 16-10). This type of visualization is commonly used in scientific publications. We can also draw error bars along both the x and the y direction in a scatterplot (Figure 16-11).

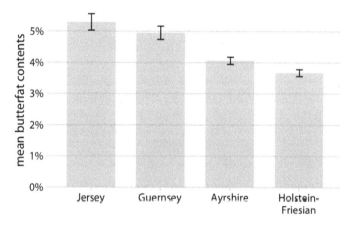

Figure 16-10. Mean butterfat contents in the milk of four cattle breeds. Error bars indicate +/– one standard error of the mean. Visualizations of this type are frequently seen in the scientific literature. While they are technically correct, they represent neither the variation within each category nor the uncertainty of the sample means particularly well. See Figure 7-11 for the variation in butterfat contents within individual breeds. Data source: Canadian Record of Performance for Purebred Dairy Cattle.

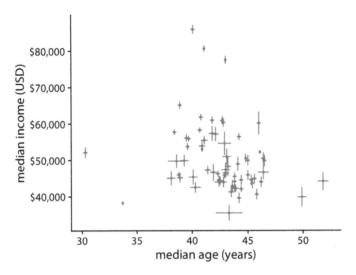

Figure 16-11. Median income versus median age for 67 counties in Pennsylvania. Error bars represent 90% confidence intervals. Data source: 2015 Five-Year American Community Survey.

Let's return to the topic of frequentists and Bayesians. Frequentists assess uncertainty with confidence intervals, whereas Bayesians calculate *posterior distributions* and *credible intervals*. The Bayesian posterior distribution tells us how likely specific parameter estimates are given the input data. The credible interval indicates a range of values in which the parameter value is expected with a given probability, as calculated from the posterior distribution. For example, a 95% credible interval corresponds to the center 95% of the posterior distribution. The true parameter value has a 95% chance of lying in the 95% credible interval.

If you are not a statistician, you may be surprised by my definition of a credible interval. You may have thought that it was actually the definition of a confidence interval. It is not. A Bayesian credible interval tells you about where the true parameter likely is, and a frequentist confidence interval tells you about where the true parameter likely is not. While this distinction may seem like semantics, there are important conceptual differences between the two approaches. Under the Bayesian approach, you use the data and your prior knowledge about the system under study (called the *prior*) to calculate a probability distribution (the *posterior*) that tells you where you can expect the true parameter value to lie. By contrast, under the frequentist approach, you first make an assumption that you intend to disprove. This assumption is called the *null hypothesis*, and it is often simply the assumption that the parameter equals zero (e.g., there is no difference between two conditions). You then calculate the probability that random sampling would generate data similar to what was observed if the null hypothesis were true. The confidence interval is a representation of this probability. If a given confidence interval excludes the parameter value under the null hypothesis (i.e., the value zero), then you can reject the null hypothesis at that confidence level. Alternatively, you can think of a confidence interval as an interval that captures the true parameter value with the specified likelihood under repeated sampling (Figure 16-12). Thus, if the true parameter value were zero, a 95% confidence interval would only exclude zero in 5% of the samples analyzed.

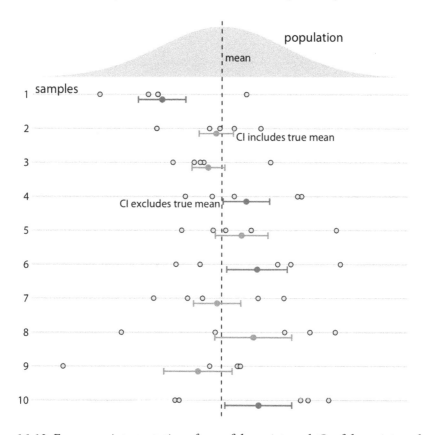

Figure 16-12. Frequency interpretation of a confidence interval. Confidence intervals (CIs) are best understood in the context of repeated sampling. For each sample, a specific confidence interval either includes (green) or excludes (orange) the true parameter, here the mean. However, if we sample repeatedly, then the confidence intervals (shown here are 68% confidence intervals, corresponding to sample mean +/– standard error) include the true mean approximately 68% of the time.

To summarize, a Bayesian credible interval makes a statement about the true parameter value, and a frequentist confidence interval makes a statement about the null hypothesis. In practice, however, Bayesian and frequentist estimates are often quite similar (Figure 16-13). Once conceptual advantage of the Bayesian approach is that it emphasizes thinking about the magnitude of an effect, whereas the frequentist thinking emphasizes a binary perspective of an effect either existing or not.

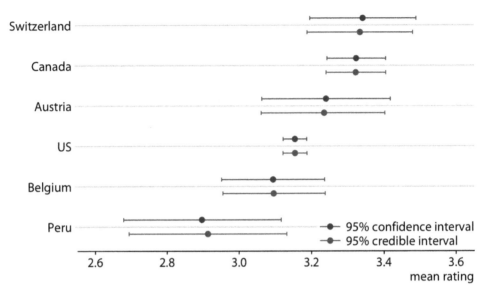

Figure 16-13. Comparison of frequentist confidence intervals and Bayesian credible intervals for mean chocolate ratings. We see that the two approaches yield similar but not exactly identical results. In particular, the Bayesian estimates display a small amount of shrinkage, which is an adjustment of the most extreme parameter estimates toward the overall mean. (Note how the Bayesian estimate for Switzerland is slightly moved to the left and the Bayesian estimate for Peru is slightly moved to the right relative to the respective frequentist estimates.) The frequentist estimates and confidence intervals shown here are identical to the results for 95% confidence shown in Figure 16-7. Data source: Brady Brelinski, Manhattan Chocolate Society.

 A Bayesian credible interval answers the question, "Where do we expect the true parameter value to lie?" A frequentist confidence interval answers the question, "How certain are we that the true parameter value is not zero?"

The central goal of Bayesian estimation is to obtain the posterior distribution. Therefore, Bayesians commonly visualize the entire distribution rather than simplifying it into a credible interval. So, in terms of data visualization, all the approaches to visualizing distributions discussed in Chapters 7, 8, and 9 are applicable. Specifically, histograms, density plots, boxplots, violins, and ridgeline plots are all commonly used to visualize Bayesian posterior distributions. Since these approaches have been discussed at length in their respective chapters, I will here show only one example, using a ridgeline plot to show Bayesian posterior distributions of mean chocolate ratings (Figure 16-14). In this specific case, I have added shading under the curve to indicate defined regions of posterior probabilities. As an alternative to shading, I could also have drawn quantile dot plots, or I could have added graded error bars underneath each distribution. Ridgeline plots with error bars underneath are called *half-eyes*, and violin plots with error bars are called *eye plots* (see "Uncertainty" on page 43).

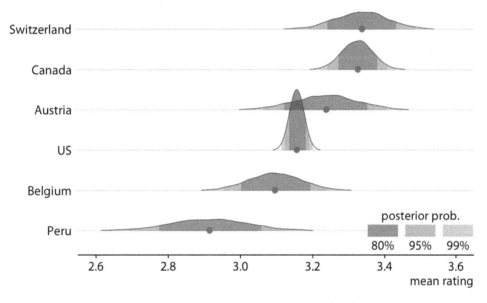

Figure 16-14. *Bayesian posterior distributions of mean chocolate bar ratings, shown as a ridgeline plot. The red dots represent the medians of each posterior distribution. Because it is difficult to convert a continuous distribution into specific confidence regions by eye, I have added shading under each curve to indicate the center 80%, 95%, and 99% of each posterior distribution. Data source: Brady Brelinski, Manhattan Chocolate Society.*

Visualizing the Uncertainty of Curve Fits

In Chapter 14, we discussed how to show a trend in a dataset by fitting a straight line or curve to the data. These trend estimates also have uncertainty, and it is customary to show the uncertainty in a trend line with a *confidence band* (Figure 16-15). The confidence band provides us with a range of different fit lines that would be compatible with the data. When students encounter a confidence band for the first time, they are often surprised that even a perfectly straight line fit produces a confidence band that is curved. The reason for the curvature is that the straight line fit can move in two distinct directions: it can move up and down (i.e., have different intercepts), and it can rotate (i.e., have different slopes). We can visually show how the confidence band arises by drawing a set of alternative fit lines randomly generated from the posterior distribution of the fit parameters. This is done in Figure 16-16, which shows 15 randomly chosen alternative fits. We see that even though each line is perfectly straight, the combination of different slopes and intercepts of each line generates an overall shape that looks just like the confidence band.

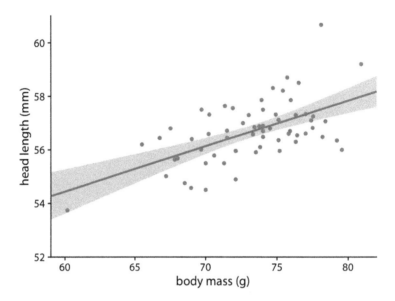

Figure 16-15. Head length versus body mass for male blue jays, as in Figure 14-7. The straight blue line represents the best linear fit to the data, and the gray band around the line shows the uncertainty in the linear fit. The gray band represents a 95% confidence level. Data source: Keith Tarvin, Oberlin College.

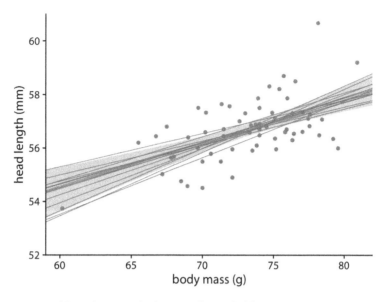

Figure 16-16. Head length versus body mass for male blue jays. In contrast to Figure 16-15, the straight blue lines now represent equally likely alternative fits randomly drawn from the posterior distribution. Data source: Keith Tarvin, Oberlin College.

To draw a confidence band, we need to specify a confidence level, and just as we saw for error bars and posterior probabilities, it can be useful to highlight different levels of confidence. This leads us to the *graded confidence band*, which shows several confidence levels at once (Figure 16-17). A graded confidence band enhances the sense of uncertainty in the reader, and it forces the reader to confront the possibility that the data might support different alternative trend lines.

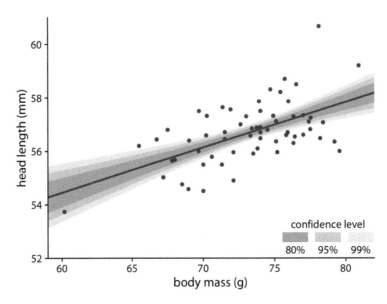

Figure 16-17. Head length versus body mass for male blue jays. As in the case of error bars, we can draw graded confidence bands to highlight the uncertainty in the estimate. Data source: Keith Tarvin, Oberlin College.

We can also draw confidence bands for nonlinear curve fits. Such confidence bands look nice but can be difficult to interpret (Figure 16-18). If we look at Figure 16-18a, we may think that the confidence band arises by moving the blue line up and down and maybe deforming it slightly. However, as Figure 16-18b reveals, the confidence band represents a family of curves that are all quite a bit more wiggly than the overall best fit shown in part (a). This is a general principle of nonlinear curve fits. Uncertainty corresponds not just to a movement of the curve up and down but also to increased wiggliness.

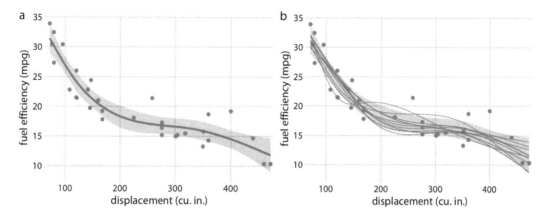

Figure 16-18. Fuel efficiency versus displacement, for 32 cars (1973–74 models). Each dot represents one car, and the smooth lines were obtained by fitting a cubic regression spline with 5 knots. (a) Best fit spline and confidence band. (b) Equally likely alternative fits drawn from the posterior distribution. Data source: Motor Trend, *1974.*

Hypothetical Outcome Plots

All static visualizations of uncertainty suffer from the problem that viewers may interpret some aspect of the uncertainty visualization as a deterministic feature of the data (a deterministic construal error, as described previously). We can avoid this problem by visualizing uncertainty through animation, by cycling through a number of different but equally likely plots. This kind of visualization is called a *hypothetical outcome plot* (HOP) [Hullman, Resnick, and Adar 2015]. While HOPs are not possible in a print medium, they can be very effective in online settings where animated visualizations can be provided in the form of GIFs or MP4 videos. HOPs can also work well in the context of an oral presentation.

To illustrate the concept of a HOP, let's go back once more to chocolate bar ratings. When you are standing in the grocery store thinking about buying some chocolate, you probably don't care about the mean flavor rating and associated uncertainty for certain groups of chocolate bars. Instead, you might want to know the answer to a simpler question, such as: if I randomly pick up a Canadian- and a US-manufactured chocolate bar, which one of the two should I expect to taste better? To arrive at an answer to this question, we could randomly select a Canadian and a US bar from the dataset, compare their ratings, record the outcome, and then repeat this process many times. If we did this, we would find that in approximately 53% of the cases the Canadian bar will be ranked higher, and in 47% of the cases either the US bar is ranked higher or the two bars are tied. We can show this process visually by cycling between several of these random draws and showing the relative ranking of the two bars for each draw (Figure 16-19).

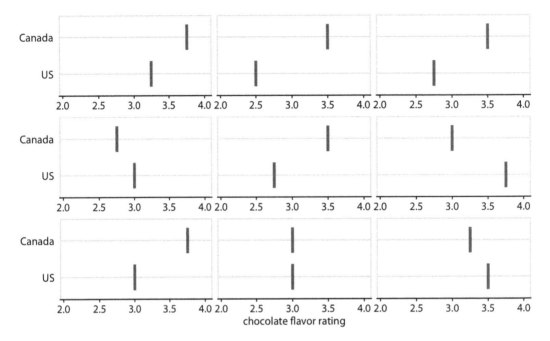

Figure 16-19. Schematic of a hypothetical outcome plot for chocolate bar ratings of Canadian- and US-manufactured bars. Each vertical green bar represents the rating for one bar, and each panel shows a comparison of two randomly chosen bars, one each from a Canadian manufacturer and a US manufacturer. In an actual hypothetical outcome plot, the display would cycle between the distinct plot panels instead of showing them side-by-side. Data source: Brady Brelinski, Manhattan Chocolate Society.

As a second example, consider the variation in shapes among equally probable trend lines in Figure 16-18b. Because all trend lines are plotted on top of one another, we primarily perceive the overall area that is covered by trend lines, which is similar to the confidence band. Perceiving individual trend lines is difficult. By turning this figure into a HOP, we can highlight individual trend lines one at a time (Figure 16-20).

When preparing a HOP, you may wonder whether it is better to make a hard switch between different outcomes (as in a slide projector) or rather smoothly animate from one outcome to the next (e.g., slowly deform the trend line for one outcome until it looks like the trend line for another outcome). While this is to some extent an open question that continues to be researched, some evidence indicates that smooth transitions make it harder to judge about the probabilities represented [Kale et al. 2018]. If you consider animating between outcomes, you may want to at least make these animations very fast, or choose an animation style where outcomes fade in and out rather than deform from one to the other.

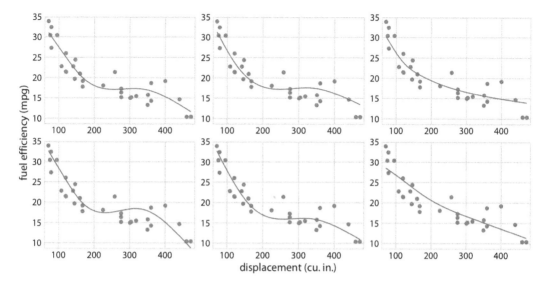

Figure 16-20. Schematic of a hypothetical outcome plot for fuel efficiency versus displacement. Each dot represents one car, and the smooth lines were obtained by fitting a cubic regression spline with 5 knots. Each line in each panel represents one alternative fit outcome, drawn from the posterior distribution of the fit parameters. In an actual hypothetical outcome plot, the display would cycle between the distinct plot panels instead of showing them side-by-side. Data source: Motor Trend, *1974.*

There is one critical aspect we need to pay attention to when preparing a HOP: we need to make sure that the outcomes we do show are representative of the true distribution of possible outcomes. Otherwise, our HOP could be rather misleading. For example, going back to the case of chocolate ratings, if I randomly selected 10 outcome pairs of chocolate bars and among those the US bar was rated higher than the Canadian bar in 7 cases, then the HOP would erroneously create the impression that US bars tend to be rated higher than Canadian bars. We can prevent this issue either by choosing a very large number of outcomes, so sampling biases are unlikely, or by verifying in some form that the outcomes that are shown are appropriate. When making Figure 16-19, I verified that the number of times the Canadian bar was shown winning was close to the true percentage of 53%.

## PART II

Principles of Figure Design

## CHAPTER 17

The Principle of Proportional Ink

In many different visualization scenarios, we represent data values by the extent of a graphical element. For example, in a bar plot, we draw bars that begin at 0 and end at the data value they represent. In this case, the data value is not only encoded in the endpoint of the bar but also in the height or length of the bar. If we drew a bar that started at a different value than 0, then the length of the bar and the bar endpoint would convey contradicting information. Such figures are internally inconsistent, because they show two different values with the same graphical element. Contrast this to a scenario where we visualize the data value with a dot. In this case, the value is only encoded in the location of the dot, not in the size or shape of the dot.

Similar issues will arise whenever we use graphical elements such as bars, rectangles, shaded areas of arbitrary shape, or any other elements that have a defined visual extent which can be either consistent or inconsistent with the data value shown. In all these cases, we need to make sure that there is no inconsistency. This concept has been termed as the *principle of proportional ink* [Bergstrom and West 2016]:

> When a shaded region is used to represent a numerical value, the area of that shaded region should be directly proportional to the corresponding value.

(It is common practice to use the word "ink" to refer to any part of a visualization that deviates from the background color. This includes lines, points, shared areas, and text. In this chapter, however, we are talking primarily about shaded areas.) Violations of this principle are quite common, in particular in the popular press and in the world of finance.

Visualizations Along Linear Axes

We first consider the most common scenario, visualization of amounts along a linear scale. Figure 17-1 shows the median income in the five counties that make up the state of Hawaii. It is a typical figure one might encounter in a newspaper article. A quick glance at the figure suggests that the county of Hawaii is incredibly poor while the county of Honolulu is much richer than the other counties. However, Figure 17-1 is quite misleading, because all the bars begin at $50,000 median income. Thus, while the endpoint of each bar correctly represents the actual median income in each county, the bar height represents the extent to which median incomes exceed $50,000, an arbitrary number. And human perception is such that the bar height is the key quantity we perceive when looking at this figure, not the location of the bar endpoint relative to the *y* axis.

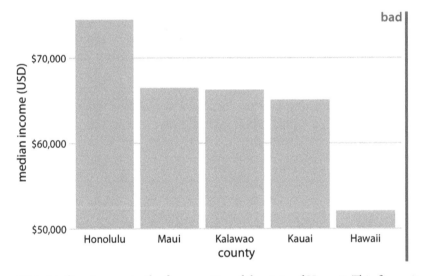

Figure 17-1. Median income in the five counties of the state of Hawaii. This figure is misleading, because the y-axis scale starts at $50,000 instead of $0. As a result, the bar heights are not proportional to the values shown, and the income differential between the county of Hawaii and the other four counties appears much bigger than it actually is. Data source: 2015 Five-Year American Community Survey.

An appropriate visualization of this dataset makes for a less exciting story (Figure 17-2). While there are differences in median income between the counties, they are nowhere near as big as Figure 17-1 suggested. Overall, the median incomes in the different counties are somewhat comparable.

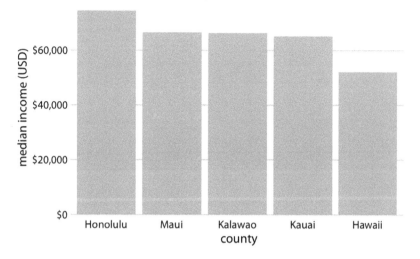

Figure 17-2. Median income in the five counties of the state of Hawaii. Here, the y-axis scale starts at $0 and therefore the relative magnitudes of the median incomes in the five counties are accurately shown. Data source: 2015 Five-Year American Community Survey.

Bars on a linear scale should always start at 0.

Similar visualization problems frequently arise in the visualization of time series, such as those of stock prices. Figure 17-3 suggests a massive collapse in the stock price of Facebook occurred around Nov. 1, 2016. In reality, the price decline was moderate relative to the total price of the stock (Figure 17-4). The y-axis range in Figure 17-3 would be questionable even without the shading underneath the curve. But with the shading, the figure becomes particularly problematic. The shading emphasizes the distance from the location of the x axis to the specific y values shown, and thus it creates the visual impression that the height of the shaded area at a given day represents the stock price of that day. Instead, it only represents the difference in the stock price from the baseline, which is $110 in Figure 17-3.

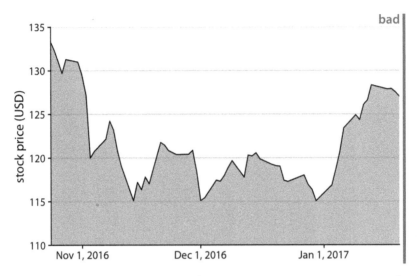

Figure 17-3. Stock price of Facebook (FB) from Oct. 22, 2016 to Jan. 21, 2017. This figure seems to imply that the FB stock price collapsed around Nov. 1, 2016. However, this is misleading, because the y axis starts at $110 instead of $0. Data source: Yahoo! Finance.

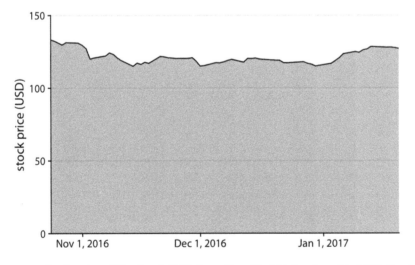

Figure 17-4. Stock price of Facebook (FB) from Oct. 22, 2016 to Jan. 21, 2017. By showing the stock price on a y scale from $0 to $150, this figure more accurately relays the magnitude of the FB price drop around Nov. 1, 2016. Data source: Yahoo! Finance.

The examples of Figures 17-2 and 17-4 could suggest that bars and shaded areas are not useful to represent small changes over time or differences between conditions, since we always have to draw the whole bar or area starting from 0. However, this is not the case. It is perfectly valid to use bars or shaded areas to show differences between conditions, as long as we make it explicit which differences we are showing. For example, we can use bars to visualize the change in median income in Hawaiian counties from 2010 to 2015 (Figure 17-5). For all counties except Kalawao, this change amounts to less than $5,000. (Kalawao is an unusual county, with fewer than 100 inhabitants, and it can experience large swings in median income from a small number of people moving into or out of the county.) And for Hawaii County, the change is negative; i.e., the median income in 2015 was lower than it was in 2010. We represent negative values by drawing bars that go in the opposite direction, extending downward from 0 rather than up.

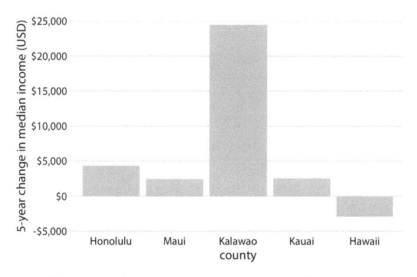

Figure 17-5. Change in median income in Hawaiian counties from 2010 to 2015. Data source: 2010 and 2015 Five-Year American Community Surveys.

Similarly, we can draw the change in Facebook stock price over time as the difference from its temporary high point on Oct. 22, 2016 (Figure 17-6). By shading an area that represents the distance from the high point, we are accurately representing the absolute magnitude of the price drop without making any implicit statement about the magnitude of the price drop relative to the total stock price.

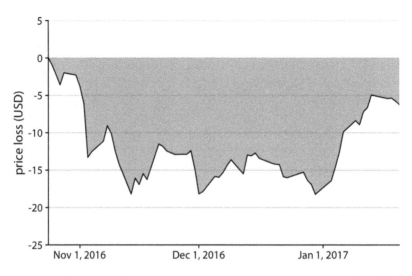

Figure 17-6. Decline in Facebook (FB) stock price relative to the price of Oct. 22, 2016. Between Nov. 1, 2016 and Jan. 1, 2017, the price remained approximately $15 lower than it was at its high point on Oct. 22, 2016. The price started to recover in January. Data source: Yahoo! Finance.

Visualizations Along Logarithmic Axes

When we are visualizing data along a linear scale, the areas of bars, rectangles, or other shapes are automatically proportional to the data values. The same is not true if we are using a logarithmic scale, because data values are not linearly spaced along the axis. Therefore, one could argue that, for example, bar graphs on a log scale are inherently flawed. On the flip side, the area of each bar will be proportional to the logarithm of the data value, and thus bar graphs on a log scale satisfy the principle of proportional ink in log-transformed coordinates. In practice, I think neither of these two arguments can resolve whether log-scale bar graphs are appropriate. Instead, the relevant question is whether we want to visualize amounts or ratios.

In Chapter 3, I have explained that a log scale is the natural scale to visualize ratios, because a unit step along a log scale corresponds to multiplication with or division by a constant factor. In practice, however, log scales are often used not specifically to visualize ratios but rather just because the numbers shown vary over many orders of magnitude. As an example, consider the gross domestic products (GDPs) of countries in Oceania. In 2007, these varied from less than a billion US dollars (USD) to over 300 billion USD (Figure 17-7). Visualizing these numbers on a linear scale would not work, because the two countries with the largest GDPs (New Zealand and Australia) would dominate the figure.

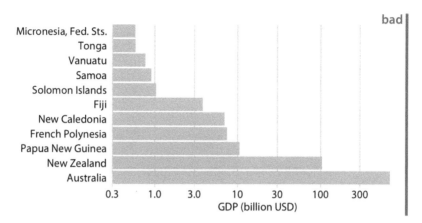

Figure 17-7. GDP in 2007 of countries in Oceania. The lengths of the bars do not accurately reflect the data values shown, since bars start at the arbitrary value of 0.3 billion USD. Data source: Gapminder.

However, the visualization with bars on a log scale (Figure 17-7) does not work either. The bars start at an arbitrary value of 0.3 billion USD, and at a minimum the figure suffers from the same problem of Figure 17-1, that the bar lengths are not representative of the data values. The added difficulty with a log scale, though, is that we cannot simply let the bars start at 0. In Figure 17-7, the value 0 would lie infinitely far to the left. Therefore, we could make our bars arbitrarily long by pushing their origin further and further away, as in Figure 17-8. This problem always arises when we try to visualize amounts (which is what the GDP values are) on a log scale.

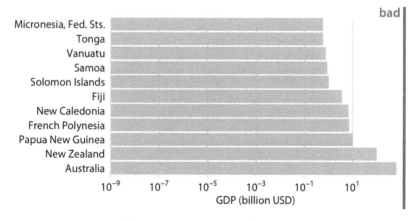

Figure 17-8. GDP in 2007 of countries in Oceania. The lengths of the bars do not accurately reflect the data values shown, since bars start at the arbitrary value of 10^{-9} billion USD. Data source: Gapminder.

For the data of Figure 17-7, I think bars are inappropriate. Instead, we can simply place a dot at the appropriate location along the scale for each country's GDP and avoid the issue of bar lengths altogether (Figure 17-9). Importantly, by placing the country names right next to the dots rather than along the *y* axis, we avoid generating the visual perception of a magnitude conveyed by the distance from the country name to the dot.

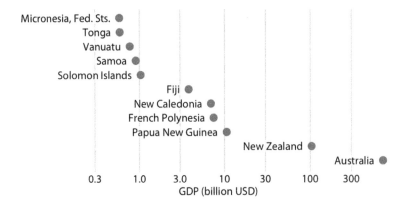

Figure 17-9. GDP in 2007 of countries in Oceania. Data source: Gapminder.

If we want to visualize ratios rather than amounts, however, bars on a log scale are a perfectly good option. In fact, they are preferable to bars on a linear scale in that case. As an example, let's visualize the GDP values of countries in Oceania relative to the GDP of Papua New Guinea. The resulting figure does a good job of highlighting the key relationships between the GDPs of the various countries (Figure 17-10). We can see that New Zealand has over 8 times the GDP of Papua New Guinea and Australia over 64 times, while Tonga and the Federated States of Micronesia each have less than 1/16th the GDP of Papua New Guinea. French Polynesia and New Caledonia are close but have slightly smaller GDPs than Papua New Guinea.

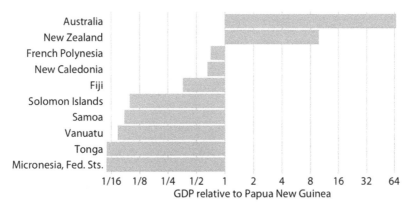

Figure 17-10. GDP in 2007 of countries in Oceania, relative to the GDP of Papua New Guinea. Data source: Gapminder.

Figure 17-10 also highlights that the natural midpoint of a log scale is 1, with bars representing numbers above 1 going in one direction and bars representing numbers below 1 going in the other direction. Bars on a log scale represent ratios and should always start at 1, and bars on a linear scale represent amounts and should always start at 0.

When bars are drawn on a log scale, they represent ratios and need to be drawn starting from 1, not 0.

Direct Area Visualizations

All the preceding examples visualized data along one linear dimension, so that each data value was encoded both by area and by location along the x or y axis. In these cases, we can consider the area encoding as incidental and secondary to the location encoding of the data value. Other visualization approaches, however, represent the data values primarily or directly by area, without a corresponding location mapping. The most common one is the pie chart (Figure 17-11). Even though technically the data values are mapped onto angles, which are represented by location along a circular axis, in practice we are typically not judging the angles of a pie chart. Instead, the dominant visual property we notice is the area of each pie wedge.

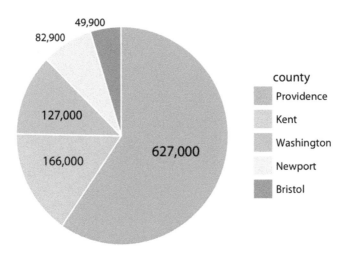

Figure 17-11. Number of inhabitants in Rhode Island counties, shown as a pie chart. Both the angle and the area of each pie wedge are proportional to the number of inhabitants in the respective county. Data source: 2010 US Decennial Census.

Because the area of each pie wedge is proportional to its angle, which is proportional to the data value the wedge represents, pie charts satisfy the principle of proportional ink. However, we perceive the area in a pie chart differently from the same area in a bar plot. The fundamental reason is that human perception primarily judges distances and not areas. Thus, if a data value is encoded entirely as a distance, as is the case with the length of a bar, we perceive it more accurately than when the data value is encoded through a combination of two or more distances that jointly create an area. To see this difference, compare Figure 17-11 to Figure 17-12, which shows the same data as bars. The difference in the number of inhabitants between Providence County and the other counties appears larger in Figure 17-12 than in Figure 17-11.

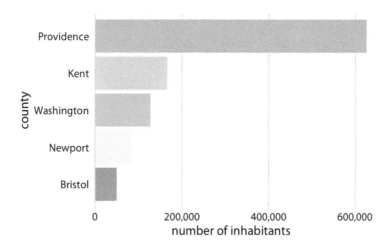

Figure 17-12. Number of inhabitants in Rhode Island counties, shown as bars. The length of each bar is proportional to the number of inhabitants in the respective county. Data source: 2010 US Decennial Census.

The problem that human perception is better at judging distances than at judging areas also arises in treemaps (Figure 17-13), which can be thought of as square versions of pie charts. Again, in comparison to Figure 17-12, the differences in the number of inhabitants among the counties appears less pronounced in Figure 17-13.

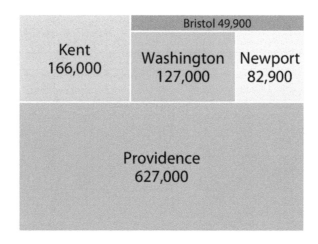

Figure 17-13. Number of inhabitants in Rhode Island counties, shown as a treemap. The area of each rectangle is proportional to the number of inhabitants in the respective county. Data source: 2010 US Decennial Census.

## CHAPTER 18

Handling Overlapping Points

When we want to visualize large or very large datasets, we often experience the challenge that simple x–y scatterplots do not work very well because many points lie on top of each other and partially or fully overlap. And similar problems can arise even in small datasets if data values were recorded with low precision or rounded, such that multiple observations have exactly the same numeric values. The technical term commonly used to describe this situation is *overplotting*, which means that we are plotting many points on top of each other. Here I describe several strategies you can pursue when encountering this challenge.

Partial Transparency and Jittering

We first consider a scenario with only a moderate number of data points but with extensive rounding. Our dataset contains fuel economy during city driving and engine displacement for 234 popular car models released between 1999 and 2008 (Figure 18-1). In this dataset, fuel economy is measured in miles per gallon (mpg) and is rounded to the nearest integer value. Engine displacement is measured in liters and is rounded to the nearest deciliter. Due to this rounding, many car models have exactly identical values. For example, there are 21 cars total with 2.0 liter engine displacement, and as a group they have only four different fuel economy values: 19, 20, 21, or 22 mpg. Therefore, in Figure 18-1 these 21 cars are represented by only four distinct points, so that 2.0 liter engines appear much less popular than they actually are. Moreover, the dataset contains two four-wheel drive cars with 2.0 liter engines, which are represented by black dots. However, these black dots are fully occluded by yellow dots, so that it looks like there are no four-wheel drive cars with a 2.0 liter engine.

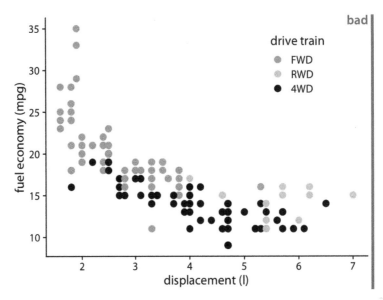

Figure 18-1. City fuel economy versus engine displacement, for popular cars released between 1999 and 2008. Each point represents one car. The point color encodes the drive train: front-wheel drive (FWD), rear-wheel drive (RWD), or four-wheel drive (4WD). The figure is labeled "bad" because many points are plotted on top of others and obscure them. Data source: US Environmental Protection Agency (EPA), https://fueleconomy.gov.

One way to ameliorate this problem is to use partial transparency. If we make individual points partially transparent, then overplotted points appear as darker points and thus the shade of the points reflects the density of points in that location of the graph (Figure 18-2).

However, making points partially transparent is not always sufficient to solve the issue of overplotting. For example, even though we can see in Figure 18-2 that some points have a darker shade than others, it is difficult to estimate how many points were plotted on top of each other in each location. In addition, while the differences in shading are clearly visible, they are not self-explanatory. A reader who sees this figure for the first time will likely wonder why some points are darker than others and will not realize that those points are in fact multiple points stacked on top of each other. A simple trick that helps in this situation is to apply a small amount of jitter to the points—i.e., to displace each point randomly by a small amount in either the *x* or the *y* direction or both. With jitter, it is immediately apparent that the darker areas arise from points that are plotted on top of each other (Figure 18-3). Also, now, for the first time the black dots that represent four-wheel drive cars with 2.0 liter engines can be seen.

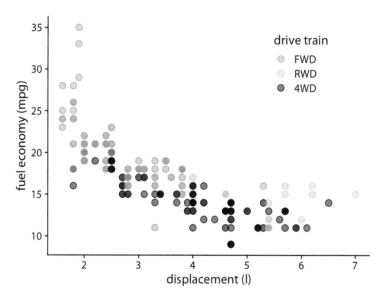

Figure 18-2. City fuel economy versus engine displacement. Because points have been made partially transparent, points that lie on top of other points can now be identified by their darker shade. Data source: EPA.

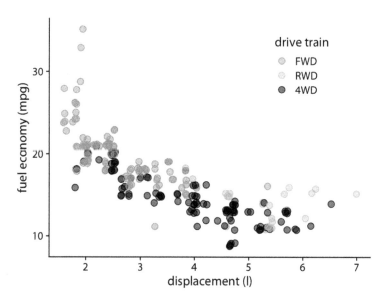

Figure 18-3. City fuel economy versus engine displacement. By adding a small amount of jitter to each point, we can increase the visibility of the overplotted points without substantially distorting the message of the plot. Data source: EPA.

One downside of jittering is that it does change the data and therefore has to be performed with care. If we jitter too much, we end up placing points in locations that are not representative of the underlying dataset. The result is a misleading visualization of the data. See Figure 18-4 as an example.

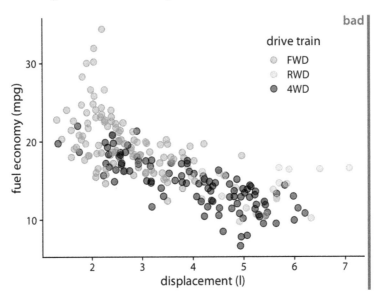

Figure 18-4. City fuel economy versus engine displacement. By adding too much jitter to the points, we have created a visualization that does not accurately reflect the underlying dataset. Data source: EPA.

2D Histograms

When the number of individual points gets very large, partial transparency (with or without jittering) will not be sufficient to resolve the overplotting issue. What will typically happen is that areas with high point density will appear as uniform blobs of dark color, while in areas with low point density the individual points are barely visible (Figure 18-5). And changing the transparency level of individual points will either ameliorate one or the other of these problems while worsening the other; no transparency setting can address both at the same time.

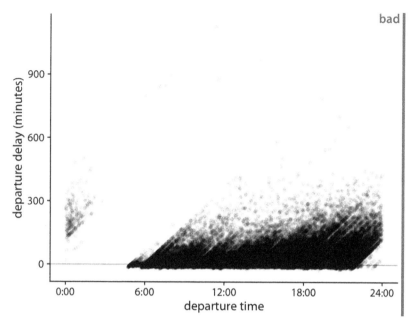

Figure 18-5. Departure delay in minutes versus flight departure time, for all flights departing Newark Airport (EWR) in 2013. Each dot represents one departure. Data source: US Dept. of Transportation, Bureau of Transportation Statistics.

Figure 18-5 shows departure delays for over 100,000 individual flights, with each dot representing one flight departure. Even though we have made the individual dots fairly transparent, the majority of them just form a black band at between 0 and 300 minutes departure delay. This band obscures whether most flights depart approximately on time or with a substantial delay (say, 50 minutes or more). At the same time, the most-delayed flights (with delays of 400 minutes or more) are barely visible due to the transparency of the dots.

In such cases, instead of plotting individual points, we can make a *2D histogram*. A 2D histogram is conceptually similar to a 1D histogram, as discussed in Chapter 7, but now we bin the data in two dimensions. We subdivide the entire x–y plane into small rectangles, count how many observations fall into each one, and then color the rectangles by those counts. Figure 18-6 shows the result of this approach for the departure delay data. This visualization highlights several important features of the flight departure data. First, the vast majority of departures during the day (from 6 a.m. to about 9 p.m.) actually depart without delay or even early (negative delay). However, a modest number of departures have a substantial delay. Moreover, the later a plane departs in the day, the more of a delay it can have. Importantly, the departure time is the actual time of departure, not the scheduled time of departure, so this figure does not necessarily tell us that planes scheduled to depart early never experience delay. What it does tell us, though, is that if a plane departs early it either has little delay or, in very rare cases, a delay of around 900 minutes.

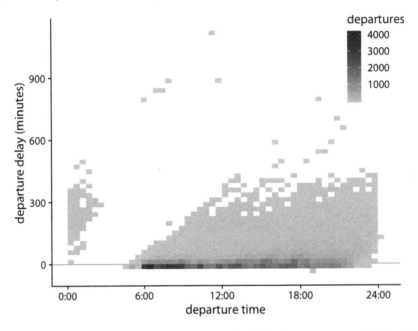

Figure 18-6. Departure delay in minutes versus the flight departure time. Each colored rectangle represents all flights departing at that time with that departure delay. Coloring represents the number of flights represented by that rectangle. Data source: US Dept. of Transportation, Bureau of Transportation Statistics.

As an alternative to binning the data into rectangles, we can bin into hexagons [Carr et al. 1987]. This approach has the advantage that the points in a hexagon are, on average, closer to the hexagon's center than the points in an equal-area square are to the center of the square. Therefore, the colored hexagons represent the data slightly more accurately than the colored rectangles. Figure 18-7 shows the flight departure data with hexagon binning rather than rectangular binning.

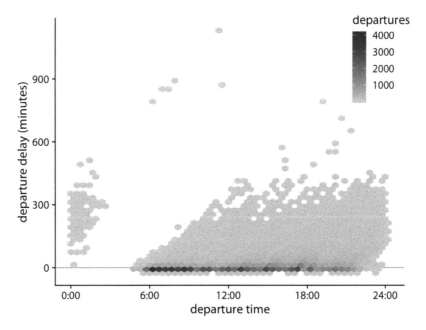

Figure 18-7. Departure delay in minutes versus the flight departure time. Each colored hexagon represents all flights departing at that time with that departure delay. Coloring represents the number of flights represented by that hexagon. Data source: US Dept. of Transportation, Bureau of Transportation Statistics.

Contour Lines

Instead of binning data points into rectangles or hexagons, we can also estimate the point density across the plot area and indicate regions of different point densities with contour lines. This technique works well when the point density changes slowly across both the *x* and the *y* dimensions.

As an example for this approach, we return to the blue jays dataset from Chapter 12. Figure 12-1 showed the relationship between head length and body mass for 123 blue jays, and there was some amount of overlap among the points. We can highlight the distribution of points more clearly by making the points smaller and partially transparent and plotting them on top of contour lines that delineate regions of similar point density (Figure 18-8). We can further enhance the perception of changes in the point density by shading the regions enclosed by the contour lines, using darker colors for regions representing higher point densities (Figure 18-9).

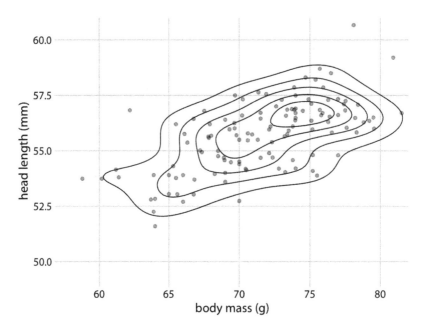

Figure 18-8. Head length versus body mass for 123 blue jays, as in Figure 12-1. Each dot corresponds to one bird, and the lines indicate regions of similar point density. The point density increases toward the center of the plot, near a body mass of 75 g and a head length between 55 mm and 57.5 mm. Data source: Keith Tarvin, Oberlin College.

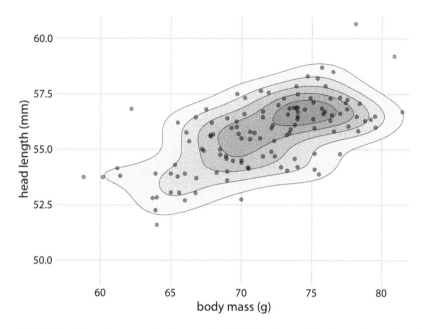

Figure 18-9. Head length versus body mass for 123 blue jays. This figure is nearly identi-cal to Figure 18-8, but now the areas enclosed by the contour lines are shaded with increasingly darker shades of gray. This shading creates a stronger visual impression of increasing point density toward the center of the point cloud. Data source: Keith Tarvin, Oberlin College.

In Chapter 12, we also looked at the relationship between head length and body mass separately for male and female birds (Figure 12-2). We can do the same with contour lines, by drawing separately colored contour lines for male and female birds (Figure 18-10).

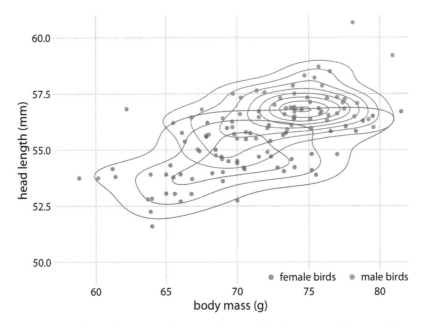

Figure 18-10. Head length versus body mass for 123 blue jays. As in Figure 12-2, we can also indicate the birds' sex by color when drawing contour lines. This figure highlights how the point distribution is different for male and female birds. In particular, male birds are more densely clustered in one region of the plot area whereas female birds are more spread out. Data source: Keith Tarvin, Oberlin College.

Drawing multiple sets of contour lines in different colors can be a powerful strategy for showing the distributions of several point clouds at once. However, this technique needs to be employed with care. It only works when the number of groups with distinct colors is small (two to three) and the groups are clearly separated. Otherwise, we may end up with a hairball of differently colored lines all crisscrossing each other and not showing any particular pattern at all.

To illustrate this potential problem, I will employ the diamonds dataset, which contains information for 53,940 diamonds, including their price, weight (carat), and cut. Figure 18-11 shows this dataset as a scatterplot. The figure exhibits severe overplotting. There are so many different-colored points on top of one another that it is impossible to discern anything beyond the overall broad outline of where diamonds fall on the price–carat spectrum.

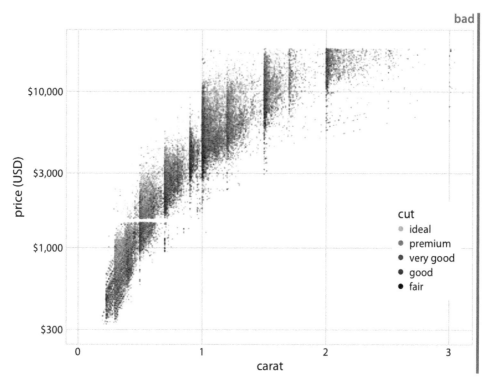

Figure 18-11. Price of diamonds versus their carat value, for 53,940 individual diamonds. Each diamond's cut is indicated by color. The plot is labeled as "bad" because the extensive overplotting makes it impossible to discern any patterns among the different diamond cuts. Data source: Hadley Wickham, ggplot2.

We could try to draw colored contour lines for the different qualities of cut, as in Figure 18-10. However, in the diamonds dataset, we have five distinct colors and the groups strongly overlap. Therefore, the contour plot (Figure 18-12) is not much better than the original scatterplot (Figure 18-11).

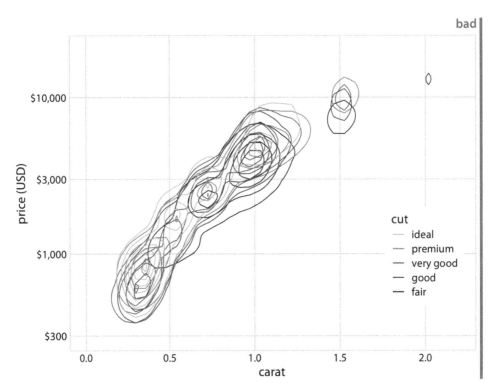

Figure 18-12. Price of diamonds versus their carat value. As in Figure 18-11, but now individual points have been replaced by contour lines. The resulting plot is still labeled "bad," because the contour lines all lie on top of each other. Neither the point distribution for individual cuts nor the overall point distribution can be discerned. Data source: Hadley Wickham, ggplot2.

What helps here is to draw the contour lines for each cut quality in its own plot panel (Figure 18-13). The purpose of drawing them all in one panel might be to enable visual comparison between the groups, but Figure 18-12 is so busy that a comparison isn't possible. Instead, in Figure 18-13, the background grid enables us to make comparisons across cut qualities by paying attention to where exactly the contour lines fall relative to the grid lines. (A similar effect could have been achieved by plotting partially transparent individual points instead of contour lines in each panel.)

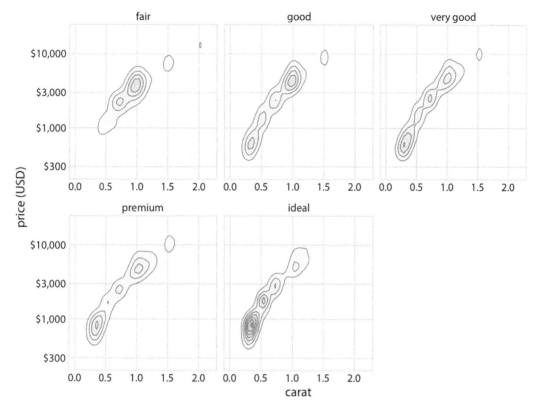

Figure 18-13. Price of diamonds versus their carat value. Here, we have taken the density contours from Figure 18-12 and drawn them separately for each cut. We can now see that better cuts (very good, premium, ideal) tend to have lower carat values than the poorer cuts (fair, good) but command a higher price per carat. Data source: Hadley Wickham, ggplot2.

We can now make out two main trends. First, the better cuts (very good, premium, ideal) tend to have lower carat values than the poorer cuts (fair, good). Recall that carat is a measure of diamond weight (1 carat = 0.2 grams). Better cuts tend to result (on average) in lighter diamonds because more material needs to be removed to create them. Second, at the same carat value, better cuts tend to command higher prices. To see this pattern, look for example at the price distribution for 0.5 carats. The distribution is shifted upwards for better cuts, and in particular it is substantially higher for diamonds with ideal cut than for diamonds with fair or good cut.

## CHAPTER 19

Common Pitfalls of Color Use

Color can be an incredibly effective tool to enhance data visualizations. At the same time, poor color choices can ruin an otherwise excellent visualization. Color needs to be applied to serve a purpose, it must be clear, and it must not distract.

Encoding Too Much or Irrelevant Information

One common mistake is trying to give color a job that is too big for it to handle, by encoding too many different items in different colors. As an example, consider Figure 19-1. It shows population growth versus population size for all 50 US states and the District of Columbia. I have attempted to identify each state by giving it its own color. However, the result is not very useful. Even though we can guess which state is which by looking at the colored points in the plot and in the legend, it takes a lot of effort to go back and forth between the two to try to match them up. There are simply too many different colors, and many of them are quite similar to each other. Even if with a lot of effort we can figure out exactly which state is which, this visualization defeats the purpose of coloring. We should use color to enhance figures and make them easier to read, not to obscure the data by creating visual puzzles.

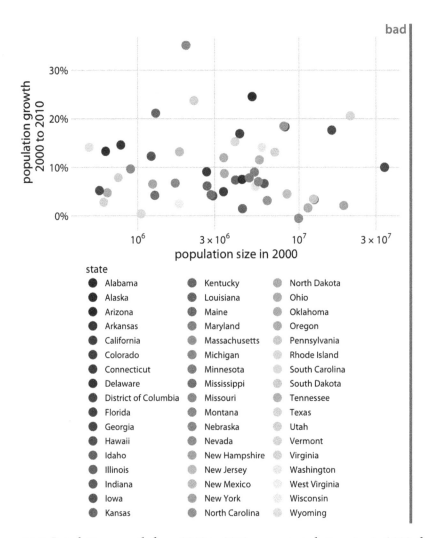

Figure 19-1. Population growth from 2000 to 2010 versus population size in 2000, for all 50 US states and the District of Columbia. Every state is marked in a different color. Because there are so many states, it is very difficult to match the colors in the legend to the dots in the scatterplot. Data source: US Census Bureau.

As a rule of thumb, qualitative color scales work best when there are three to five different categories that need to be colored. Once we reach 8 to 10 different categories or more, the task of matching colors to categories becomes too burdensome to be useful, even if the colors remain sufficiently different to be distinguishable in principle. For the dataset of Figure 19-1, it is probably best to use color only to indicate the geographic region of each state and to identify individual states by direct labeling—i.e., by placing appropriate text labels adjacent to the data points (Figure 19-2). Even though we cannot label every individual state without making the figure too crowded, direct labeling is the right choice for this figure. In general, for figures such as this one, we don't need to label every single data point. It is sufficient to label a representative subset, for example a set of states we specifically want to call out in the text that will accompany the figure. We always have the option to also provide the underlying data as a table if we want to make sure the reader has access to it in its entirety.

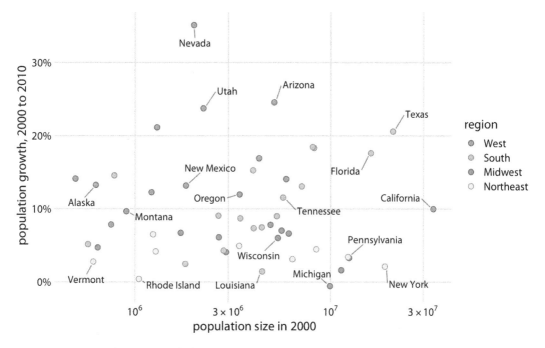

Figure 19-2. Population growth from 2000 to 2010 versus population size in 2000. In contrast to Figure 19-1, I have now colored states by region and have directly labeled a subset of states. The majority of states have been left unlabeled to prevent overcrowding in the figure. Data source: US Census Bureau.

 Use direct labeling instead of colors when you need to distinguish between more than about eight categorical items.

A second common problem is coloring for the sake of coloring, without having a clear purpose for the colors. As an example, consider Figure 19-3, which is a variation of Figure 4-2. However, now instead of coloring the bars by geographic regions, I have given each bar its own color, so that in aggregate the bars create a rainbow effect.

This may look like an interesting visual effect, but it is not creating any new insight into the data or making the figure easier to read.

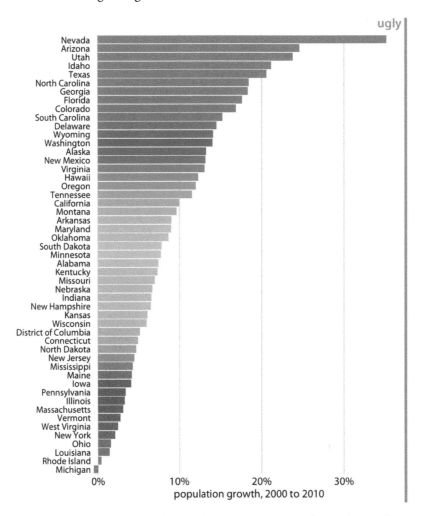

Figure 19-3. Population growth in the US from 2000 to 2010. The rainbow coloring of states serves no purpose and is distracting. Furthermore, the colors are overly saturated. Data source: US Census Bureau.

Besides the gratuitous use of different colors, Figure 19-3 has a second color-related problem: the chosen colors are too saturated and intense. This color intensity makes the figure difficult to look at. For example, it is difficult to read the names of the states without having our eyes drawn to the large, strongly colored areas right next to the state names. Similarly, it is difficult to compare the endpoints of the bars to the underlying grid lines.

Avoid large filled areas of overly saturated colors. They make it difficult for your reader to carefully inspect your figure.

Using Nonmonotonic Color Scales to Encode Data Values

In Chapter 4, I listed two critical conditions for designing sequential color scales that can represent data values: the colors need to clearly indicate which data values are larger or smaller than which other ones, and the differences between colors need to visualize the corresponding differences between data values. Unfortunately, several existing color scales—including very popular ones—violate one or both of these conditions. The most popular such scale is the rainbow scale (Figure 19-4). It runs through all possible colors in the color spectrum. This means the scale is effectively circular; the colors at the beginning and the end are nearly the same (dark red). If these two colors end up next to each other in a plot, we do not instinctively perceive them as representing data values that are maximally apart. In addition, the scale is highly nonmonotonic. It has regions where colors change very slowly and others where colors change rapidly. This lack of monotonicity becomes particularly apparent if we look at the color scale converted to grayscale (Figure 19-4). The scale goes from medium dark to light to very dark and back to medium dark, and there are large stretches where lightness changes very little followed by relatively narrow stretches with large changes in lightness.

rainbow scale

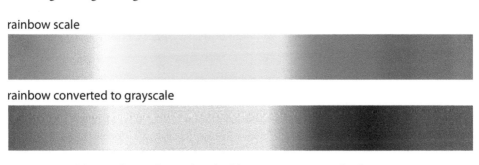

rainbow converted to grayscale

Figure 19-4. The rainbow color scale is highly nonmonotonic. This becomes apparent when the colors are converted to gray values. From left to right, the scale goes from moderately dark to light to very dark and back to moderately dark. In addition, the changes in lightness are nonuniform. The lightest part of the scale (corresponding to the colors yellow, light green, and cyan) takes up almost a third of the entire scale, while the darkest part (corresponding to dark blue) is concentrated in a narrow region of the scale.

In a visualization of actual data, the rainbow scale tends to obscure data features and/or highlight arbitrary aspects of the data (Figure 19-5). As an aside, the colors in the rainbow scale are also overly saturated. Looking at Figure 19-5 for any extended period of time can be quite uncomfortable.

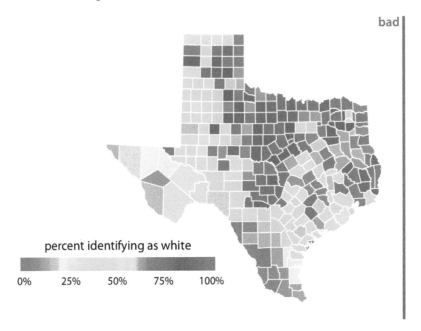

Figure 19-5. Percentage of people identifying as white in Texas counties. The rainbow color scale is not an appropriate scale to visualize continuous data values, because it tends to place emphasis on arbitrary features of the data. Here, it emphasizes counties in which approximately 75% of the population identify as white. Data source: 2010 US Decennial Census.

Not Designing for Color-Vision Deficiency

Whenever we are choosing colors for a visualization, we need to keep in mind that a good proportion of our readers may have some form of color-vision deficiency (i.e., are colorblind). These readers may not be able to distinguish colors that look clearly different to most other people. People with impaired color vision are not literally unable to see any colors, however. Instead, they will typically have difficulty distinguishing certain types of colors, such as red and green (red–green color-vision deficiency) or blue and green (blue–yellow color-vision deficiency). The technical terms for these deficiencies are *deuteranomaly/deuteranopia* and *protanomaly/protanopia* for the red–green variant (where people have difficulty perceiving either green or red, respectively) and *tritanomaly/tritanopia* for the blue–yellow variant (where people have difficulty perceiving blue). The terms ending in "anomaly" refer to some impairment in the perception of the respective color, and the terms ending in "anopia" refer to complete absence of perception of that color. Approximately 8% of males and 0.5%

of females suffer from some sort of color-vision deficiency (CVD); deuteranomaly is the most common form whereas tritanomaly is relatively rare.

As discussed in Chapter 4, there are three fundamental types of color scales used in data visualization: sequential scales, diverging scales, and qualitative scales. Of these three, sequential scales will generally not cause any problems for people with CVD, since a properly designed sequential scale should present a continuous gradient from dark to light colors. Figure 19-6 shows the Heat scale from Figure 4-3 in simulated versions of deuteranomaly, protanomaly, and tritanomaly. While none of these CVD-simulated scales look like the original, they all present a clear gradient from dark to light and they all work well to convey the magnitude of a data value.

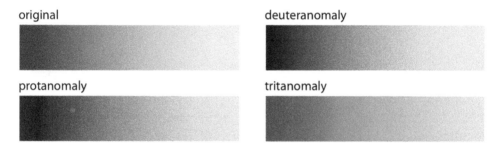

Figure 19-6. Color-vision deficiency simulation of the sequential color scale Heat, which runs from dark red to light yellow. From left to right and top to bottom, we see the original scale and the scale as seen under deuteranomaly, protanomaly, and tritanomaly simulations. Even though the specific colors look different under the three types of CVD, in each case we can see a clear gradient from dark to light. Therefore, this color scale is safe to use for viewers with CVD.

Things become more complicated for diverging scales, because popular color contrasts can be indistinguishable to people with CVD. In particular, the colors red and green provide about the strongest contrast for people with normal color vision but become nearly indistinguishable for deutans (people with deuteranomaly) or protans (people with protanomaly) (Figure 19-7). Similarly, blue-green contrasts are visible for deutans and protans but become indistinguishable for tritans (people with tritanomaly) (Figure 19-8).

These examples might suggest that it is nearly impossible to find two contrasting colors that are safe under all forms of CVD. However, the situation is not that dire. It is often possible to make slight modifications to the colors such that they have the desired character while also being safe for viewers with CVD. For example, the ColorBrewer PiYG (pink to yellow-green) scale from Figure 4-5 looks red–green to people with normal color vision yet remains distinguishable for people with CVD (Figure 19-9).

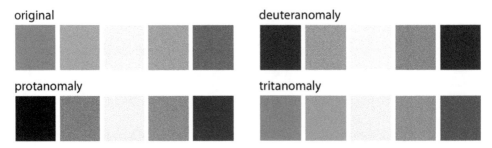

Figure 19-7. A red–green contrast becomes indistinguishable under red–green CVD (deuteranomaly or protanomaly).

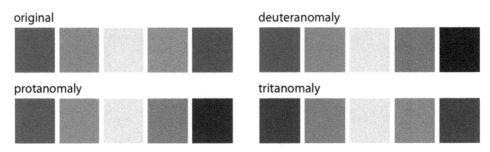

Figure 19-8. A blue–green contrast becomes indistinguishable under blue–yellow CVD (tritanomaly).

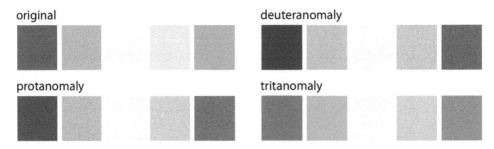

Figure 19-9. The ColorBrewer PiYG (pink to yellow-green) scale from Figure 4-5 looks like a red–green contrast to people with regular color vision but works for people with all forms of color-vision deficiency. It works because the reddish color is actually pink (a mix of red and blue) while the greenish color also contains yellow. The difference in the blue component between the two colors can be picked up by deutans or protans, and the difference in the red component can be picked up by tritans.

Things are most complicated for qualitative scales, because there we need many different colors and they all need to be distinguishable from each other under all forms of CVD. My preferred qualitative color scale, which I use extensively throughout this book, was developed specifically to address this challenge (Figure 19-10). By providing eight different colors, the palette works for nearly any scenario with discrete colors. As discussed at the beginning of this chapter, you should probably not color-code more than eight different items in a plot anyway.

Figure 19-10. Qualitative color palette for all color-vision deficiencies [Okabe and Ito 2008]. The alphanumeric codes represent the colors in RGB space, encoded as hexadecimals. In many plot libraries and image manipulation programs, you can just enter these codes directly. If your software does not take hexadecimals directly, you can also use the values in Table 19-1.

Table 19-1. Colorblind-friendly color scale [Okabe and Ito 2008].

Name	Hex code	Hue	C, M, Y, K (%)	R, G, B (0–255)	R, G, B (%)
Orange	#E69F00	41°	0, 50, 100, 0	230, 159, 0	90, 60, 0
Sky blue	#56B4E9	202°	80, 0, 0, 0	86, 180, 233	35, 70, 90
Bluish green	#009E73	164°	97, 0, 75, 0	0, 158, 115	0, 60, 50
Yellow	#F0E442	56°	10, 5, 90, 0	240, 228, 66	95, 90, 25
Blue	#0072B2	202°	100, 50, 0, 0	0, 114, 178	0, 45, 70
Vermilion	#D55E00	27°	0, 80, 100, 0	213, 94, 0	80, 40, 0
Reddish purple	#CC79A7	326°	10, 70, 0, 0	204, 121, 167	80, 60, 70
Black	#000000	N/A	0, 0, 0, 100	0, 0, 0	0, 0, 0

While there are several good, CVD-safe color scales readily available, we need to recognize that they are not magic bullets. It is very possible to use a CVD-safe scale and yet produce a figure a person with CVD cannot decipher. One critical parameter is the size of the colored graphical elements. Colors are much easier to distinguish when they are applied to large areas than to small ones or thin lines [Stone, Albers Szafir, and Setlur 2014], and this effect is exacerbated under CVD (Figure 19-11). In addition to the various color design considerations discussed in this chapter and in Chapter 4, I recommend to view color figures under CVD simulations to get a sense of what they may look like for a person with CVD. There are several online services and desktop apps available that allow you to run arbitrary figures through a CVD simulation.

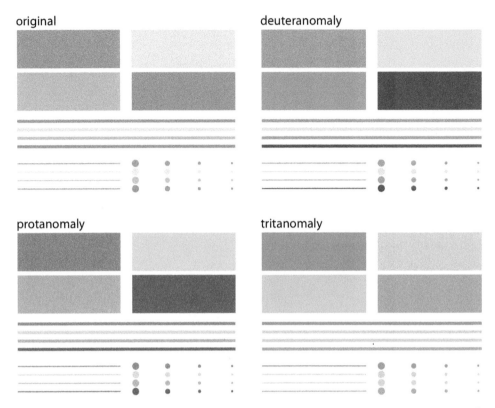

Figure 19-11. Colored elements become difficult to distinguish at small sizes. The top-left panel (labeled "original") shows four rectangles, four thick lines, four thin lines, and four groups of points, all colored in the same four colors. We can see that the colors become more difficult to distinguish the smaller or thinner the visual elements are. This problem becomes exacerbated in the CVD simulations, where the colors are already more difficult to distinguish even for the large graphical elements.

 To make sure your figures work for people with CVD, don't just rely on specific color scales. Instead, test your figures in a CVD simulator.

CHAPTER 20

Redundant Coding

In Chapter 19, we saw that color cannot always convey information as effectively as we might wish. If we have many different items we want to identify, doing so by color may not work. It will be difficult to match the colors in the plot to the colors in the legend (Figure 19-1). And even if we only need to distinguish two or three different items, color may fail if the colored items are very small (Figure 19-11) and/or the colors look similar for people suffering from color-vision deficiency (Figures 19-7 and 19-8). The general solution in all these scenarios is to use color to enhance the visual appearance of the figure without relying entirely on color to convey key information. I refer to this design principle as *redundant coding*, because it prompts us to encode data redundantly, using multiple different aesthetic dimensions.

Designing Legends with Redundant Coding

Scatterplots of several groups of data are frequently designed such that the points representing different groups differ only in their color. As an example, consider Figure 20-1, which shows the sepal width versus the sepal length of three different *Iris* species. (Sepals are the outer leaves of flowers in flowering plants.) The points representing the different species differ in their colors, but otherwise all points look exactly the same. Even though this figure contains only three distinct groups of points, it is difficult to read even for people with normal color vision. The problem arises because the data points for the two species *Iris virginica* and *Iris versicolor* intermingle, and their two respective colors, green and blue, are not particularly distinct from each other.

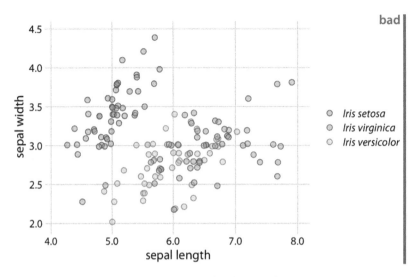

Figure 20-1. Sepal width versus sepal length for three different Iris *species (*Iris setosa, Iris virginica, *and* Iris versicolor*). Each point represents the measurements for one plant sample. A small amount of jitter has been applied to all point positions to prevent overplotting. The figure is labeled "bad" because the* virginica *points in green and the* versicolor *points in blue are difficult to distinguish from each other. Data source: [Fisher 1936].*

Surprisingly, the green and blue points look more distinct for people with red–green color-vision deficiency (deuteranomaly or protanomaly) than for people with normal color vision (compare Figure 20-2, top row, to Figure 20-1). On the other hand, for people with blue–yellow deficiency (tritanomaly), the blue and green points look very similar (Figure 20-2, bottom left). And if we print out the figure in grayscale (i.e., we *desaturate* the figure), we cannot distinguish any of the *Iris* species (Figure 20-2, bottom right).

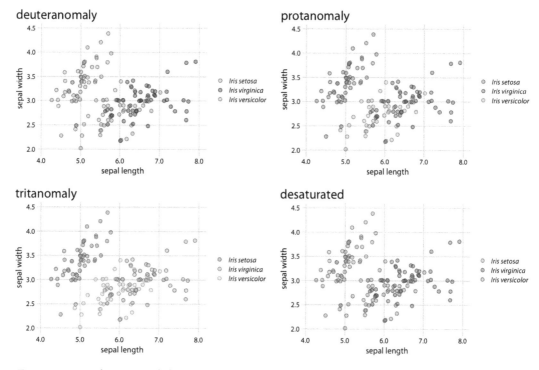

Figure 20-2. Color-vision deficiency simulation of Figure 20-1. Data source: [Fisher 1936].

There are two simple improvements we can make to Figure 20-1 to alleviate these issues. First, we can swap the colors used for *Iris setosa* and *Iris versicolor*, so that the blue is no longer directly next to the green (Figure 20-3). Second, we can use three different symbol shapes, so that the points all look different. With these two changes, both the original version of the figure (Figure 20-3) and the versions under color-vision deficiency and in grayscale (Figure 20-4) become legible.

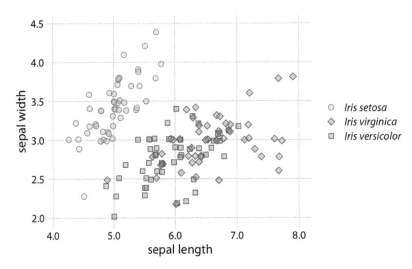

Figure 20-3. Sepal width versus sepal length for three different Iris *species. Compared to Figure 20-1, we have swapped the colors for* Iris setosa *and* Iris versicolor *and we have given each* Iris *species its own point shape. Data source: [Fisher 1936].*

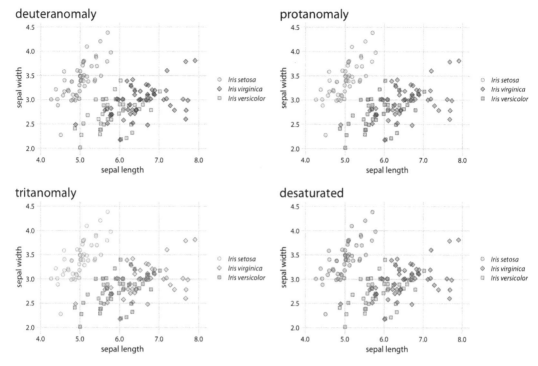

Figure 20-4. Color-vision deficiency simulation of Figure 20-3. Because of the use of different point shapes, even the fully desaturated grayscale version of the figure is legible. Data source: [Fisher 1936].

Changing the point shape is a simple strategy for scatterplots, but it doesn't necessarily work for other types of plots. In line plots, we could change the line type (solid, dashed, dotted, etc.; see also Figure 2-1), but using dashed or dotted lines often yields sub-optimal results. In particular, dashed or dotted lines usually don't look good unless they are perfectly straight or only gently curved, and in either case they create visual noise. Also, it frequently requires significant mental effort to match different types of dash or dot–dash patterns from the plot to the legend. So what do we do with a visualization such as Figure 20-5, which uses lines to show the change in stock price over time for four different major tech companies?

Figure 20-5. Stock price over time for four major tech companies. The stock price for each company has been normalized to equal 100 in June 2012. This figure is labeled as "bad" because it takes considerable mental energy to match the company names in the legend to the data curves. Data source: Yahoo! Finance.

The figure contains four lines representing the stock prices of the four different companies. The lines are color-coded using a colorblind-friendly color scale. Thus, it should be relatively straightforward to associate each line with the corresponding company—yet it is not. The problem here is that the data lines have a visual order. The yellow line, representing Facebook, is perceived as the highest line, and the black line, representing Apple, is perceived as the lowest, with Alphabet and Microsoft in between, in that order. Yet the order of the four companies in the legend is Alphabet, Apple, Facebook, Microsoft (alphabetical order). Thus, the perceived order of the data lines differs from the order of the companies in the legend, and it takes a surprising amount of mental effort to match data lines with company names.

This problem arises commonly with plotting software that autogenerates legends. The plotting software has no concept of the visual order the viewer will perceive. Instead, the software sorts the legend by some other order, most commonly alphabetical. We can fix this problem by manually reordering the entries in the legend so they match the perceived ordering in the data (Figure 20-6). The result is a figure that makes it much easier to match the legend to the data.

Figure 20-6. Stock price over time for four major tech companies. Compared to Figure 20-5, the entries in the legend have now been ordered such that they match the perceived visual order of the data lines, with Facebook the highest and Apple the lowest. Data source: Yahoo! Finance.

If there is a visual ordering in your data, make sure to match it in the legend.

Matching the legend order to the data order is always helpful, but the benefits are particularly obvious under color-vision deficiency simulation (Figure 20-7). For example, it helps in the tritanomaly version of the figure, where the blue and the green become difficult to distinguish (Figure 20-7, bottom left). It also helps in the grayscale version (Figure 20-7, bottom right). Even though the two colors for Facebook and Alphabet have virtually the same gray value, we can see that Microsoft and Apple are represented by darker colors and take the bottom two spots. Therefore, we correctly assume that the highest line corresponds to Facebook and the second-highest line to Alphabet.

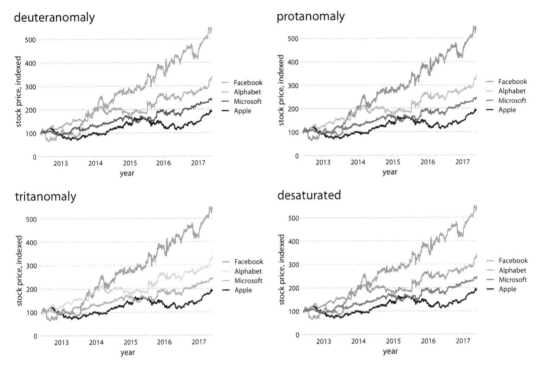

Figure 20-7. Color-vision deficiency simulation of Figure 20-6. Data source: Yahoo! Finance.

Designing Figures Without Legends

Even though legend legibility can be improved by encoding data redundantly, in multiple aesthetics, legends always put an extra mental burden on the reader. In reading a legend, the reader needs to pick up information in one part of the visualization and then transfer it over to a different part. We can typically make our readers' lives easier if we eliminate the legend altogether. Eliminating the legend does not mean, however, that we simply don't provide one and instead write sentences such as "The yellow dots represent *Iris versicolor*" in the figure caption. Eliminating the legend means that we design the figure in such a way that it is immediately obvious what the various graphical elements represent, even if no explicit legend is present.

The general strategy we can employ is called *direct labeling*, whereby we incorporate appropriate text labels or other visual elements that serve as guideposts to the rest of the figure. We have previously encountered direct labeling in Chapter 19 (Figure 19-2), as an alternative to drawing a legend with over 50 distinct colors. To apply the direct labeling concept to the stock price figure, we place the name of each company right next to the end of its respective data line (Figure 20-8).

Figure 20-8. Stock price over time for four major tech companies. The stock price for each company has been normalized to equal 100 in June 2012. Data source: Yahoo! Finance.

Whenever possible, design your figures so they don't need a separate legend.

We can also apply the direct labeling concept to the *Iris* data from the beginning of this chapter, specifically Figure 20-3. Because it is a scatterplot of many points that separate into three different groups, we need to directly label the groups rather than the individual points. One solution is to draw ellipses that enclose the majority of the points and then label the ellipses (Figure 20-9).

For density plots, we can similarly direct-label the curves rather than providing a color-coded legend (Figure 20-10). In both Figures 20-9 and 20-10, I have colored the text labels in the same colors as the data. Colored labels can greatly enhance the direct labeling effect, but they can also turn out poorly. If the text labels are printed in a color that is too light, then the labels become difficult to read. And because text consists of very thin lines, colored text often appears to be lighter than an adjacent filled area of the same color. I generally circumvent these issues by using two different shades of each color, a light one for filled areas and a dark one for lines, outlines, and text. If you carefully inspect Figure 20-9 or 20-10, you will see how each data point or shaded area is filled with a light color and has an outline drawn in a darker color of the same hue. The text labels are drawn in the same darker colors.

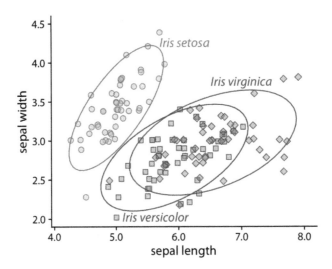

Figure 20-9. Sepal width versus sepal length for three different Iris *species. The points representing different* Iris *species have been directly labeled with colored ellipses and text labels. Compared to Figure 20-3, I have removed the background grid here because the figure was becoming too busy. Data source: [Fisher 1936].*

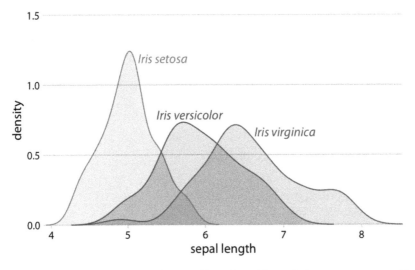

Figure 20-10. Density estimates of the sepal lengths of three different Iris *species. Each density estimate is directly labeled with the respective species name. Data source: [Fisher 1936].*

We can also use density plots such as the one in Figure 20-10 as a legend replacement, by placing the density plots into the margins of a scatterplot (Figure 20-11). This allows us to direct-label the marginal density plots rather than the central scatterplot and hence results in a figure that is somewhat less cluttered than Figure 20-9 with its directly labeled ellipses.

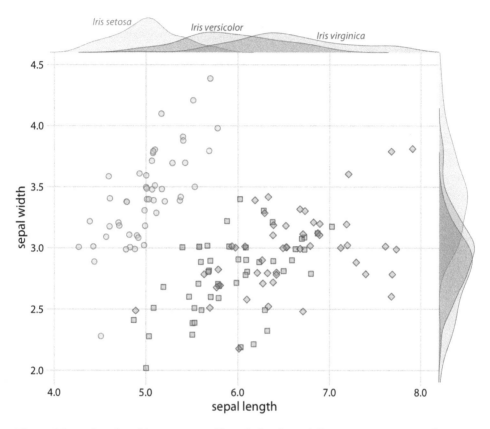

Figure 20-11. Sepal width versus sepal length for three different Iris *species, with marginal density estimates of each variable for each species. Data source: [Fisher 1936].*

And finally, whenever we encode a single variable in multiple aesthetics, we don't normally want multiple separate legends for the different aesthetics. Instead, there should be a single legend-like visual element that conveys all the mappings at once. In the case where we map the same variable onto a position along a major axis and onto color, this implies that the reference color bar should run along and be integrated into the same axis. Figure 20-12 shows a case where we map temperature to both a position along the x axis and to color, and where we therefore have integrated the color legend into the x axis.

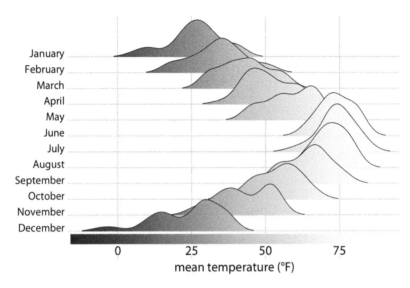

Figure 20-12. Temperatures in Lincoln, NE, in 2016. This figure is a variation of Figure 9-9. Temperature is now shown both by location along the x axis and by color, and a color bar along the x axis visualizes the scale that converts temperatures into colors. Data source: Weather Underground.

## CHAPTER 21

Multipanel Figures

When datasets become large and complex, they often contain much more information than can reasonably be shown in a single figure panel. To visualize such datasets, it can be helpful to create multipanel figures. These are figures that consist of multiple figure panels where each one shows some subset of the data. There are two distinct categories of such figures, small multiples and compound figures. *Small multiples* are plots consisting of multiple panels arranged in a regular grid. Each panel shows a different subset of the data but all panels use the same type of visualization. *Compound figures* consist of separate figure panels assembled in an arbitrary arrangement (which may or may not be grid-based) and showing entirely different visualizations, or possibly even different datasets.

We have encountered both types of multipanel figures in many places throughout this book. In general, these figures are intuitive and straightforward to interpret. However, when preparing such figures, there are a few issues we need to pay attention to, such as appropriate axis scaling, alignment, and consistency between separate panels.

Small Multiples

The term "small multiple" was popularized by [Tufte 1990]. An alternative term, "trellis plot," was popularized around the same time by Cleveland, Becker, and colleagues at Bell Labs ([Cleveland 1993]; [Becker, Cleveland, and Shyu 1996]). Regardless of the terminology, the key idea is to slice the data into parts according to one or more data dimensions, visualize each data slice separately, and then arrange the individual visualizations into a grid. Columns, rows, or individual panels in the grid are labeled by the values of the data dimensions that define the data slices. More recently, this technique is also sometimes referred to as "faceting," named after the methods that create such plots in the widely used ggplot2 plot library (e.g., the ggplot2 function `facet_grid()`) [Wickham 2016].

As a first example, we will apply this technique to the dataset of *Titanic* passengers. We can subdivide this dataset by the class in which each passenger traveled and by whether a passenger survived or not. Within each of these six slices of data, there are both male and female passengers, and we can visualize their numbers using bars. The result is six bar plots, which we arrange in two columns (one for passengers who died and one for those who survived) of three rows (one for each class) (Figure 21-1). The columns and rows are labeled, so it is immediately obvious which of the six plots corresponds to each combination of survival status and class.

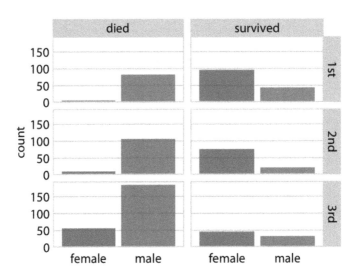

Figure 21-1. Breakdown of passengers on the Titanic *by gender, survival, and class in which they traveled (1st, 2nd, or 3rd). Data source: Encyclopedia Titanica.*

This visualization provides an intuitive and interpretable visualization of the fate of *Titanic*'s passengers. We see immediately that most men died and most women survived. Further, among the women who died nearly all were traveling in third class.

Small multiples are a powerful tool to visualize very large amounts of data at once. Figure 21-1 uses six separate panels, but we can use many more. Figure 21-2 shows the relationship between the average ranking of a movie on the Internet Movie Database (IMDB) and the number of votes the movie has received, separately for movies released over a 100-year time period. Here, the dataset is sliced by only one dimension, the year, and panels for each year are arranged in rows from top left to bottom right. This visualization shows that there is an overall relationship between average ranking and number of votes, such that movies with more votes tend to have higher rankings. However, the strength of this trend varies with year, and for movies released in the early 2000s there is no relationship or even a negative one.

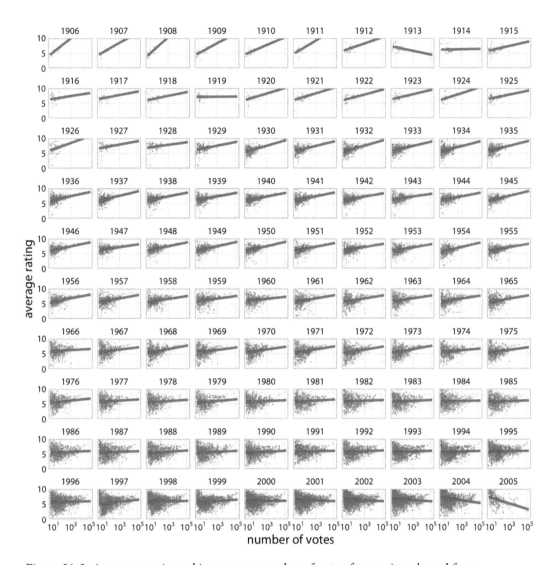

Figure 21-2. Average movie rankings versus number of votes, for movies released from 1906 to 2005. Blue dots represent individual movies, and orange lines represent the linear regression of the average ranking of each movie versus the logarithm of the number of votes the movie has received. In most years, movies with a higher number of votes have, on average, a higher average ranking. However, this trend weakened toward the end of the 20th century, and a negative relationship can be seen for movies released in the early 2000s. Data source: IMDB (http://imdb.com).

For such large plots to be easily understandable, it is important that each panel uses the same axis ranges and scaling. The human mind expects this to be the case. When it is not, there is a good chance that a reader will misinterpret what the figure shows. For example, consider Figure 21-3, which presents how the proportion of bachelor's degrees awarded in different degree areas has changed over time. The figure shows each of the nine degree areas that have represented, on average, more than 4% of all degrees awarded between 1971 and 2015. The *y* axis of each panel is scaled such that the curve for each degree field covers the entire *y*-axis range. As a consequence, a cursory examination of Figure 21-3 suggests that the nine degree areas are all equally popular and have all experienced variation in popularity of a similar magnitude.

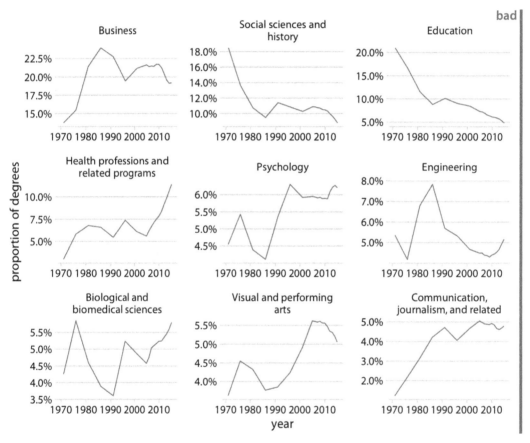

Figure 21-3. Trends in bachelor's degrees conferred by US institutions of higher learning. Shown are all degree areas that represent, on average, more than 4% of all degrees. This figure is labeled as "bad" because all panels use different y-axis ranges. This choice obscures the relative sizes of the different degree areas and it overexaggerates the changes that have happened in some of the degree areas. Data source: National Center for Education Statistics.

Placing all the panels onto the same y axis reveals, however, that this interpretation is misleading (Figure 21-4). Some degree areas are much more popular than others, and similarly some areas have grown or shrunk in popularity much more than others. For example, degrees in education have declined sharply, whereas the proportion of visual and performing arts degrees awarded has remained approximately constant or maybe seen a small increase.

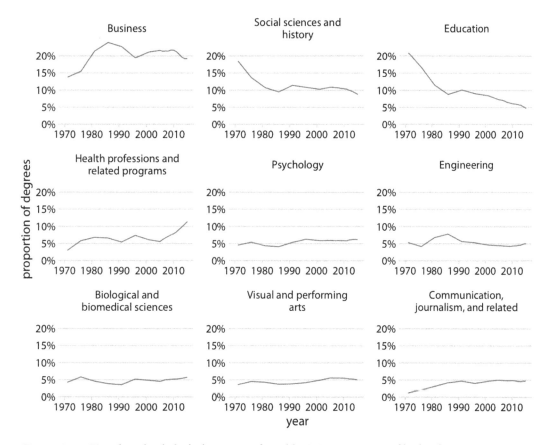

Figure 21-4. Trends in bachelor's degrees conferred by US institutions of higher learning. Shown are all degree areas that represent, on average, more than 4% of all degrees. Data source: National Center for Education Statistics.

I generally recommend against using different axis scalings in separate panels of a small multiples plot. However, on occasion, this problem truly cannot be avoided. If you encounter such a scenario, then I think at a minimum you need to draw the reader's attention to this issue in the figure caption. For example, you could add a sentence such as: "Notice that the y-axis scalings differ among the different panels of this figure."

It is also important to think about the ordering of the individual panels in a small multiples plot. The plot will be easier to interpret if the ordering follows some logical principle. In Figure 21-1, I arranged the rows from the highest class (first class) to the lowest class (third class). In Figure 21-2, I arranged the panels by increasing years from the top left to the bottom right. In Figure 21-4, I arranged the panels by decreasing average degree popularity, such that the most popular degrees are in the top row and/or to the left and the least popular degrees are in the bottom row and/or to the right.

 Always arrange the panels in a small multiples plot in a meaningful and logical order.

Compound Figures

Not every figure with multiple panels fits the pattern of small multiples. Sometimes we simply want to combine several independent panels into a figure that conveys one overarching point. In this case, we can take the individual plots and arrange them in rows, columns, or other more complex arrangements, and call the entire arrangement one figure. For an example, see Figure 21-5, which continues the analysis of trends in bachelor's degrees conferred by US institutions of higher learning. Panel (a) of Figure 21-5 shows the growth in total number of degrees awarded from 1971 to 2015, a time span during which the number approximately doubled. Panel (b) instead shows the change in the percent of degrees awarded over the same time period in the five most popular degree areas. We can see that social sciences, history, and education have experienced massive declines from 1971 to 2015, whereas business and health professions have seen substantial growth.

Notice how unlike in my small multiples examples, the individual panels of the compound figure are labeled alphabetically. It is conventional to use lower- or uppercase letters from the Latin alphabet for this labeling, which is needed to uniquely specify a particular panel. For example, when I want to talk about the part of Figure 21-5 showing the changes in percent of degrees awarded, I can refer to panel (b) of that figure or simply to Figure 21-5b. Without labeling, I would have to awkwardly talk about the "right panel" or the "left panel" of Figure 21-5, and referring to specific panels would be even more awkward for more complex panel arrangements. Labeling is not needed and not normally done for small multiples because there each panel is uniquely specified by the faceting variable(s) that are provided as figure labels.

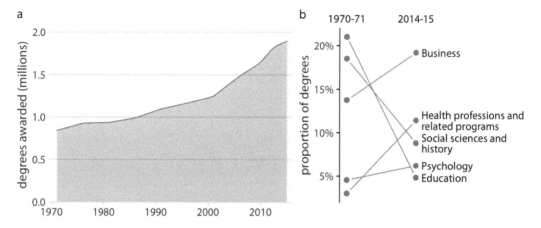

Figure 21-5. Trends in bachelor's degrees conferred by US institutions of higher learning. (a) From 1970 to 2015, the total number of degrees awarded nearly doubled. (b) Among the most popular degree areas, social sciences, history, and education experienced a major decline, while business and health professions grew in popularity. Data source: National Center for Education Statistics.

When labeling the different panels of a compound figure, pay attention to how the labels fit into the overall figure design. I often see figures where the labels look like they were slapped on after the fact by a different person. It's not uncommon to see labels made overly large and prominent, placed in an awkward location, or typeset in a different font than the rest of the figure. (See Figure 21-6 for an example.) The labels should not be the first thing you see when you look at a compound figure. In fact, they don't need to stand out at all. We generally know which figure panel has which label, since the convention is to start in the top-left corner with "a" and label consecutively from left to right and top to bottom. I think of these labels as equivalent to page numbers. You don't normally read the page numbers, and there is no surprise in which page has which number, but on occasion it can be helpful to use page numbers to refer to a particular place in a book or article.

We also need to pay attention to how the individual panels of a compound figure fit together. It is possible to make a set of figure panels that individually are fine but jointly don't work. In particular, we need to employ a consistent visual language. By "visual language," I mean the colors, symbols, fonts, and so on that we use to display the data. Keeping the language consistent means, in a nutshell, that the same things look the same or at least substantively similar across figures.

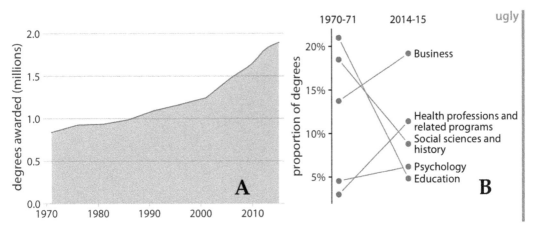

Figure 21-6. Variation of Figure 21-5 with poor labeling. The panel labels are too large and thick, they are in the wrong font, and they are placed in an awkward location. Also, while labeling with capital letters is fine and is in fact quite common, labeling needs to be consistent across all figures in a document. In this book, the convention is that multipanel figures use lowercase labels, and thus this figure is inconsistent with the other figures in this book. Data source: National Center for Education Statistics.

Let's look at an example that violates this principle. Figure 21-7 is a three-panel figure visualizing a dataset about the physiology and body composition of male and female athletes. Panel (a) shows the number of men and women in the dataset, panel (b) shows the counts of red and white blood cells for men and women, and panel (c) shows the body fat percentages of men and women, broken down by sport. Each panel individually is an acceptable figure. However, in combination the three panels do not work, because they don't share a common visual language. First, panel (a) uses the same blue color for both male and female athletes, panel (b) uses it only for male athletes, and panel (c) uses it for female athletes. Moreover, panels (b) and (c) introduce additional colors, but these colors differ between the two panels. It would have been better to use the same two colors consistently for male and female athletes, and to apply the same coloring scheme to panel (a) as well. Second, in panels (a) and (b) women are on the left and men on the right, but in panel (c) the order is reversed. The order of the boxplots in panel (c) should be switched so it matches panels (a) and (b).

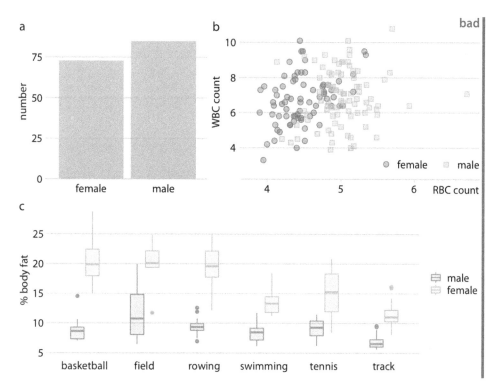

Figure 21-7. Physiology and body composition of male and female athletes. (a) The data-set encompasses 73 female and 85 male professional athletes. (b) Male athletes tend to have higher red blood cell (RBC, reported in units of 10^{12} per liter) counts than female athletes, but there are no such differences for white blood cell counts (WBC, reported in units of 10^9 per liter). (c) Male athletes tend to have a lower body fat percentage than female athletes performing in the same sport. This figure is labeled "bad" because parts (a), (b), and (c) do not use a consistent visual language. Data source: [Telford and Cunningham 1991].

Figure 21-8 fixes all these issues. In this figure, female athletes are consistently shown in orange and to the left of male athletes, who are shown in blue. Notice how much easier it is to read this figure than Figure 21-7. When we use a consistent visual language, it doesn't take much mental effort to determine which visual elements in the different panels represent women and which men. Figure 21-7, on the other hand, can be quite confusing. In particular, on first glance it may generate the impression that men tend to have higher body fat percentages than women. Notice also that we need only a single legend in Figure 21-8 but needed two in Figure 21-7. Since the visual language is consistent, the same legend works for panels (b) and (c).

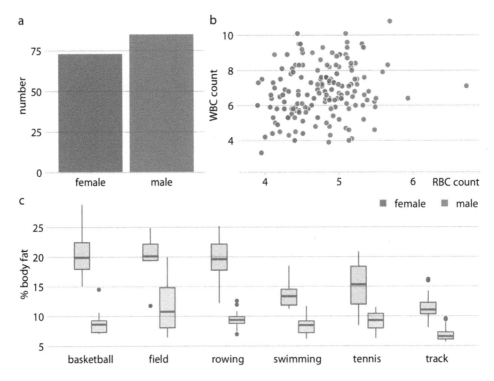

Figure 21-8. Physiology and body composition of male and female athletes. This figure shows the exact same data as Figure 21-7, but now uses a consistent visual language. Data for female athletes is always shown to the left of the corresponding data for male athletes, and genders are consistently color-coded throughout all elements of the figure. Data source: [Telford and Cunningham 1991].

Finally, we need to pay attention to the alignment of individual figure panels in a compound figure. The axes and other graphical elements of the individual panels should all be aligned to each other. Getting the alignment right can be quite tricky, in particular if individual panels are prepared separately, possibly by different people and/or in different programs, and then pasted together in an image manipulation program. To draw your attention to such alignment issues, Figure 21-9 shows a variation of Figure 21-8 where now all figure elements are slightly out of alignment. I have added axis lines to all panels of Figure 21-9 to emphasize these alignment problems. Notice how no axis line is aligned with any other axis line for any other panel of the figure.

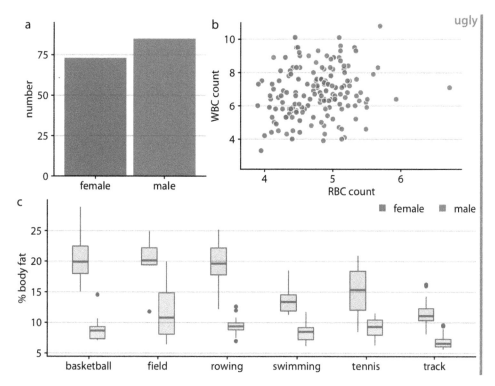

Figure 21-9. Variation of Figure 21-8 where all figure panels are slightly misaligned. Misalignments are ugly and should be avoided. Data source: [Telford and Cunningham 1991].

## CHAPTER 22

Titles, Captions, and Tables

A data visualization is not a piece of art meant to be looked at only for its aesthetically pleasing features. Instead, its purpose is to convey information and make a point. To reliably achieve this goal when preparing visualizations, we have to place the data into context and provide accompanying titles, captions, and other annotations. In this chapter, I will discuss how to properly title and label figures. I will also discuss how to present data in table form.

Figure Titles and Captions

One critical component of every figure is the title. Every figure needs a title. The job of the title is to accurately convey to the reader what the figure is about, what point it makes. However, the figure title may not necessarily appear where you were expecting to see it. Consider Figure 22-1. Its title is "Corruption and human development: the most developed countries experience the least corruption." This title is not shown above the figure. Instead, the title is provided as the first part of the caption block, underneath the figure display. This is the style I am using throughout this book. I consistently show figures without integrated titles and with separate captions. (An exception are the stylized plot examples in Chapter 5, which instead have titles and no captions.)

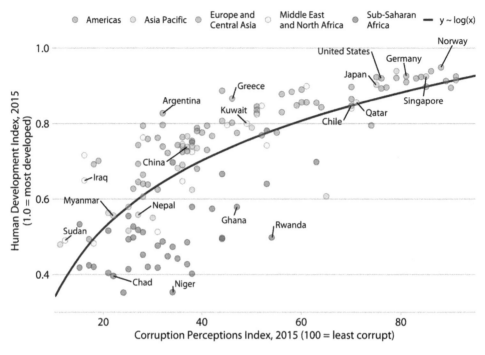

Figure 22-1. Corruption and human development: the most developed countries experience the least corruption. Original figure concept: [The Economist online 2011]. Data sources: Transparency International & UN Human Development Report.

Alternatively, I could incorporate the figure title—as well as other elements of the caption, such as the data source statement—into the main display (Figure 22-2). In a direct comparison, you may find Figure 22-2 more attractive than Figure 22-1, and you may wonder why I choose to use the latter style throughout this book. I do so because the two styles have different application areas, and figures with integrated titles are not appropriate for conventional book layouts. The underlying principle is that a figure can have only one title. Either the title is integrated into the actual figure display or it is provided as the first element of the caption underneath the figure. And if a publication is laid out such that each figure has a regular caption block underneath the display item, then the title *must* be provided in that block of text. For this reason, in the context of conventional book or article publishing, we do not normally integrate titles into figures. Figures with integrated titles, subtitles, and data source statements are appropriate, however, if they are meant to be used as standalone infographics or to be posted on social media or on a web page without accompanying caption text.

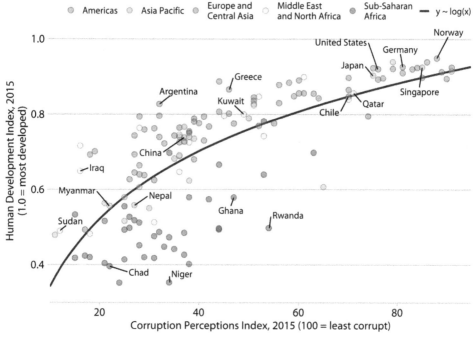

Corruption and human development
The most developed countries experience the least corruption

Data sources: Transparency International & UN Human Development Report

Figure 22-2. Infographic version of Figure 22-1. The title, subtitle, and data source statements have been incorporated into the figure. This figure could be posted on the web as is or otherwise used without a separate caption block.

If your document layout uses caption blocks underneath each figure, then place the figure titles as the first element of each caption block, not on top of the figures.

One of the most common mistakes I see in figure captions is the omission of a proper figure title as the first element of the caption. Take a look back at the caption to Figure 22-1. It begins with "Corruption and human development." It *does not* begin with "This figure shows how corruption is related to human development." The first part of the caption is always the title, not a description of the contents of the figure. A title does not have to be a complete sentence, though short sentences making a clear assertion can serve as titles. For example, for Figure 22-1, a title such as "The most developed countries are the least corrupt" would have worked fine.

Axis and Legend Titles

Just like every plot needs a title, axes and legends need titles as well. (Axis titles are often colloquially referred to as *axis labels*.) Axis and legend titles and labels explain what the displayed data values are and how they map to plot aesthetics.

To present an example of a plot where all axes and legends are appropriately labeled and titled, I have taken the blue jay dataset discussed at length in Chapter 12 and visualized it as a bubble plot (Figure 22-3). In this plot, the axis titles indicate that the *x* axis shows body mass in grams and the *y* axis shows head length in millimeters. Similarly, the legend titles show that point coloring indicates the birds' sex and point size indicates the birds' skull size in millimeters. I emphasize that for all numerical variables (body mass, head length, and skull size) the relevant titles not only state the variables shown but also the units in which the variables are measured. This is good practice and should be done whenever possible. Categorical variables (such as sex) do not require units.

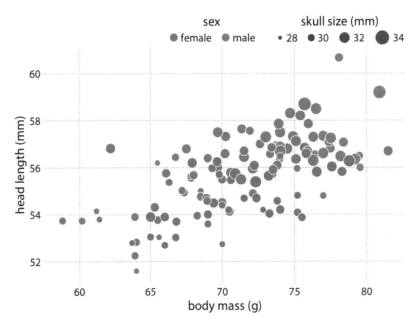

Figure 22-3. Head length versus body mass for 123 blue jays. The birds' sex is indicated by color, and the birds' skull size by symbol size. Head length measurements include the length of the bill while skull size measurements do not. Data source: Keith Tarvin, Oberlin College.

There are cases, however, when axis or legend titles can be omitted, namely when the labels themselves are fully explanatory. For example, a legend showing two differently colored dots labeled "female" and "male" already indicates that color encodes sex. The title "sex" is not required to clarify this fact, and indeed throughout this book I have often omitted the legend title for legends indicating sex or gender (see e.g., Figures 6-10, 12-2, or 21-1). Similarly, country names will generally not require a title stating what they are (Figure 6-11), nor will movie titles (Figure 6-1) or years (Figure 22-4).

Figure 22-4. Stock price over time for four major tech companies. The stock price for each company has been normalized to equal 100 in June 2012. This figure is a slightly modified version of Figure 20-6 in Chapter 20. Here, the x axis representing time does not have a title. It is obvious from the context that the numbers 2013, 2014, etc. refer to years. Data source: Yahoo! Finance.

However, we have to be careful when omitting axis or legend titles, because it is easy to misjudge what is and isn't obvious from the context. I frequently see graphs in the popular press that push omitting axis titles to a point that would make me uncomfortable. For example, some publications might produce a figure such as Figure 22-5, assuming that the meaning of the axes is obvious from the plot title and subtitle (here: "stock price over time for four major tech companies" and "the stock price for each company has been normalized to equal 100 in June 2012"). I disagree with the perspective that the context defines the axes. Because a caption typically doesn't include words such as "the x/y axis shows," some amount of guesswork is always required to interpret the figure. In my own experience, figures without properly labeled axes tend to leave me with a nagging feeling of uncertainty—even if I'm 95% certain I understand what is shown, I don't feel 100% certain. As a general principle, I think it is a bad practice to make your readers guess what you mean. Why would you want to create a feeling of uncertainty in your readers?

Figure 22-5. Stock price over time for four major tech companies. The stock price for each company has been normalized to equal 100 in June 2012. This variant of Figure 22-4 has been labeled as "bad" because the y axis now does not have a title either, and what the values shown along the y axis represent is not immediately obvious from the context. Data source: Yahoo! Finance.

On the flip side, we can overdo the labeling. If the legend lists the names of four well-known companies, the legend title "company" is redundant and doesn't add anything useful (Figure 22-6). Similarly, even though we generally should report units for all quantitative variables, if the x axis shows a few recent years, titling it as "time (years AD)" is awkward.

Finally, in some cases it is acceptable to omit not only the axis title but the entire axis. Pie charts typically don't have explicit axes (e.g., Figure 10-1), and neither do tree-maps (Figure 11-4). Mosaic plots or bar charts can be shown without one or both axes if the meaning of the plot is otherwise clear (Figures 6-10 and 11-3). Omitting explicit axes with axis ticks and tick labels signals to the reader that the qualitative features of the graph are more important than the specific data values.

Figure 22-6. Stock price over time for four major tech companies. The stock price for each company has been normalized to equal 100 in June 2012. This variant of Figure 22-4 has been labeled as "ugly" because it is labeled excessively. In particular, providing a unit ("years AD") for the values along the x axis is awkward and unnecessary. Data source: Yahoo! Finance.

Tables

Tables are an important tool for visualizing data. Yet because of their apparent simplicity, they may not always receive the attention they deserve. I have shown a handful of tables throughout this book; for example, Tables 6-1, 7-1, and 19-1. Take a moment and locate these tables, look at how they are formatted, and compare them to a table you or a colleague has recently made. In all likelihood, there are important differences. In my experience, absent proper training in table formatting, few people will instinctively make the right formatting choices. In self-published documents, poorly formatted tables are even more prevalent than poorly designed figures. Also, most software commonly used to create tables provides defaults that are not recommended. For example, my version of Microsoft Word provides 105 predefined table styles, and of these at least 70 or 80 violate some of the table rules I'm going to discuss here. So, if you pick a Microsoft Word table layout at random, you have an approximately 80% chance of picking one that has issues. And if you pick the default, you will end up with a poorly formatted table every time.

Some key rules for table layout are the following:

1. Do not use vertical lines.

2. Do not use horizontal lines between data rows. (Horizontal lines as a separator between the title row and the first data row or as a frame for the entire table are fine.)

3. Text columns should be left aligned.

4. Number columns should be right aligned and should use the same number of decimal digits throughout.

5. Columns containing single characters should be centered.

6. The header fields should be aligned with their data; i.e., the heading for a text column will be left aligned and the heading for a number column will be right aligned.

Figure 22-7 reproduces Table 6-1 in four different ways, two of which (a, b) violate several of these rules and two of which (c, d) do not.

a   ugly

Rank	Title	Amount
1	Star Wars: The Last Jedi	$71,565,498
2	Jumanji: Welcome to the Jungle	$36,169,328
3	Pitch Perfect 3	$19,928,525
4	The Greatest Showman	$8,805,843
5	Ferdinand	$7,316,746

b   ugly

Rank	Title	Amount
1	Star Wars: The Last Jedi	$71,565,498
2	Jumanji: Welcome to the Jungle	$36,169,328
3	Pitch Perfect 3	$19,928,525
4	The Greatest Showman	$8,805,843
5	Ferdinand	$7,316,746

c

Rank	Title	Amount
1	Star Wars: The Last Jedi	$71,565,498
2	Jumanji: Welcome to the Jungle	$36,169,328
3	Pitch Perfect 3	$19,928,525
4	The Greatest Showman	$8,805,843
5	Ferdinand	$7,316,746

d

Rank	Title	Amount
1	Star Wars: The Last Jedi	$71,565,498
2	Jumanji: Welcome to the Jungle	$36,169,328
3	Pitch Perfect 3	$19,928,525
4	The Greatest Showman	$8,805,843
5	Ferdinand	$7,316,746

Figure 22-7. Examples of poorly and appropriately formatted tables, using the data from Table 6-1 in Chapter 6. (a) This table violates numerous conventions of proper table formatting, including using vertical lines, using horizontal lines between data rows, and using centered data columns. (b) This table suffers from all problems of (a), and also creates visual noise by alternating between very dark and very light rows. Also, the table header is not strongly visually separated from the table body. (c) This is an appropriately formatted table with a minimal design. (d) Colors can be used effectively to group data into rows, but the color differences should be subtle. The table header can be set off by using a stronger color. Data source: Box Office Mojo (http://www.boxofficemojo.com). Used with permission.

When authors draw tables with horizontal lines between data rows, the intent is usually to help the eye follow the individual rows. However, unless the table is very wide and sparse, this visual aid is not normally needed. We don't draw horizontal lines between rows in a piece of regular text either. The cost of horizontal (or vertical) lines is visual clutter. Compare parts (a) and (c) of Figure 22-7. Part (c) is much easier to read than part (a). If we feel that a visual aid separating table rows is necessary, then alternating lighter and darker shading of rows tends to work well without creating much clutter (Figure 22-7d).

Finally, there is a key distinction between figures and tables in where the caption is located relative to the display item. For figures, it is customary to place the caption underneath, whereas for tables it is customary to place it above. This caption placement is guided by the way in which readers process figures and tables. For figures, readers tend to first look at the graphical display and then read the caption for context, hence the caption makes sense below the figure. By contrast, tables tend to be processed like text, from top to bottom, and reading the table contents before reading the caption will frequently not be useful. Hence, captions are placed above the table.

## CHAPTER 23

Balance the Data and the Context

We can broadly subdivide the graphical elements in any visualization into elements that represent data and elements that do not. The former are elements such as the points in a scatterplot, the bars in a histogram or bar plot, or the shaded areas in a heatmap. The latter are elements such as plot axes, axis ticks and labels, axis titles, legends, and plot annotations. These elements generally provide context for the data and/or visual structure to the plot. When designing a plot, it can be helpful to think about the amount of ink (Chapter 17) used to represent the data and context. A common recommendation is to reduce the amount of non-data ink, and following this advice can often yield less cluttered and more elegant visualizations. At the same time, context and visual structure are important, and overly minimizing the plot elements that provide them can result in figures that are difficult to read, confusing, or simply not that compelling.

Providing the Appropriate Amount of Context

The idea that distinguishing between data and non-data ink may be useful was popularized by Edward Tufte in his book *The Visual Display of Quantitative Information* [Tufte 2001]. Tufte introduces the concept of the "data–ink ratio," which he defines as the "proportion of a graphic's ink devoted to the non-redundant display of data information." He then writes (emphasis mine):

> Maximize the data–ink ratio, *within reason*.

I have emphasized the phrase "within reason" because it is critical and frequently forgotten. In fact, I think that Tufte himself forgets it in the remainder of his book, where he advocates overly minimalistic designs that, in my opinion, are neither elegant nor easy to decipher. If we interpret the phrase "maximize the data–ink ratio" to mean "remove clutter and strive for clean and elegant designs," then I think it is reasonable advice. But if we interpret it as "do everything you can to remove non-data ink," then it will result in poor design choices. If we go too far in either direction we will end up with ugly figures. However, away from the extremes there is a wide range of designs that are all acceptable and may be appropriate in different settings.

To explore the extremes, let's consider a figure that has far too much non-data ink (Figure 23-1). The colored points in the plot panel (the framed center area containing data points) are data ink. Everything else is non-data ink. The non-data ink includes a frame around the entire figure, a frame around the plot panel, and a frame around the legend. None of these frames are needed. We also see a prominent and dense background grid that draws attention away from the actual data points. By removing the frames and minor grid lines and by drawing the major grid lines in a light gray, we arrive at Figure 23-2. In this version of the figure, the actual data points stand out much more clearly, and they are perceived as the most important component of the figure.

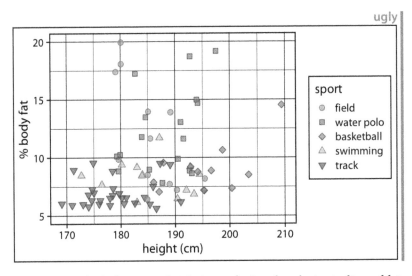

Figure 23-1. Percent body fat versus height in professional male Australian athletes. Each point represents one athlete. This figure devotes way too much ink to non-data. There are unnecessary frames around the entire figure, around the plot panel, and around the legend. The coordinate grid is very prominent, and its presence draws attention away from the data points. Data source: [Telford and Cunningham 1991].

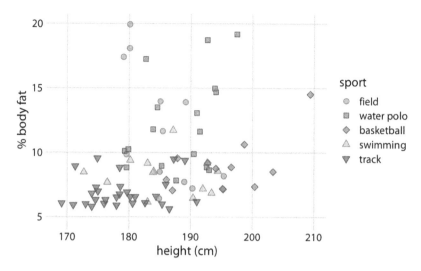

Figure 23-2. Percent body fat versus height in professional male Australian athletes. This figure is a cleaned-up version of Figure 23-1. Unnecessary frames have been removed, minor grid lines have been removed, and major grid lines have been drawn in light gray to stand back relative to the data points. Data source: [Telford and Cunningham 1991].

At the other extreme, we might end up with a figure such as Figure 23-3, which is a minimalist version of Figure 23-2. In this figure, the axis tick labels and titles have been made so faint that they are hard to see. If we just glance at the figure we will not immediately perceive what data is actually shown. We only see points floating in space. Moreover, the legend annotations are so faint that the points in the legend could be mistaken for data points. This effect is amplified because there is no visual separation between the plot area and the legend. Notice how the background grid in Figure 23-2 both anchors the points in space and sets off the data area from the legend area. Both of these effects have been lost in Figure 23-3.

In Figure 23-2, I am using an open background grid and no axis lines or frame around the plot panel. I like this design because it conveys to the viewer that the range of possible data values extends beyond the axis limits. For example, even though Figure 23-2 shows no athlete taller than 210 cm, such an athlete could conceivably exist. However, some authors prefer to delineate the extent of the plot panel, by drawing a frame around it (Figure 23-4). Both options are reasonable, and which is preferable is primarily a matter of personal opinion. One advantage of the framed version is that it visually separates the legend from the plot panel.

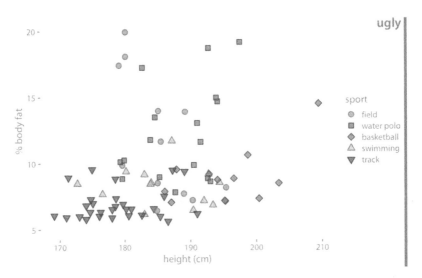

Figure 23-3. Percent body fat versus height in professional male Australian athletes. In this example, the concept of removing non-data ink has been taken too far. The axis tick labels and title are too faint and are barely visible. The data points seem to float in space. The points in the legend are not sufficiently set off from the data points, and the casual observer might think they are part of the data. Data source: [Telford and Cunningham 1991].

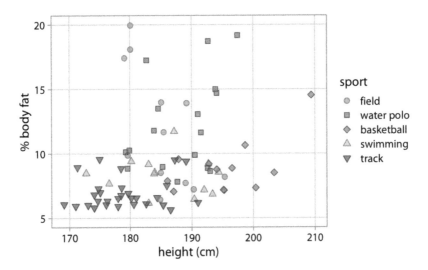

Figure 23-4. Percent body fat versus height in professional male Australian athletes. This figure adds a frame around the plot panel of Figure 23-2, and this frame helps separate the legend from the data. Data source: [Telford and Cunningham 1991].

Figures with too little non-data ink commonly suffer from the effect that figure elements appear to float in space, without clear connection or reference to anything. This problem tends to be particularly severe in small multiples plots. Figure 23-5 shows a small multiples plot comparing six different bar plots, but it looks more like a piece of modern art than a useful data visualization. The bars are not anchored to a baseline and the individual plot facets are not clearly delineated. We can resolve these issues by adding a light gray background and thin horizontal grid lines to each facet (Figure 23-6).

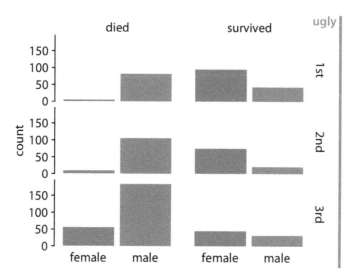

Figure 23-5. Survival of passengers on the Titanic, *broken down by gender and class. This small multiples plot is too minimalistic. The individual facets are not framed, so it's difficult to see which part of the figure belongs to which facet. Further, the individual bars are not anchored to a baseline, and they seem to float. Data source: Encyclopedia Titanica.*

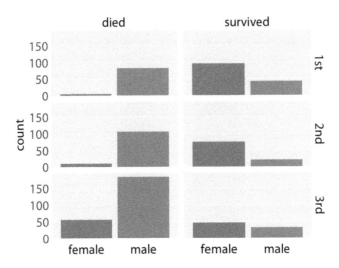

Figure 23-6. Survival of passengers on the Titanic, *broken down by gender and class. This is an improved version of Figure 23-5. The gray background in each facet clearly delineates the six groupings (survived or died in 1st, 2nd, or 3rd class) that make up this plot. Thin horizontal lines in the background provide a reference for the bar heights and facilitate comparison of bar heights among facets. Alternatively, we could put a frame around each individual plot panel and use gray bars to highlight the grouping variables (see Figure 21-1). Data source: Encyclopedia Titanica.*

Background Grids

Grid lines in the background of a plot can help the reader discern specific data values and compare values in one part of a plot to values in another part. At the same time, grid lines can add visual noise, in particular when they are prominent or densely spaced. Reasonable people can disagree about whether to use a grid or not, and if so how to format it and how densely to space it. Throughout this book I am using a variety of different grid styles, to highlight that there isn't necessarily one best choice.

The R software ggplot2 has popularized a style using a fairly prominent background grid of white lines on a gray background. Figure 23-7 shows an example in this style. The figure displays the change in stock price of four major tech companies over a five-year window, from 2012 to 2017. With apologies to the ggplot2 author Hadley Wickham, for whom I have the utmost respect, I don't find the white-on-gray background grid particularly attractive. To my eye, the gray background can detract from the actual data, and a grid with major and minor lines can be too dense. I also find the gray squares in the legend confusing.

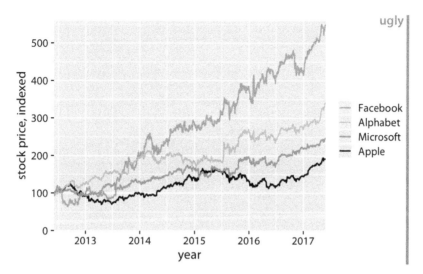

Figure 23-7. Stock price over time for four major tech companies. The stock price for each company has been normalized to equal 100 in June 2012. This figure mimics the ggplot2 default look, with white major and minor grid lines on a gray background. In this particular example, I think the grid lines overpower the data lines, and the result is a figure that is not well balanced and that doesn't place sufficient emphasis on the data. Data source: Yahoo! Finance.

Arguments in favor of the gray background include that it both helps the plot to be perceived as a single visual entity and prevents the plot from appearing as a white box in surrounding dark text [Wickham 2016]. I completely agree with the first point, and it was the reason I used gray backgrounds in Figure 23-6. For the second point, I'd like to caution that the perceived darkness of text will depend on the font size, font face, and line spacing, and the perceived darkness of a figure will depend on the absolute amount and color of ink used, including all data ink. A scientific paper typeset in dense, 10-point Times New Roman will look much darker than a coffee table book typeset in 14-point Palatino with one-and-a-half line spacing. Likewise, a scatterplot of 5 data points in yellow will look much lighter than a scatterplot of 10,000 data points in black. If you want to use a gray figure background, consider the color intensity of your figure foreground, as well as the expected layout and typography of the text around your figures, and adjust the choice of your background gray accordingly. Otherwise, it could happen that your figures end up standing out as dark boxes among the surrounding lighter text. Also, keep in mind that the colors you use to plot your data need to work with the gray background. We tend to perceive colors differently against different backgrounds, and a gray background requires darker and more saturated foreground colors than a white background.

We can go all the way in the opposite direction and remove both the background and the grid lines (Figure 23-8). In this case, we need visible axis lines to frame the plot and keep it as a single visual unit. For this particular figure, I think this choice is a worse option, and I have labeled it as "bad." In the absence of any background grid whatsoever, the curves seem to float in space, and it's difficult to reference the final values on the right to the axis ticks on the left.

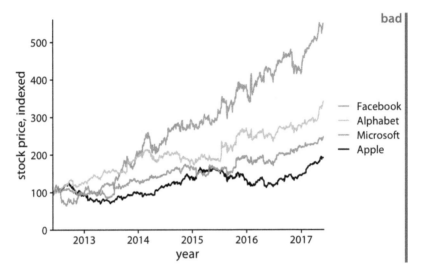

Figure 23-8. Indexed stock price over time for four major tech companies. In this variant of Figure 23-7, the data lines are not sufficiently anchored. This makes it difficult to ascertain to what extent they have deviated from the index value of 100 at the end of the covered time interval. Data source: Yahoo! Finance.

At the absolute minimum, we need to add one horizontal reference line. Since the stock prices in Figure 23-8 are indexed to 100 in June 2012, marking this value with a thin horizontal line at $y = 100$ helps a lot (Figure 23-9). Alternatively, we can use a minimal "grid" of horizontal lines. For a plot where we are primarily interested in the change in y values, vertical grid lines are not needed. Moreover, grid lines positioned at only the major axis ticks will often be sufficient, and the axis line can be omitted or made very thin since the horizontal lines mark the extent of the plot (Figure 23-10).

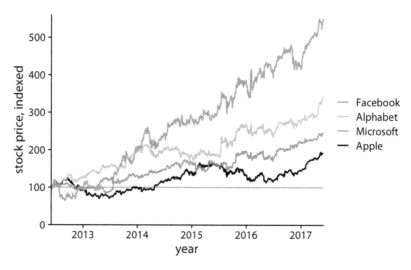

Figure 23-9. Indexed stock price over time for four major tech companies. Adding a thin horizontal line at the index value of 100 to Figure 23-8 helps provide an important reference throughout the entire time period the plot spans. Data source: Yahoo! Finance.

Figure 23-10. Indexed stock price over time for four major tech companies. Adding thin horizontal lines at all major y-axis ticks provides a better set of reference points than just the one horizontal line of Figure 23-9. This design also removes the need for prominent x- and y-axis lines, since the evenly spaced horizontal lines create a visual frame for the plot panel. Data source: Yahoo! Finance.

For such a minimal grid, we generally draw the lines orthogonally to the direction along which the numbers of interest vary. Therefore, if instead of plotting the stock price over time we plot the five-year increase, as horizontal bars, then we will want to use vertical lines instead (Figure 23-11).

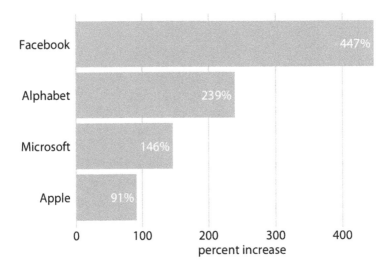

Figure 23-11. Percent increase in stock price from June 2012 to June 2017, for four major tech companies. Because the bars run horizontally, vertical grid lines are appropriate here. Data source: Yahoo! Finance.

 Grid lines that run perpendicular to the key variable of interest tend to be the most useful.

For bar graphs such as Figure 23-11, Tufte recommends drawing white grid lines on top of the bars instead of dark grid lines underneath [Tufte 2001]. These white grid lines have the effect of separating the bars into distinct segments of equal length (Figure 23-12). I'm of two minds on this style. On the one hand, research into human perception suggests that breaking bars into discrete segments helps the viewer to perceive bar lengths [Haroz, Kosara, and Franconeri 2015]. On the other hand, to my eye the bars look like they are falling apart and don't form a visual unit. In fact, I used this style purposefully in Figure 6-10 to visually separate stacked bars representing male and female passengers. Which effect dominates may depend on the specific choices of bar width, distance between bars, and thickness of the white grid lines. Thus, if you intend to use this style, I encourage you to vary these parameters until you have a figure that creates the desired visual effect.

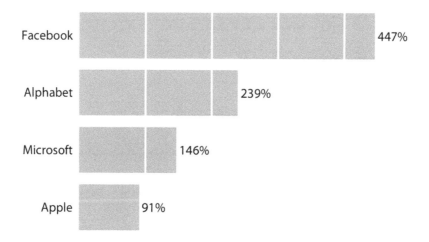

Facebook 447%

Alphabet 239%

Microsoft 146%

Apple 91%

Figure 23-12. Percent increase in stock price from June 2012 to June 2017, for four major tech companies. White grid lines on top of bars can help the reader perceive the relative lengths of the bars. At the same time, they can also create the perception that the bars are falling apart. Data source: Yahoo! Finance.

I would like to point out another downside of Figure 23-12. I had to move the percentage values outside the bars, because the labels didn't fit into the final segments of several of the bars. However, this choice inappropriately visually elongates the bars and should be avoided whenever possible.

Background grids along both axis directions are most appropriate for scatterplots where there is no primary axis of interest. Figure 23-2 at the beginning of this chapter provides an example. When a figure has a full background grid, axis lines are generally not needed.

Paired Data

For figures where the relevant comparison is the $x = y$ line, such as in scatterplots of paired data, I prefer to draw a diagonal line rather than a grid. For example, consider Figure 23-13, which compares gene expression levels in a mutant virus to the nonmutated (wild-type) variant. The diagonal line allows us to see immediately which genes are expressed higher or lower in the mutant relative to the wild type. The same observation is much harder to make when the figure has a background grid and no diagonal line (Figure 23-14). Thus, even though Figure 23-14 looks pleasing, I label it as bad. In particular, gene *10A*, which has a significantly reduced expression level in the mutant relative to the wild-type virus (Figure 23-13), does not visually stand out in Figure 23-14.

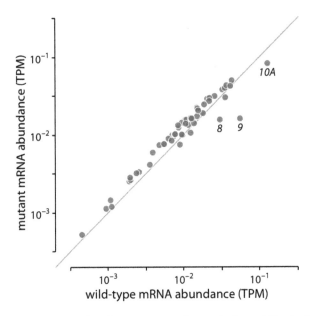

Figure 23-13. Gene expression levels in a mutant bacteriophage T7 relative to wild type. Gene expression levels are measured by mRNA abundances, in transcripts per million (TPM). Each dot corresponds to one gene. In the mutant bacteriophage T7, the promoter in front of gene 9 was deleted, and this resulted in reduced mRNA abundances of gene 9 as well as the neighboring genes 8 and 10A (highlighted). Data source: [Paff et al. 2018].

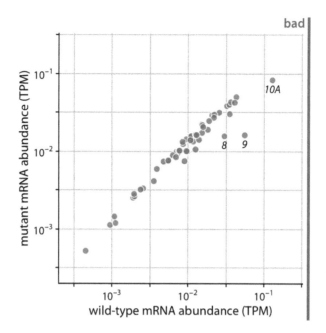

Figure 23-14. Gene expression levels in a mutant bacteriophage T7 relative to wild type. By plotting this dataset against a background grid instead of a diagonal line, we are obscuring which genes are higher or lower in the mutant than in the wild-type bacteriophage. Data source: [Paff et al. 2018].

Of course, we could take the diagonal line from Figure 23-13 and add it on top of the background grid of Figure 23-14, to ensure that the relevant visual reference is present. However, the resulting figure is getting quite busy (Figure 23-15). I had to make the diagonal line darker so it would stand out against the background grid, but now the data points almost seem to fade into the background. We could ameliorate this issue by making the data points larger or darker, but all considered I'd rather choose Figure 23-13.

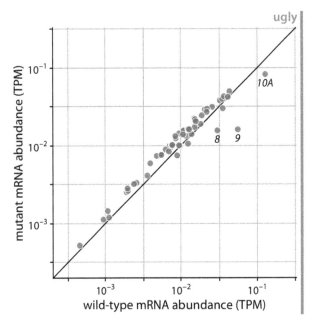

Figure 23-15. Gene expression levels in a mutant bacteriophage T7 relative to wild type. This figure combines the background grid from Figure 23-14 with the diagonal line from Figure 23-13. In my opinion, this figure is visually too busy compared to Figure 23-13, and I would prefer Figure 23-13. Data source: [Paff et al. 2018].

Summary

Both overloading a figure with non-data ink and excessively erasing non-data ink can result in poor figure design. We need to find a healthy medium, where the data points are the main emphasis of the figure while sufficient context is provided about what data is shown, where the points lie relative to each other, and what they mean.

With respect to backgrounds and background grids, there is no one choice that is preferable in all contexts. I recommend being judicious about grid lines. Think carefully about which specific grid or guide lines are most informative for the plot you are making, and then only show those. I prefer minimal, light grids on a white background, since white is the default neutral color on paper and supports nearly any foreground color. However, a shaded background can help the plot appear as a single visual entity, and this may be particularly useful in small multiples plots. Finally, we have to consider how all these choices relate to visual branding and identity. Many magazines and websites like to have an immediately recognizable in-house style, and a shaded background and specific choice of background grid can help create a unique visual identity.

Use Larger Axis Labels

If you take away only one single lesson from this book, make it this one: pay attention to your axis labels, axis tick labels, and other assorted plot annotations. Chances are they are too small. In my experience, nearly all graphing software and plot libraries have poor defaults. If you use the default values, you're almost certainly making a poor choice.

For example, consider Figure 24-1. I see figures like this all the time. The axis labels, axis tick labels, and legend labels are all incredibly small. We can barely see them, and we may have to zoom into the page to read the annotations in the legend.

A somewhat better version of this figure is shown as Figure 24-2. I think the fonts are still too small, and that's why I have labeled the figure as ugly. However, we are moving in the right direction. This figure might be passable under some circumstances. My main criticism here is not so much that the labels aren't legible as that the figure is not balanced; the text elements are too small compared to the rest of the figure.

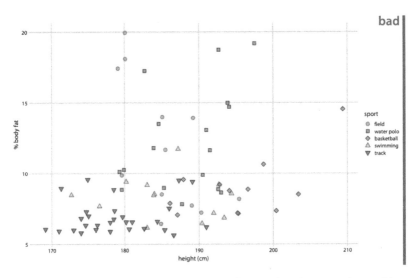

Figure 24-1. Percent body fat versus height in professional male Australian athletes. (Each point represents one athlete.) This figure suffers from the common affliction that the text elements are way too small and are barely legible. Data source: [Telford and Cunningham 1991].

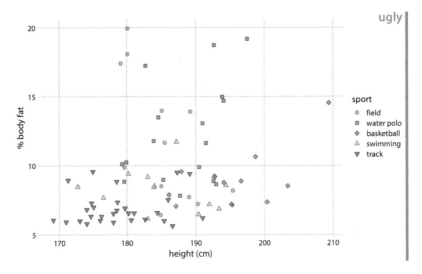

Figure 24-2. Percent body fat versus height in male athletes. This figure is an improvement over Figure 24-1, but the text elements remain too small and the figure is not balanced. Data source: [Telford and Cunningham 1991].

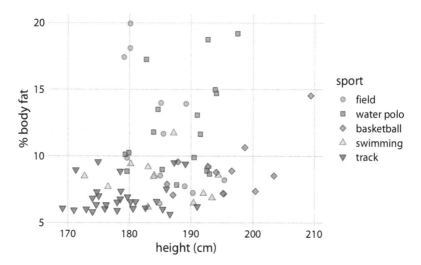

Figure 24-3. Percent body fat versus height in male athletes. All figure elements are appropriately scaled. Data source: [Telford and Cunningham 1991].

Figure 24-3 uses the default settings I'm applying throughout this book. I think it is well balanced; the text is legible, and it fits with the overall size of the figure.

Importantly, we can overdo it and make the labels too big (Figure 24-4). Sometimes we need big labels—for example, if the figure is meant to be reduced in size—but the various elements of the figure (in particular, label text and plot symbols) need to fit together. In Figure 24-4, the points used to visualize the data are too small relative to the text. Once we fix this issue, the figure becomes acceptable again (Figure 24-5).

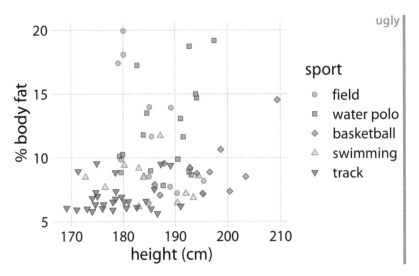

Figure 24-4. Percent body fat versus height in male athletes. The text elements are fairly large, and their size may be appropriate if the figure is meant to be reproduced at a very small scale. However, the figure overall is not balanced; the points are too small relative to the text elements. Data source: [Telford and Cunningham 1991].

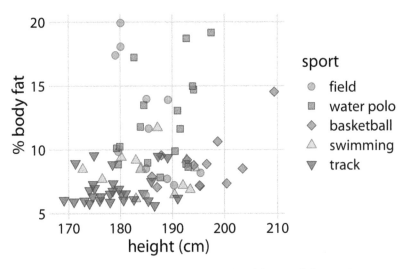

Figure 24-5. Percent body fat versus height in male athletes. All figure elements are sized such that the figure is balanced and can be reproduced at a small scale. Data source: [Telford and Cunningham 1991].

You may look at Figure 24-5 and find everything too big. However, keep in mind that it is meant to be scaled down. Scale the figure down so that it is only two to three inches in width, and it looks just fine. In fact, at that scaling this is the only figure in this chapter that looks good.

 Always look at scaled-down versions of your figures to make sure the axis labels are appropriately sized.

I think there is a simple psychological reason for why we routinely make figures whose axis labels are too small, and it relates to large, high-resolution computer monitors. We routinely preview figures on the computer screen, and often we do so while the figure takes up a large amount of space on the screen. In this viewing mode, even comparatively small text seems perfectly fine and legible, and large text can seem awkward and overpowering. In fact, if you take the first figure from this chapter and magnify it to the point where it fills your entire screen, you will likely think that it looks just fine. The solution is to always make sure that you look at your figures at a realistic print size. You can either zoom out so they are only three to five inches in width on your screen, or stand well back and check whether the figure still looks good from a substantial distance.

## CHAPTER 25

Avoid Line Drawings

Whenever possible, visualize your data with solid, colored shapes rather than with lines that outline those shapes. Solid shapes are more easily perceived as coherent objects, are less likely to create visual artifacts or optical illusions, and more immediately convey amounts than do outlines. In my experience, visualizations using solid shapes are both clearer and more pleasant to look at than equivalent versions that use line drawings. Thus, I avoid line drawings as much as possible. However, I want to emphasize that this recommendation does not supersede the principle of proportional ink (Chapter 17).

Line drawings have a long history in the field of data visualization because throughout most of the 20th century, scientific visualizations were drawn by hand and had to be reproducible in black and white. This precluded the use of areas filled with solid colors, including solid grayscale fills. Instead, filled areas were sometimes simulated by applying hatch, cross-hatch, or stipple patterns. Early plotting software imitated the hand-drawn simulations and similarly made extensive use of line drawings, dashed or dotted line patterns, and hatching. While modern visualization tools and modern reproduction and publishing platforms have none of the earlier limitations, many plotting applications still default to outlines and empty shapes rather than filled areas. To raise your awareness of this issue, here I'll show you several examples of the same figures drawn with both lines and filled shapes.

The most common and at the same time most inappropriate use of line drawings is seen in histograms and bar plots. The problem with bars drawn as outlines is that it is not immediately apparent which side of any given line is inside a bar and which side is outside. As a consequence, in particular when there are gaps between bars, we end up with a confusing visual pattern that detracts from the main message of the figure (Figure 25-1). Filling the bars with a light color, or with gray if color reproduction is not possible, avoids this problem (Figure 25-2).

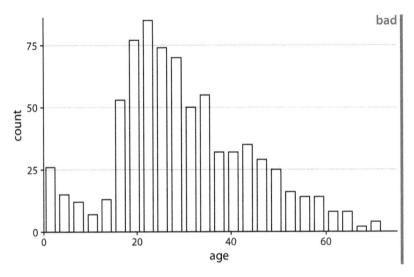

Figure 25-1. Histogram of the ages of Titanic *passengers, drawn with empty bars. The empty bars create a confusing visual pattern. In the center of the histogram, it is difficult to tell which parts are inside of bars and which parts are outside. Data source: Encyclopedia Titanica.*

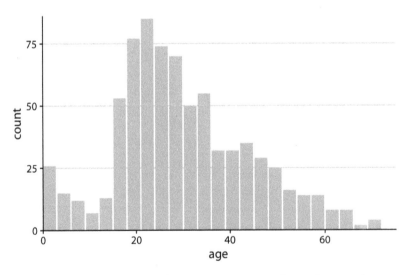

Figure 25-2. Histogram of the ages of Titanic *passengers. This is the same histogram as in Figure 25-1, now drawn with filled bars. The shape of the age distribution is much more easily discernible in this variation of the figure. Data source: Encyclopedia Titanica.*

Next, let's take a look at an old-school density plot. I'm showing density estimates for the sepal length distributions of three species of *Iris*, drawn entirely in black and white as a line drawing (Figure 25-3). The distributions are shown just by their outlines, and because the figure is in black and white I'm using different line styles to distinguish them. This figure has two main problems. First, the dashed line styles do not provide a clear separation between the area under the curve and the area above it. While the human visual system is quite good at connecting the individual line elements into a continuous line, the dashed lines nevertheless look porous and do not serve as a strong boundary for the enclosed area. Second, because the lines intersect and the areas they enclose are not shaded, it is difficult to segment the different densities from the six distinct shape outlines. This effect would have been even stronger had I used solid rather than dashed lines for all three distributions.

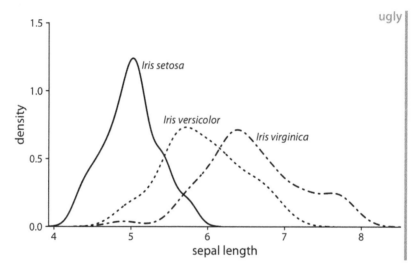

Figure 25-3. *Density estimates of the sepal lengths of three different* Iris *species. The broken line styles used for* Iris versicolor *and* Iris virginica *detract from the perception that the areas under the curves are distinct from the areas above them. Data source: [Fisher 1936].*

We can attempt to address the problem of porous boundaries by using colored lines rather than dashed lines (Figure 25-4). However, the density areas in the resulting plot still have little visual presence. Overall, I find the version with filled areas (Figure 25-5) the most clear and intuitive. It is important, however, to make the filled areas partially transparent, so that the complete distribution for each species is visible.

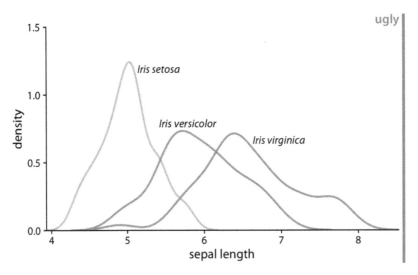

Figure 25-4. Density estimates of the sepal lengths of three different Iris species. By using solid, colored lines we have solved the problem of Figure 25-3 that the areas below and above the lines seem to be connected. However, we still don't have a strong sense of the size of the area under each curve. Data source: [Fisher 1936].

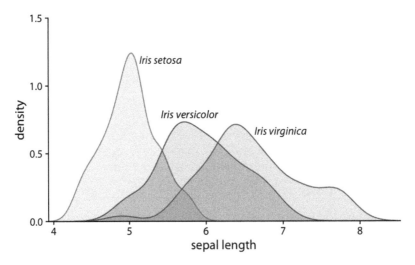

Figure 25-5. Density estimates of the sepal lengths of three different Iris species, shown as partially transparent shaded areas. The shading helps us perceive the three density curves as three distinct objects. Data source: [Fisher 1936].

Line drawings also arise in the context of scatterplots, when different point types are drawn as open circles, triangles, crosses, etc. As an example, consider Figure 25-6. The figure contains a lot of visual noise, and the different point types do not strongly separate from each other. Drawing the same figure with solidly colored shapes addresses this issue (Figure 25-7).

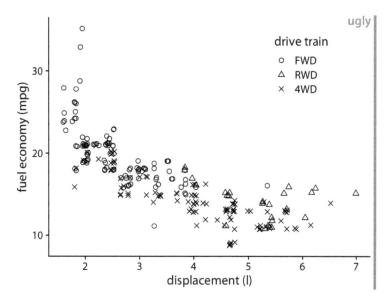

Figure 25-6. *City fuel economy versus engine displacement, for cars with front-wheel drive (FWD), rear-wheel drive (RWD), and all-wheel drive (4WD). The different point styles, all black-and-white line-drawn symbols, create substantial visual noise and make it difficult to read the figure. Data source: US Environmental Protection Agency (EPA), https://fueleconomy.gov.*

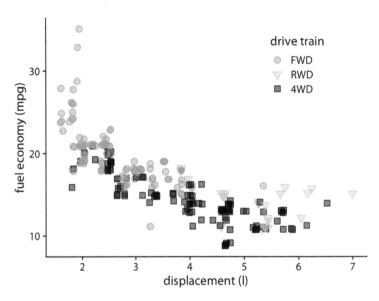

Figure 25-7. City fuel economy versus engine displacement. By using both different colors and different solid shapes for the different drive-train variants, this figure visually separates the drive-train variants while remaining reproducible in grayscale if needed. Data source: EPA.

I strongly prefer solid points over open points, because the solid points have much more visual presence. The argument that I sometimes hear in favor of open points is that they help with overplotting, since the empty areas in the middle of each point allow us to see other points that may be lying underneath. In my opinion, the benefit of being able to see overplotted points does not, in general, outweigh the detriment of the added visual noise of open symbols. There are other approaches for dealing with overplotting; see Chapter 18 for some suggestions.

Finally, let's consider boxplots. Boxplots are commonly drawn with empty boxes, as in Figure 25-8. I prefer a light shading for the box, as in Figure 25-9. The shading separates the box from the plot background, and it helps in particular when we're showing many boxplots right next to each other, as is the case in Figures 25-8 and 25-9. In Figure 25-8, the large number of boxes and lines can again create the illusion of background areas outside of boxes being actually on the inside of some other shape, just as we saw in Figure 25-1. This problem is eliminated in Figure 25-9. I have sometimes heard the critique that shading the inside of the box gives too much weight to the center 50% of the data, but I don't buy that argument. It is inherent to the boxplot, shaded box or not, to give more weight to the center 50% of the data than to the rest. If you don't want this emphasis, then don't use a boxplot. Instead, use a violin plot, jittered points, or a sina plot (Chapter 9).

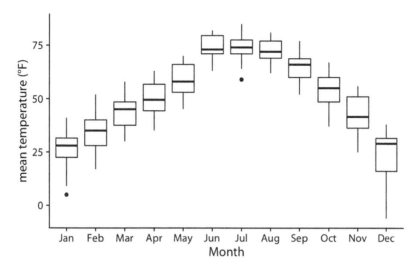

Figure 25-8. Distributions of daily mean temperatures in Lincoln, NE, in 2016. Boxes are drawn in the traditional way, without shading. Data source: Weather Underground.

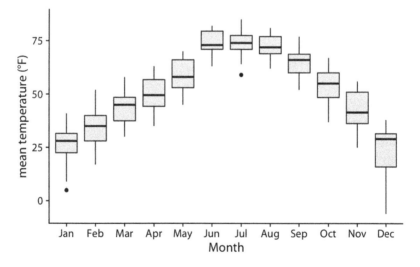

Figure 25-9. Distributions of daily mean temperatures in Lincoln, NE, in 2016. By giving the boxes a light gray shading, we can make them stand out better against the background. Data source: Weather Underground.

## CHAPTER 26

Don't Go 3D

3D plots are quite popular, in particular in business presentations but also among academics. They are also almost always inappropriately used. It is rare that I see a 3D plot that couldn't be improved by turning it into a regular 2D figure. In this chapter, I will explain why 3D plots have problems, why they generally are not needed, and in what limited circumstances 3D plots may be appropriate.

Avoid Gratuitous 3D

Many visualization tools enable you to spruce up your plots by turning the plots' graphical elements into three-dimensional objects. Most commonly, we see pie charts turned into disks rotated in space, bar plots turned into columns, and line plots turned into bands. Notably, in none of these cases does the third dimension convey any actual data. 3D is used simply to decorate and adorn the plot. I consider this use of 3D as gratuitous. It is unequivocally bad and should be erased from the visual vocabulary of data scientists.

The problem with gratuitous 3D is that the projection of 3D objects into two dimensions for printing or display on a monitor distorts the data. The human visual system tries to correct for this distortion as it maps the 2D projection of a 3D image back into a 3D space. However, this correction can only ever be partial. As an example, let's take a simple pie chart with two slices, one representing 25% of the data and one 75%, and rotate this pie in space (Figure 26-1). As we change the angle at which we're looking at the pie, the size of each slice seems to change as well. In particular, the 25% slice, which is located in the front of the pie, seems to take up much more than 25% of the area when we look at the pie from a flat angle (Figure 26-1a).

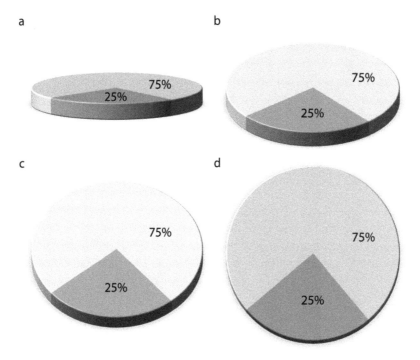

Figure 26-1. The same 3D pie chart shown from four different angles. Rotating a pie into the third dimension makes pie slices in the front appear larger than they really are and pie slices in the back appear smaller. Here, in parts (a), (b), and (c), the blue slice corresponding to 25% of the data visually occupies more than 25% of the area representing the pie. Only part (d) is an accurate representation of the data.

Similar problems arise for other types of 3D plot. Figure 26-2 shows the breakdown of *Titanic* passengers by class and gender using 3D bars. Because of the way the bars are arranged relative to the axes, the bars all look shorter than they actually are. For example, there were 322 passengers total traveling in first class, yet Figure 26-2 suggests that the number was less than 300. This illusion arises because the columns representing the data are located at a distance from the two back surfaces on which the gray horizontal lines are drawn. To see this effect, consider extending any of the bottom edges of one of the columns until it hits the lowest gray line, which represents 0. Then, imagine doing the same to any of the top edges, and you'll see that all the columns are taller than they appear at first glance. (See Figure 6-10 in Chapter 6 for a more reasonable 2D version of this figure.)

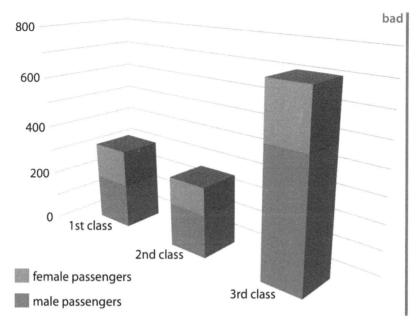

Figure 26-2. Numbers of female and male passengers on the Titanic *traveling in 1st, 2nd, and 3rd class, shown as a 3D stacked bar plot. The total numbers of passengers in 1st, 2nd, and 3rd class are 322, 279, and 711, respectively (see Figure 6-10). Yet in this plot, the 1st class bar appears to represent fewer than 300 passengers, the 3rd class bar appears to represent fewer than 700 passengers, and the 2nd class bar seems to be closer to 210 passengers than the actual 279 passengers. Furthermore, the 3rd class bar visually dominates the figure and makes the number of passengers in 3rd class appear larger than it actually is.*

Avoid 3D Position Scales

While visualizations with gratuitous 3D can easily be dismissed as bad, it is less clear what to think of visualizations using three genuine position scales (x, y, and z) to represent data. In this case, the use of the third dimension serves an actual purpose. Nevertheless, the resulting plots are frequently difficult to interpret, and in my mind they should be avoided.

Consider a 3D scatterplot of fuel efficiency versus displacement and power for 32 cars. We saw this dataset previously in Chapter 2 (Figure 2-5). Here, we plot displacement along the x axis, power along the y axis, and fuel efficiency along the z axis, and we represent each car with a dot (Figure 26-3). Even though this 3D visualization is shown from four different perspectives, it is difficult to envision how exactly the points are distributed in space. I find part (d) of Figure 26-3 particularly confusing. It almost seems to show a different dataset, even though nothing has changed other than the angle from which we look at the dots.

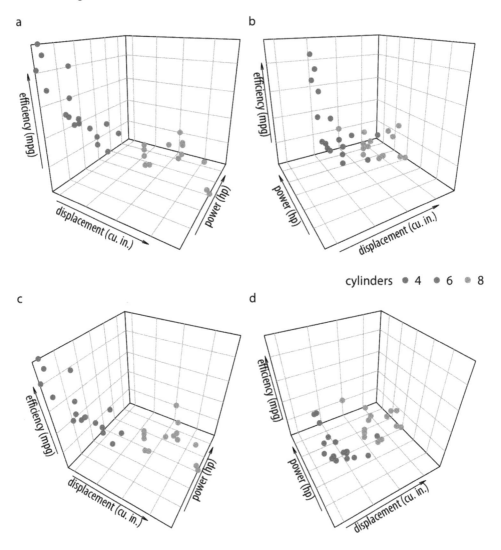

Figure 26-3. Fuel efficiency versus displacement and power for 32 cars (1973–74 models). Each dot represents one car, and the dot color represents the number of cylinders of the car. The four panels (a)–(d) show exactly the same data but use different perspectives. Data source: Motor Trend, 1974.

The fundamental problem with such 3D visualizations is that they require two separate, successive data transformations. The first transformation maps the data from the data space into the 3D visualization space, as discussed in Chapters 2 and 3 in the context of position scales. The second one maps the data from the 3D visualization space into the 2D space of the final figure. (This second transformation obviously does not occur for visualizations shown in a true 3D environment, such as when shown as physical sculptures or 3D-printed objects. My primary objection here is to 3D visualizations shown on 2D displays.) The second transformation is noninvertible, because each point on the 2D display corresponds to a line of points in the 3D visualization space. Therefore, we cannot uniquely determine where in 3D space any particular data point lies.

Our visual system nevertheless attempts to invert the 3D to 2D transformation. However, this process is unreliable, fraught with error, and strongly dependent on appropriate cues in the image that convey some sense of three-dimensionality. When we remove these cues the inversion becomes entirely impossible. This can be seen in Figure 26-4, which is identical to Figure 26-3 except all depth cues have been removed. The result is four random arrangements of points that we cannot interpret at all and that aren't even easily relatable to each other. Could you tell which points in part (a) correspond to which points in part (b)? I certainly cannot.

Instead of applying two separate data transformations, one of which is noninvertible, I think it is generally better to just apply one appropriate, invertible transformation and map the data directly into 2D space. It is rarely necessary to add a third dimension as a position scale, since variables can also be mapped onto color, size, or shape scales. For example, in Chapter 2, I plotted five variables of the fuel-efficiency dataset at once yet used only two position scales (Figure 2-5).

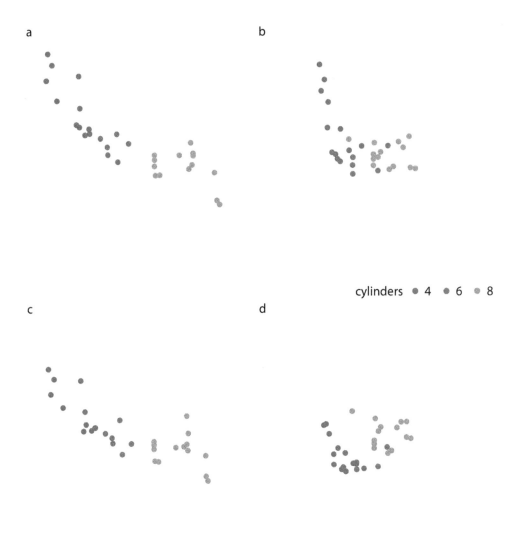

a   b

cylinders ● 4 ● 6 ● 8

c   d

Figure 26-4. Fuel efficiency versus displacement and power for 32 cars (1973–74 models). The four panels (a)–(d) correspond to the same panels in Figure 26-3, but all the grid lines providing depth cues have been removed. Data source: Motor Trend, 1974.

Here, I want to show two alternative ways of plotting exactly the variables used in Figure 26-3. First, if we primarily care about fuel efficiency as the response variable, we can plot it twice, once against displacement and once against power (Figure 26-5). Second, if we are more interested in how displacement and power relate to each other, with fuel efficiency as a secondary variable of interest, we can plot power versus displacement and map fuel efficiency onto the size of the dots (Figure 26-6). Both figures are more useful and less confusing than Figure 26-3.

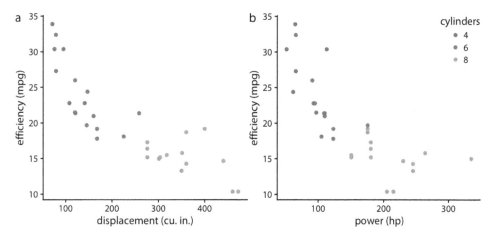

Figure 26-5. *Fuel efficiency versus displacement (a) and power (b) for 32 cars. Data source:* Motor Trend, *1974.*

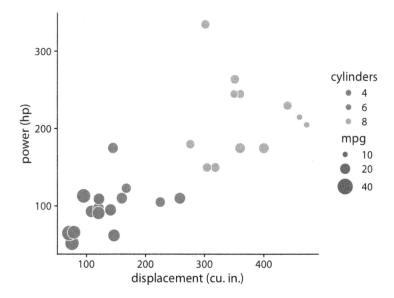

Figure 26-6. *Power versus displacement for 32 cars, with fuel efficiency represented by dot size. Data source:* Motor Trend, *1974.*

You may wonder whether the problem with 3D scatterplots is that the actual data representation, the dots, do not themselves convey any 3D information. What happens, for example, if we use 3D bars instead? Figure 26-7 shows a typical dataset that one might visualize with 3D bars, the mortality rates in 1940 Virginia stratified by age group and by gender and housing location. We can see that indeed the 3D bars help us interpret the plot. It is unlikely that one might mistake a bar in the foreground for one in the background, or vice versa. Nevertheless, the problems discussed in the context of Figure 26-2 exist here as well. It is difficult to judge exactly how tall the individual bars are, and it is also difficult to make direct comparisons. For example, was the mortality rate of urban females in the 65–69 age group higher or lower than that of urban males in the 60–64 age group?

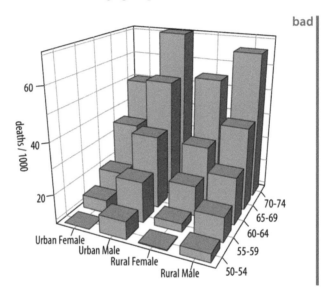

Figure 26-7. Mortality rates in Virginia in 1940, visualized as a 3D bar plot. Mortality rates are shown for four groups of people (urban and rural females and males) and five age categories (50–54, 55–59, 60–64, 65–69, 70–74), and they are reported in units of deaths per 1,000 persons. This figure is labeled as "bad" because the 3D perspective makes the plot difficult to read. Data source: [Molyneaux, Gilliam, and Florant 1947].

In general, it is better to use small multiples plots (Chapter 21) instead of 3D visualizations. The Virginia mortality dataset requires only four panels when shown as a small multiples plot (Figure 26-8). I consider this figure clear and easy to interpret. It is immediately obvious that mortality rates were higher among men than among women, and also that urban males seem to have had higher mortality rates than rural males, whereas no such trend is apparent for urban and rural females.

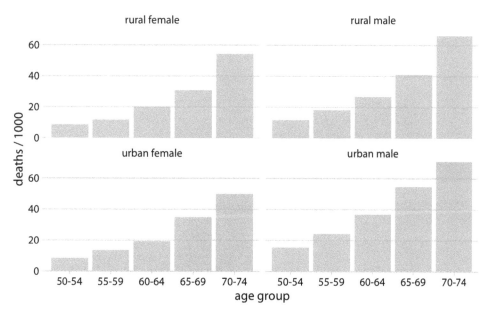

Figure 26-8. Mortality rates in Virginia in 1940, visualized as a small multiples plot. Mortality rates are shown for four groups of people (urban and rural females and males) and five age categories (50–54, 55–59, 60–64, 65–69, 70–74), and they are reported in units of deaths per 1,000 persons. Data source: [Molyneaux, Gilliam, and Florant 1947].

Appropriate Use of 3D Visualizations

Visualizations using 3D position scales can sometimes be appropriate, however. First, the issues described in the preceding section are of lesser concern if the visualization is interactive and can be rotated by the viewer, or if it is shown in a VR or augmented reality environment where it can be inspected from multiple angles. Second, even if the visualization isn't interactive, showing it slowly rotating, rather than as a static image from one perspective, will allow the viewer to discern where in 3D space different graphical elements reside. The human brain is very good at reconstructing a 3D scene from a series of images taken from different angles, and the slow rotation of the graphic provides exactly these images.

Finally, it makes sense to use 3D visualizations when we want to show actual 3D objects and/or data mapped onto them. For example, showing the topographic relief of a mountainous island is a reasonable choice (Figure 26-9). Similarly, if we want to visualize the evolutionary sequence conservation of a protein mapped onto its structure, it makes sense to show the structure as a 3D object (Figure 26-10). In either case, however, these visualizations would still be easier to interpret if they were shown as rotating animations. While this is not possible in traditional print publications, it can be done easily when posting figures on the web or when giving presentations.

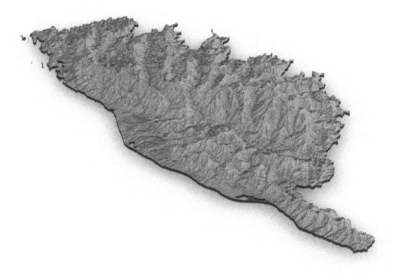

Figure 26-9. Relief of the Island of Corsica in the Mediterranean Sea. Data source: Copernicus Land Monitoring Service.

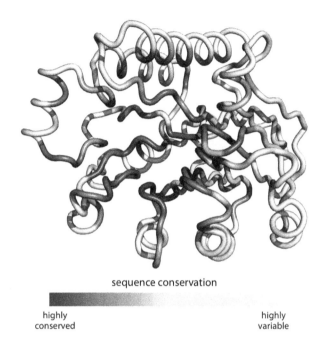

sequence conservation

highly
conserved

highly
variable

Figure 26-10. Patterns of evolutionary variation in a protein. The colored tube represents the backbone of the protein Exonuclease III from the bacterium Escherichia coli. *The coloring indicates the evolutionary conservation of the individual sites in this protein, with dark coloring indicating conserved amino acids and light coloring indicating variable amino acids. Data source: [Marcos and Echave 2015].*

## PART III

Miscellaneous Topics

## CHAPTER 27

Understanding the Most Commonly Used Image File Formats

Anybody who is making figures for data visualization will eventually have to know a few things about how figures are stored on the computer. There are many different image file formats, and each has its own set of benefits and disadvantages. Choosing the right file format and the right workflow can alleviate many figure preparation headaches.

My own preference is to use PDF for high-quality publication-ready files and generally whenever possible, PNG for online documents and other scenarios where bitmap graphics are required, and JPEG as the final resort if the PNG files are too large. In the following sections, I explain the key differences between these file formats and their respective benefits and drawbacks.

Bitmap and Vector Graphics

The most important difference between the various graphics formats is whether they are bitmap or vector (Table 27-1). *Bitmaps* or *raster graphics* store the image as a grid of individual points (called pixels), each with a specified color. By contrast, *vector graphics* store the geometric arrangement of individual graphical elements in the image. Thus, a vector image contains information such as "there's a black line from the top-left corner to the bottom-right corner, and a red line from the bottom-left corner to the top-right corner," and the actual image is recreated on the fly as it is displayed on screen or printed.

Table 27-1. Commonly used image file formats

Acronym	Name	Type	Application
PDF	Portable Document Format	Vector	General purpose
EPS	Encapsulated PostScript	Vector	General purpose, outdated; use PDF
SVG	Scalable Vector Graphics	Vector	Online use
PNG	Portable Network Graphics	Bitmap	Optimized for line drawings
JPEG/JPG	Joint Photographic Experts Group	Bitmap	Optimized for photographic images
TIFF	Tagged Image File Format	Bitmap	Print production, accurate color reproduction
RAW	Raw Image File	Bitmap	Digital photography, needs post-processing
GIF	Graphics Interchange Format	Bitmap	Outdated for static figures, OK for animations

Vector graphics are also called "resolution-independent," because they can be magnified to arbitrary size without losing detail or sharpness. See Figure 27-1 for a demonstration.

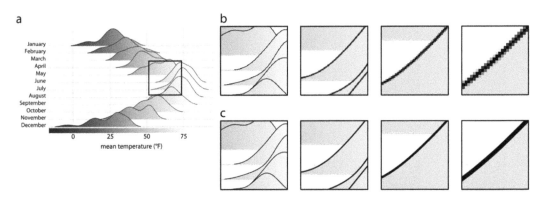

Figure 27-1. Illustration of the key difference between vector graphics and bitmaps. (a) Original image. The black square indicates the area we are magnifying in parts (b) and (c). (b) Increasing magnification of the highlighted area from part (a) when the image has been stored as a bitmap graphic. We can see how the image becomes increasingly pixelated as we zoom in further. (c) Increasing magnification of a vector representation of the image. The image maintains perfect sharpness at arbitrary magnification levels.

Vector graphics have two downsides that can and often do cause trouble in real-world applications. First, because vector graphics are redrawn on the fly by the graphics program with which they are displayed, it can happen that there are differences in how the same graphic looks in two different programs, or on two different computers. This problem occurs most frequently with text, for example when the required font is not available and the rendering software substitutes a different font. Font substitutions will typically allow the viewer to read the text as intended, but the resulting image rarely looks good. There are ways to avoid these problems, such as outlining or embedding all fonts in a PDF file, but they may require special software and/or special technical knowledge to achieve. By contrast, bitmap images will always look the same.

Second, for very large and/or complex figures, vector graphics can grow to enormous file sizes and be slow to render. For example, a scatterplot of millions of data points will contain the x and y coordinates of every individual point, and each point needs to be drawn when the image is rendered, even if points overlap and/or are hidden by other graphical elements. As a consequence, the file may be many megabytes in size, and it may take the rendering software some time to display the figure. When I was a postdoc in the early 2000s, I once created a PDF file that at the time took almost an hour to display in Acrobat Reader. While modern computers are much faster and rendering times of many minutes are all but unheard of these days, even a rendering time of a few seconds can be disruptive if you want to embed your figure into a larger document and your PDF reader grinds to a halt every time you display the page with that one offending figure. Of course, on the flip side, simple figures with only a small number of elements (a few data points and some text, say) will often be much smaller as vector graphics than as bitmaps, and the viewing software may even render such figures faster than it would the corresponding bitmap images.

Lossless and Lossy Compression of Bitmap Graphics

Most bitmap file formats employ some form of data compression to keep file sizes manageable. There are two fundamental types of compression: lossless and lossy. Lossless compression guarantees that the compressed image is pixel-for-pixel identical to the original image, whereas lossy compression accepts some image degradation in return for smaller file sizes.

To understand when using either lossless or lossy compression is appropriate, it is helpful to have a basic understanding of how these different compression algorithms work. Let's first consider lossless compression. Imagine an image with a black background, where large areas of the image are solid black and thus many black pixels appear right next to each other. Each black pixel can be represented by three zeros in a row, 0 0 0, representing zero intensities in the red, green, and blue color channels of the image. The areas of black background in the image correspond to thousands of zeros in the image file. Now assume somewhere in the image are 1,000 consecutive black pixels, corresponding to 3,000 zeros. Instead of writing out all these zeros, we could simply store the total number of zeros we need, for example by writing 3000 0. In this way, we have conveyed the exact same information with only two numbers, the count (here, 3000) and the value (here, 0). Over the years, many clever tricks along these lines have been developed, and modern lossless image formats (such as PNG) can store bitmap data with impressive efficiency. However, all lossless compression algorithms perform best when images have large areas of uniform color, and therefore Table 27-1 lists PNG as optimized for line drawings.

Photographic images rarely have multiple pixels of identical color and brightness right next to each other. Instead, they have gradients and other somewhat regular patterns on many different scales. Therefore, lossless compression of these images often doesn't work very well, and lossy compression has been developed as an alternative. The key idea of lossy compression is that some details in an image are too subtle for the human eye to see, and those can be discarded without obvious degradation in the image quality. For example, consider a gradient of 1,000 pixels, each with a slightly different color value. Chances are the gradient will look nearly the same if it is drawn with only 200 different colors and each group of 5 adjacent pixels is the exact same color.

The most widely used lossy image format is JPEG (Table 27-1), and indeed many digital cameras output images as JPEG by default. JPEG compression works exceptionally well for photographic images, and huge reductions in file size can often be obtained with very little degradation in image quality. However, JPEG compression fails when images contain sharp edges, such as those created by line drawings or by text. In those cases, JPEG compression can result in very noticeable artifacts (Figure 27-2).

Even if JPEG artifacts are sufficiently subtle that they are not immediately visible to the naked eye, they can cause trouble, for example in print production. Therefore, it is a good idea to avoid the JPEG format whenever possible. In particular, you should avoid it for images containing line drawings or text, as is the case for data visualizations or screenshots. The appropriate format for those images is PNG or TIFF. I use the JPEG format exclusively for photographic images. If an image contains both photographic elements and line drawings or text, you should still use PNG or TIFF. The worst-case scenario with those file formats is that your image files grow large, whereas the worst-case scenario with JPEG is that your final product looks ugly.

a

432KB

Cinque Torri,
Dolomites

81KB

Cinque Torri,
Dolomites

43KB

Cinque Torri,
Dolomites

25KB

Cinque Torri,
Dolomites

b

Cinque Torri, Dolomites

background not
perfectly white

artifacts around text

pixelated gradients

blurry details

Figure 27-2. Illustration of JPEG artifacts. (a) The same image is reproduced multiple times using increasingly severe JPEG compression. The resulting file size is shown in red text above each image. A reduction in file size by a factor of 10, from 432 KB in the original image to 43 KB in the compressed image, results in only a minor perceptible reduction in image quality. However, a further reduction in file size by a factor of 2, to a mere 25 KB, leads to numerous visible artifacts. (b) Zooming in to the most highly compressed image reveals the various compression artifacts. Photo credit: Claus O. Wilke.

Converting Between Image Formats

It is generally possible to convert any image format into any other image format. For example, on a Mac, you can open an image with Preview and then export to a number of different formats. In this process, though, important information can get lost, and information is never regained. For example, after saving a vector graphic into a bitmap format (say, a PDF file as a JPEG), the resolution independence that is a key feature of the vector graphic has been lost. Conversely, saving a JPEG image into a PDF file does not magically turn the image into a vector graphic. The image will still be a bitmap image, just stored inside the PDF file. Similarly, converting a JPEG file into a PNG file does not remove any artifacts that may have been introduced by the JPEG compression algorithm.

It is therefore a good rule of thumb to always store the original image in the format that maintains maximum resolution, accuracy, and flexibility. Thus, for data visualizations, either create your figures as PDF and then convert them into PNG or JPEG when necessary, or store them as high-resolution PNGs. Similarly, for images that are only available as bitmaps, such as digital photographs, store them in a format that doesn't use lossy compression—or, if that can't be done, compress them as little as possible. Also, store the images in as high a resolution as possible, and downscale when needed.

## CHAPTER 28

Choosing the Right Visualization Software

Throughout this book, I have purposefully avoided one critical question of data visualization: what tools should we use to generate our figures? This question can generate heated discussions, as many people have strong emotional bonds to the specific tools they are familiar with. I have often seen people vigorously defend their own preferred tools instead of investing time in learning a new approach, even if the new approach has objective benefits. And I will say that sticking with the tools you know is not entirely unreasonable. Learning any new tool will require time and effort, and you will have to go through a painful transition period where getting things done with the new tool is much more difficult than it was with the old tool. Whether going through this period is worth the effort can usually only be evaluated in retrospect, after one has invested in learning the new tool. Therefore, regardless of the pros and cons of different tools and approaches, the overriding principle is that you need to pick a tool that works for you. If you can make the figures you want to make, without excessive effort, then that's all that matters.

The best visualization software is the one that allows you to make the figures you need.

Having said this, I do think there are general principles we can use to assess the relative merits of different approaches to producing visualizations. These principles roughly break down by how reproducible the visualizations are, how easy it is to rapidly explore the data, and to what extent the visual appearance of the output can be tweaked.

Reproducibility and Repeatability

In the context of scientific experiments, we refer to work as *reproducible* if the overarching scientific finding of the work will remain unchanged if a different research group performs the same type of study. For example, if one research group finds that a new pain medication reduces perceived headache pain significantly without causing noticeable side effects and a different group subsequently studies the same medication on a different patient group and has the same findings, then the work is reproducible. By contrast, work is *repeatable* if very similar or identical measurements can be obtained by the same person repeating the exact same measurement procedure on the same equipment. For example, if I weigh my dog and find she weighs 41 lbs and then I weigh her again on the same scales and find again that she weighs 41 lbs, then this measurement is repeatable.

With minor modifications, we can apply these concepts to data visualization. A visualization is reproducible if the plotted data is available and any data transformations that may have been applied before plotting are exactly specified. For example, if you make a figure and then send me the exact data that you plotted, then I can prepare a figure that looks substantially similar. We may be using slightly different fonts or colors or point sizes to display the same data, so the two figures may not be exactly identical, but your figure and mine convey the same message and therefore are reproductions of each other. A visualization is repeatable, on the other hand, if it is possible to recreate the exact same visual appearance, down to the last pixel, from the raw data. Strictly speaking, repeatability requires that even if there are random elements in the figure, such as jitter (Chapter 18), those elements were specified in a repeatable way and can be regenerated at a future date. For random data, repeatability generally requires that we specify a particular random number generator for which we set and record a seed.

Throughout this book, we have seen many examples of figures that reproduce but don't repeat other figures. For example, Chapter 25 shows several sets of figures that each show the same data but that look somewhat different. Similarly, Figure 28-1a is a repeat of Figure 9-7, down to the random jitter that was applied to each data point, whereas Figure 28-1b is only a reproduction of that figure. Figure 28-1b has different jitter than Figure 9-7, and it also uses a sufficiently different visual design that the two figures look quite distinct, even if they convey the same information about the data.

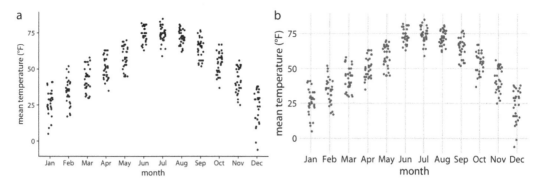

Figure 28-1. Repeat and reproduction of a figure. Part (a) is a repeat of Figure 9-7. The two figures are identical down to the random jitter that was applied to each point. By contrast, part (b) is a reproduction but not a repeat. In particular, the jitter in part (b) differs from the jitter in part (a) or in Figure 9-7. Data source: Weather Underground.

Both reproducibility and repeatability can be difficult to achieve when we're working with interactive plotting software. Many interactive programs allow you to transform or otherwise manipulate the data but don't keep track of every individual data transformation you perform, only of the final product. If you make a figure using this kind of program, and then somebody asks you to reproduce the figure or create a similar one with a different dataset, you might have difficulty doing so. During my years as a postdoc and a young assistant professor, I used an interactive program for all my scientific visualizations, and this exact issue came up several times. For example, I had made several figures for a scientific manuscript. When I wanted to revise the manuscript a few months later and needed to reproduce a slightly altered version of one of the figures, I realized that I wasn't quite sure anymore how I had made the original figure in the first place. This experience has taught me to stay away from interactive programs as much as possible. I now make figures programmatically, by writing code (scripts) that generates the figures from the raw data. Programmatically generated figures will generally be repeatable by anybody who has access to the generating scripts and the programming language and specific libraries used.

Data Exploration Versus Data Presentation

There are two distinct phases of data visualization, and they have very different requirements. The first is data exploration. Whenever you start working with a new dataset, you need to look at it from different angles and try various ways of visualizing it, just to develop an understanding of the dataset's key features. In this phase, speed and efficiency are of the essence. You need to try different types of visualizations, different data transformations, and different subsets of the data. The faster you can iterate through different ways of looking at the data, the more you will explore, and the higher the likelihood is that you will notice an important feature in the data that you might otherwise have overlooked. The second phase is data presentation. You enter it once you understand your dataset and know what aspects of it you want to show to your audience. The key objective in this phase is to prepare a high-quality, publication-ready figure that can be printed in an article or book, included in a presentation, or posted on the internet.

In the exploration stage, whether the figures you make look appealing is secondary. It's fine if the axis labels are missing, the legend is messed up, or the symbols are too small, as long as you can evaluate the various patterns in the data. What is critical, however, is how easy it is for you to change how the data is shown. To truly explore the data, you should be able to rapidly move from a scatterplot to overlapping density distribution plots to boxplots to a heatmap. In Chapter 2, we saw that all visualizations consist of mappings from data onto aesthetics. A well-designed data exploration tool will allow you to easily change which variables are mapped onto which aesthetics, and it will provide a wide range of different visualization options within a single coherent framework. In my experience, however, many visualization tools (and in particular libraries for programmatic figure generation) are not set up in this way. Instead, they are organized by plot type, where each different type of plot requires somewhat different input data and has its own idiosyncratic interface. Such tools can get in the way of efficient data exploration, because it's difficult to remember how all the different plot types work. I encourage you to carefully evaluate whether your visualization software allows for rapid data exploration or whether it tends to get in the way. If it more frequently tends to get in the way, you may benefit from exploring alternative visualization options.

Once we have determined how exactly we want to visualize our data, what data transformations we want to make, and what type of plot to use, we will commonly want to prepare a high-quality figure for publication. At this point, we have several different avenues we can pursue. First, we can finalize the figure using the same software platform we used for initial exploration. Second, we can switch to a platform that provides us finer control over the final product, even if that platform makes it harder to explore. Third, we can produce a draft figure with visualization software and then manually post-process it with an image manipulation or illustration program such as Photoshop or Illustrator. Fourth, we can manually redraw the entire figure from scratch, either with pen and paper or using an illustration program.

All these avenues are reasonable. However, I would like to caution against manually sprucing up figures in routine data analysis pipelines or for scientific publications. Manual steps in the figure preparation pipeline make repeating or reproducing a figure inherently difficult and time-consuming. And in my experience from working in the natural sciences, we rarely make a figure just once. Over the course of a study, we may redo experiments, expand the original dataset, or repeat an experiment several times with slightly altered conditions. I've seen it many times that late in the publication process, when we think everything is done and finalized, we end up introducing a small modification to how we analyze our data, and consequently all the figures have to be redrawn. And I've also seen, in similar situations, that a decision is made not to redo the analysis or not to redraw the figures, either due to the effort involved or because the people who made the original figures have moved on and aren't available anymore. In all these scenarios, an unnecessarily complicated and nonreproducible data visualization pipeline interferes with producing the best possible science.

Having said this, I have no principled concern about hand-drawn figures or figures that have been manually post-processed, for example to change axis labels, add annotations, or modify colors. These approaches can yield beautiful and unique figures that couldn't easily be made in any other way. In fact, as sophisticated and polished computer-generated visualizations are becoming increasingly commonplace, I observe that manually drawn figures are making somewhat of a resurgence (see Figure 28-2 for an example). I think this is the case because such figures represent a unique and personalized take on what might otherwise be a somewhat sterile and routine presentation of data.

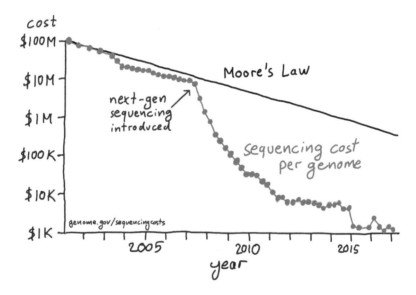

Figure 28-2. After the introduction of next-gen sequencing methods, the sequencing cost per genome has declined much more rapidly than predicted by Moore's law. This hand-drawn figure reproduces a widely publicized visualization prepared by the National Institutes of Health. Data source: National Human Genome Research Institute.

Separation of Content and Design

Good visualization software should allow you to think separately about the content and the design of your figures. By content, I refer to the specific dataset shown, the data transformations applied (if any), the specific mappings from data onto aesthetics, the scales, the axis ranges, and the type of plot (scatterplot, line plot, bar plot, boxplot, etc.). Design, on the other hand, describes features such as the foreground and background colors, font specifications (e.g., font size, face, and family), symbol shapes and sizes, whether or not the figure has a background grid, and the placement of legends, axis ticks, axis titles, and plot titles. When I work on a new visualization, I usually determine first what the content should be, using the kind of rapid exploration described in the previous section. Once the content is set, I may tweak the design, or more likely I will apply a predefined design that I like and/or that gives the figure a consistent look in the context of a larger body of work.

In the software I have used for this book, ggplot2, separation of content and design is achieved via *themes*. A theme specifies the visual appearance of a figure, and it is easy to take an existing figure and apply different themes to it (Figure 28-3). Themes can be written by third parties and distributed as R packages. Through this mechanism, a thriving ecosystem of add-on themes has developed around ggplot2, and it covers a wide range of different styles and application scenarios. If you're making figures with ggplot2, you can almost certainly find an existing theme that satisfies your design needs.

Separation of content and design allows data scientists and designers to each focus on what they do best. Most data scientists are not designers, and therefore their primary concern should be the data, not the design of a visualization. Likewise, most designers are not data scientists, and they should be able to provide a unique and appealing visual language for figures without having to worry about specific data, appropriate transformations, and so on. The same principle of separating content and design has long been followed in the publishing world of books, magazines, newspapers, and websites, where writers provide content but layout and design are handled by a separate group of people who specialize in this area and who ensure that the publication appears in a visually consistent and appealing style. This principle is logical and useful, but it is not yet that widespread in the data visualization world.

In summary, when choosing your visualization software, think about how easily you can reproduce figures and redo them with updated or otherwise changed datasets, whether you can rapidly explore different visualizations of the same data, and to what extent you can tweak the visual design separately from generating the figure content. Depending on your skill level and comfort with programming, it may be beneficial to use different visualization tools at the data exploration and data presentation stages, and you may prefer to do the final visual tweaking interactively or by hand. If you have to make figures interactively, in particular with software that does not keep track of all the data transformations and visual tweaks you have applied, consider taking careful notes on how you make each figure, so that all your work remains reproducible.

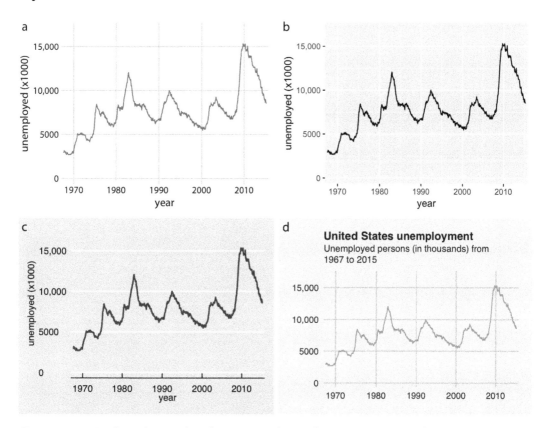

Figure 28-3. Number of unemployed persons in the US from 1970 to 2015. The same figure is displayed using four different ggplot2 themes: (a) the default theme for this book; (b) the default theme of ggplot2, the plotting software I have used to make all the figures in this book; (c) a theme that mimics visualizations shown in the Economist; *(d) a theme that mimics visualizations shown by* FiveThirtyEight. FiveThirtyEight *often foregoes axis labels in favor of plot titles and subtitles, and therefore I have adjusted the figure accordingly. Data source: US Bureau of Labor Statistics.*

## CHAPTER 29

Telling a Story and Making a Point

Most data visualization is done for the purpose of communication. We have an insight about a dataset, and we have a potential audience, and we would like to convey our insight to our audience. To communicate our insight successfully, we will have to present the audience with a meaningful and exciting story. The need for a story may seem disturbing to scientists and engineers, who may equate it with making things up, putting a spin on things, or overselling results. However, this perspective misses the important role that stories play in reasoning and memory. We get excited when we hear a good story, and we get bored when the story is bad or when there is none. Moreover, any communication creates a story in the audience's minds. If we don't provide a clear story ourselves, then our audience will make one up. In the best-case scenario, the story they make up is reasonably close to our own view of the material presented. However, it can be and often is much worse. The made-up story could be "this is boring," "the author is wrong," or "the author is incompetent."

Your goal in telling a story should be to use facts and logical reasoning to get your audience interested and excited. Let me tell you a story about the theoretical physicist Stephen Hawking. He was diagnosed with motor neuron disease at age 21—one year into his PhD—and was given two years to live. Hawking did not accept this predicament and started pouring all his energy into doing science. He ended up living to be 76, became one of the most influential physicists of his time, and did all of his seminal work while being severely disabled. I'd argue that this is a compelling story. It's also entirely fact-based and true.

What Is a Story?

Before we can discuss strategies for turning visualizations into stories, we need to understand what a story actually is. A story is a set of observations, facts, or events, true or invented, that are presented in a specific order such that they create an emotional reaction in the audience. The emotional reaction is created through the buildup of tension at the beginning of the story followed by some type of resolution toward the end of the story. We refer to the flow from tension to resolution as the *story arc*, and every good story has a clear, identifiable arc.

Experienced writers know that there are standard patterns for storytelling that resonate with how humans think. For example, we can tell a story using the Opening–Challenge–Action–Resolution format. In fact, this is the format I used for the Hawking story. I opened the story by introducing the topic, the physicist Stephen Hawking. Next I presented the challenge, the diagnosis of motor neuron disease at age 21. Then came the action, his fierce dedication to science. Finally I presented the resolution, that Hawking led a long and successful life and ended up becoming one of the most influential physicists of his time. Other story formats are also commonly used. Newspaper articles frequently follow the Lead–Development–Resolution format, or, even shorter, just Lead–Development, where the lead gives away the main point up front and the subsequent material provides further details. If we wanted to tell the Hawking story in this format, we might start out with a sentence such as "The influential physicist Stephen Hawking, who revolutionized our understanding of black holes and of cosmology, outlived his doctors' prognosis by 53 years and did all of his most influential work while being severely disabled." This is the lead. In the development, we could follow up with a more in-depth description of Hawking's life, illness, and devotion to science. Yet another format is Action–Background–Development–Climax–Ending, which develops the story a little more rapidly than Opening–Challenge–Action–Resolution but not as rapidly as Lead–Development. In this format, we might open with a sentence such as "The young Stephen Hawking, facing a debilitating disability and the prospect of an early death, decided to pour all his efforts into his science, determined to make his mark while he still could." The purpose of this format is to draw in the audience and to create an emotional connection early on, but without immediately giving away the final resolution.

My goal in this chapter is not to describe these standard forms of storytelling in more detail. There are excellent resources that cover this material; for scientists and analysts, I particularly recommend Joshua Schimel's book *Writing Science* [Schimel 2011]. Instead, I want to discuss how we can bring data visualizations into the story arc. Most importantly, we need to realize that a single (static) visualization will rarely tell an entire story. A visualization may illustrate the opening, the challenge, the action, or the resolution, but it is unlikely to convey all these parts of the story at once. To tell a complete story, we will usually need multiple visualizations. For example, when giving a presentation, we may first show some background or motivational material, then a figure that creates a challenge, and eventually some other figure that provides the resolution. Likewise, in a research paper, we may present a sequence of figures that jointly create a convincing story arc. It is, however, also possible to condense an entire story arc into a single figure. Such a figure must contain a challenge and a resolution at the same time, and it is comparable to a story arc that starts with a lead.

To provide a concrete example of incorporating figures into stories, I will now tell a story on the basis of two figures. The first creates the challenge and the second serves as the resolution. The context of my story is the growth of preprints in the biological sciences (see also Chapter 13). Preprints are manuscripts in draft form that scientists share with their colleagues before formal peer review and official publication. Scientists have been sharing manuscript drafts for as long as scientific manuscripts have existed. However, in the early 1990s, with the advent of the internet, physicists realized that it was much more efficient to store and distribute manuscript drafts in a central repository. They invented the preprint server, a web server where scientists can upload, download, and search for manuscript drafts.

The preprint server physicists developed and still use today is called arXiv.org. Shortly after it was established, arXiv.org started to branch out and become popular in related quantitative fields, including mathematics, astronomy, computer science, statistics, quantitative finance, and quantitative biology. Here, I am interested in the preprint submissions to the quantitative biology (q-bio) section of arXiv.org. The number of submissions per month grew exponentially from 2007 to late 2013, but then the growth suddenly stopped (Figure 29-1). Something must have happened in late 2013 that radically changed the landscape in preprint submissions for quantitative biology. What caused this drastic change in submission growth?

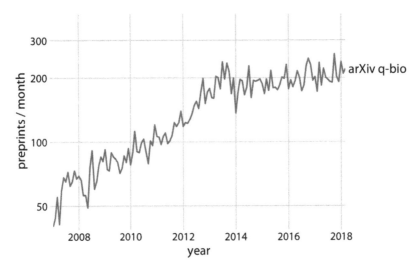

Figure 29-1. Growth in monthly submissions to the quantitative biology (q-bio) section of the preprint server arXiv.org. A sharp transition in the rate of growth can be seen around 2014. While growth was rapid up to 2014, almost no growth occurred from 2014 to 2018. Note that the y axis is logarithmic, so a linear increase in y corresponds to exponential growth in preprint submissions. Data source: Jordan Anaya, http://www.prepubmed.org/.

I will argue that late 2013 marks the point in time when preprints took off in biology, and ironically this caused the q-bio archive to slow its growth. In November 2013, the biology-specific preprint server bioRxiv was launched by Cold Spring Harbor Laboratory (CSHL) Press. CSHL Press is a publisher that is highly respected among biologists. The backing of CSHL Press helped tremendously with the acceptance of preprints in general and bioRxiv in particular among biologists. The same biologists that would have been quite suspicious of arXiv.org were much more comfortable with bioRxiv. As a result bioRxiv quickly gained acceptance among biologists, to a degree that arXiv had never managed. In fact, soon after its launch, bioRxiv started experiencing rapid, exponential growth in monthly submissions, and the slowdown in q-bio submissions exactly coincides with the start of this exponential growth of bioRxiv (Figure 29-2). It appears to be the case that many quantitative biologists who otherwise might have deposited a preprint with q-bio decided to deposit it with bioRxiv instead.

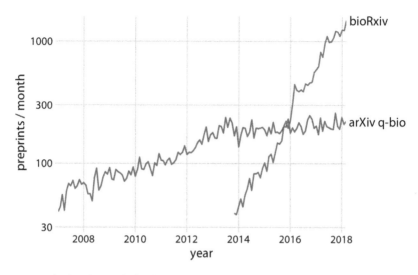

Figure 29-2. The leveling off of submission growth to q-bio coincided with the introduction of the bioRxiv server. Shown are the growth in monthly submissions to the q-bio section of the general-purpose preprint server arXiv.org and to the dedicated biology preprint server bioRxiv. The bioRxiv server went live in November 2013, and its submission rate has grown exponentially since. It seems likely that many scientists who otherwise would have submitted preprints to q-bio chose to submit to bioRxiv instead. Data source: Jordan Anaya, http://www.prepubmed.org/.

This is my story about preprints in biology. I purposefully told it with two figures, even though the first (Figure 29-1) is fully contained within the second (Figure 29-2). I think this story has the strongest impact when broken into two pieces, and this is how I would present it in a talk. However, Figure 29-2 alone can be used to tell the entire story, and the single-figure version might be more suitable to a medium where the audience can be expected to have short attention span, such as in a social media post.

Make a Figure for the Generals

For the remainder of this chapter, I will discuss strategies for making individual figures and sets of figures that help your audience to connect with your story and remain engaged throughout your entire story arc. First, and most importantly, you need to show your audience figures they can actually understand. It is entirely possible to follow all the recommendations I have provided throughout this book and still prepare figures that confuse. When this happens, you may have fallen victim to two common misconceptions: first, that the audience can see your figures and immediately infer the points you are trying to make, and second, that the audience can rapidly process complex visualizations and understand the key trends and relationships that are shown. Neither of these assumptions is true. We need to do everything we can to help our readers understand the meaning of our visualizations and see the same patterns in the data that we see. This usually means less is more. Simplify your figures as much as possible. Remove all features that are tangential to your story. Only the important points should remain. I refer to this concept as "making a figure for the generals."

For several years, I was in charge of a large research project funded by the US Army. For our annual progress reports, I was instructed by the program managers to not include a lot of figures, and that any figure I did include should show very clearly how our project was succeeding. A general, the program managers told me, should be able to look at each figure and immediately see how what we were doing was improving upon or exceeding prior capabilities. Yet when my colleagues who were part of this project sent me figures for the annual progress report, many of the figures did not meet this criterion. The figures usually were overly complex, were labeled in confusing, technical terms, or did not make any obvious point at all. Most scientists are not trained to make figures for the generals.

 Never assume your audience can rapidly process complex visual displays.

Some might hear this story and conclude that the generals are not very smart or just not that into science. I think that's exactly the wrong take-home message. The generals are simply very busy. They can't spend 30 minutes trying to decipher a cryptic figure. When they give millions of dollars of taxpayer funds to scientists to do basic research, the least they can expect in return is a handful of clear demonstrations that something worthwhile and interesting was accomplished. This story should also not be misconstrued as being about military funding in particular. The generals are a metaphor for anybody you may want to reach with your visualization: a scientific reviewer for your paper or grant proposal, a newspaper editor, or your supervisor or your supervisor's boss at the company where you're working. If you want your story to come across, you need to make figures that are appropriate for your generals.

The first thing that will get in the way of making a figure for the generals is, ironically, the ease with which modern visualization software allows us to make sophisticated data visualizations. With nearly limitless power of visualization, it becomes tempting to keep piling on more dimensions of data. And in fact, I see a trend in the world of data visualization to make the most complex, multifaceted visualizations possible. These visualizations may look very impressive, but they are unlikely to convey a meaningful story. Consider Figure 29-3, which shows the arrival delays for all flights departing out of the New York City area in 2013. I suspect it will take you a while to process this figure.

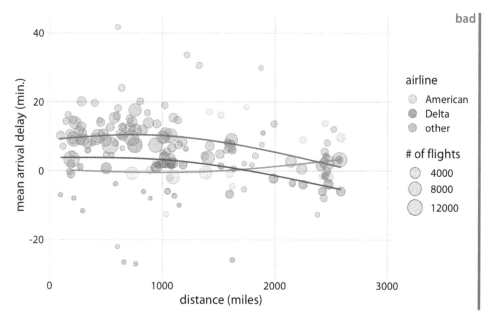

Figure 29-3. Mean arrival delay versus distance from New York City. Each point represents one destination, and the size of each point represents the number of flights from one of the three major New York City airports (Newark, JFK, or LaGuardia) to that destination in 2013. Negative delays imply that the flight arrived early. Solid lines represent the mean trends between arrival delay and distance. Delta has consistently lower arrival delays than other airlines, regardless of distance traveled. American has among the lowest delays, on average, for short distances, but has among the highest delays for longer distances traveled. This figure is labeled as "bad" because it is overly complex. Most readers will find it confusing and will not intuitively grasp what it is the figure is showing. Data source: US Dept. of Transportation, Bureau of Transportation Statistics.

I think the most important feature of Figure 29-3 is that American and Delta have the shortest arrival delays. This insight is much better conveyed in a simple bar graph (Figure 29-4). Therefore, Figure 29-4 is the correct figure to show if the story is about arrival delays of airlines, even if making that graph doesn't challenge your data visualization skills. And if you're then wondering whether these airlines have small delays because they don't fly that much out of the New York City area, you could present a second bar graph highlighting that both American and Delta are major carriers in this area (Figure 29-5). Both of these bar graphs discard the distance variable shown in Figure 29-3. This is OK. We don't need to visualize data dimensions that are tangential to our story, even if we have them and even if we could make a figure that showed them. Simple and clear is better than complex and confusing. When you're trying to show too much data at once, you may end up not showing anything.

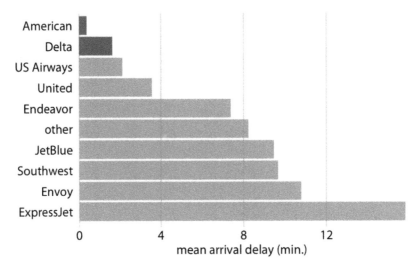

Figure 29-4. Mean arrival delay for flights out of the New York City area in 2013, by airline. American and Delta have the lowest mean arrival delays of all airlines flying out of the New York City area. Data source: US Dept. of Transportation, Bureau of Transportation Statistics.

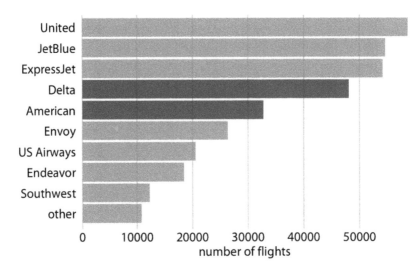

Figure 29-5. Number of flights out of the New York City area in 2013, by airline. Delta and American are the fourth and fifth largest carriers by flights out of the New York City area. Data source: US Dept. of Transportation, Bureau of Transportation Statistics.

Build Up Toward Complex Figures

Sometimes, however, we do want to show more complex figures that contain a large amount of information at once. In those cases, we can make things easier for our readers if we first show them a simplified version of the figure before we show the final one in its full complexity. The same approach is also strongly recommended for presentations. Never jump straight to a highly complex figure; first show an easily digestible subset of the information.

This recommendation is particularly relevant if the final figure is a small multiples plot (Chapter 21) showing a grid of subplots with similar structure. The full grid is much easier to digest if the audience has first seen a single subplot by itself. For example, Figure 29-6 shows the aggregate numbers of United Airlines departures out of Newark Airport (EWR) in 2013, broken down by weekday. Once we have seen and digested this figure, it's much easier to process the same information for 10 airlines and 3 airports at once (Figure 29-7).

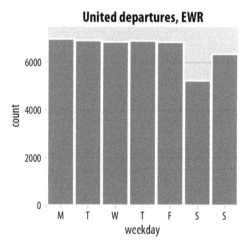

Figure 29-6. United Airlines departures out of Newark Airport (EWR) in 2013, by weekday. Most weekdays show approximately the same number of departures, but there are fewer departures on weekends. Data source: US Dept. of Transportation, Bureau of Transportation Statistics.

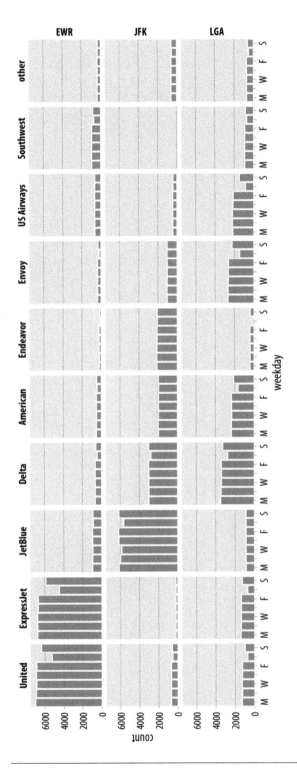

Figure 29-7. Departures out of airports in the New York City area in 2013, broken down by airline, airport, and weekday. United Airlines and ExpressJet make up most of the departures out of Newark Airport (EWR); JetBlue, Delta, American, and Endeavor make up most of the departures out of JFK; and Delta, American, Envoy, and US Airways make up most of the departures out of LaGuardia (LGA). Most but not all airlines have fewer departures on weekends than during the workweek. Data source: US Dept. of Transportation, Bureau of Transportation Statistics.

Make Your Figures Memorable

Simple and clean figures such as simple bar plots have the advantage that they avoid distractions, are easy to read, and let your audience focus on the most important points you want to bring across. However, the simplicity can come with a disadvantage: figures can end up looking generic. They don't have any features that stand out and make them memorable. If I showed you 10 bar graphs in quick succession you'd have a hard time keeping them apart and afterwards remembering what you saw. For example, if you take a quick look at Figure 29-8, you will notice the visual similarity to Figure 29-5 from earlier in this chapter. However, the two figures have nothing in common other than that they are bar graphs. Figure 29-5 showed the number of flights out of the New York City area by airline, whereas Figure 29-8 shows the most popular pets in US households. Neither figure has any element that helps you intuitively perceive what topic the figure covers, and therefore neither figure is particularly memorable.

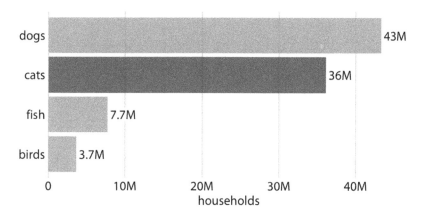

Figure 29-8. Number of households having one or more of the most popular pets: dogs, cats, fish, or birds. This bar graph is perfectly clear but not necessarily particularly memorable. The "cats" column has been highlighted solely to create visual similarity with Figure 29-5. Data source: 2012 US Pet Ownership & Demographics Sourcebook, American Veterinary Medical Association.

Research on human perception shows that more visually complex and unique figures are more memorable [Bateman et al. 2010]; [Borgo et al. 2012]. However, visual uniqueness and complexity do not just affect memorability, as they may hinder a person's ability to get a quick overview of the information or make it difficult to distinguish small differences in values. At the extreme, a figure could be very memorable but utterly confusing. Such a figure would not be a good data visualization, even if it works well as a stunning piece of art. At the other extreme, figures may be very clear but forgettable and boring, and those figures may not have the impact we might hope for either. In general, we want to strike a balance between the two extremes and make our figures both memorable and clear. (The intended audience matters as well, however. If a figure is intended for a technical scientific publication, we will generally worry less about memorability than if the figure is intended for a broadly read newspaper or blog.)

We can make a figure more memorable by adding visual elements that reflect features of the data, such as drawings or pictograms of the things or objects that the dataset is about. One approach that is commonly taken is to show the data values themselves in the form of repeated images, such that each copy of an image corresponds to a defined amount of the represented variable. For example, we can replace the bars in Figure 29-8 with repeated images of a dog, a cat, a fish, and a bird, drawn to a scale such that each complete animal corresponds to 5 million households (Figure 29-9). Thus, visually, Figure 29-9 still functions as a bar plot, but we now have added some visual complexity that makes the figure more memorable, and we have also shown the data using images that directly reflect what the data means. After only a quick glance at the figure, you may be able to remember that there were many more dogs and cats than fish or birds. Importantly, in such visualizations, we want to use the images to represent the data, rather than using images simply to adorn the visualization or to annotate the axes. In psychological experiments, the latter choices tend to be distracting rather than helpful [Haroz, Kosara, and Franconeri 2015].

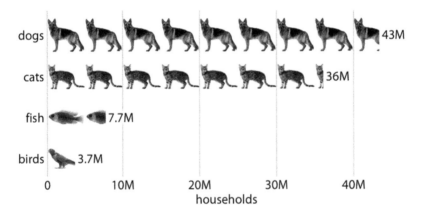

Figure 29-9. Number of households having one or more of the most popular pets, shown as an isotype plot. Each complete animal represents 5 million households that have that kind of pet. Data source: 2012 US Pet Ownership & Demographics Sourcebook, American Veterinary Medical Association.

Visualizations such as Figure 29-9 are often called *isotype plots*. The word "isotype" was introduced as an acronym of International System Of TYpographic Picture Education, and strictly speaking it refers to logo-like simplified pictograms that represent objects, animals, plants, or people [Haroz, Kosara, and Franconeri 2015]. However, I think it makes sense to use the term isotype plot more broadly to apply to any type of visualization where repeated copies of the same image are used to indicate the magnitude of a value. After all, the prefix "iso" means "the same" and "type" can mean a particular kind, class, or group.

Be Consistent but Don't Be Repetitive

When discussing compound figures in Chapter 21, I mentioned that it is important to use a consistent visual language for the different parts of a larger figure. The same is true across figures. If we make three figures that are all part of one larger story, then we need to design those figures so they look like they belong together. Using a consistent visual language does not mean, however, that everything should look exactly the same. On the contrary, it is important that figures describing different analyses look visually distinct, so that your audience can easily recognize where one analysis ends and another one starts. This is best achieved by using different visualization approaches for different parts of the overarching story. If you have used a bar plot already, next use a scatterplot, or a boxplot, or a line plot. Otherwise, the different analyses will blur together in your audience's mind, and your audience will have a hard time distinguishing one part of the story from another. For example, if we redesign Figure 21-8 from "Compound Figures" on page 260 so it uses only bar plots, the result is noticeably less distinct and more confusing (Figure 29-10).

 When preparing a presentation or report, aim to use a different type of visualization for each distinct analysis.

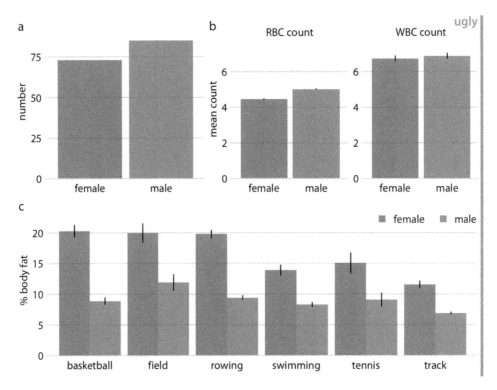

Figure 29-10. Physiology and body composition of male and female athletes. Error bars indicate the standard error of the mean. This figure is overly repetitive. It shows the same data as Figure 21-8 and it uses a consistent visual language, but all the subfigures use the same type of visualization (bar plots). This makes it difficult for the reader to process that parts (a), (b), and (c) show entirely different results. Data source: [Telford and Cunningham 1991].

Sets of repetitive figures are often a consequence of multipart stories where each part is based on the same type of raw data. In those scenarios, it can be tempting to use the same type of visualization for each part. However, in aggregate, these figures will not hold the audience's attention. As an example, let's consider a story about the price of Facebook stock, in two parts: (i) the Facebook stock price has increased rapidly from 2012 to 2017, and (ii) the price increase has outpaced that of other large tech companies. You might want to visualize these two statements with two figures showing stock price over time, as demonstrated in Figure 29-11. However, while Figure 29-11a serves a purpose and should remain as is, Figure 29-11b is at the same time repetitive and obscures the main point. We don't particularly care about the exact temporal evolution of the stock price of Alphabet, Apple, or Microsoft; we just want to highlight that it grew less than the stock price of Facebook.

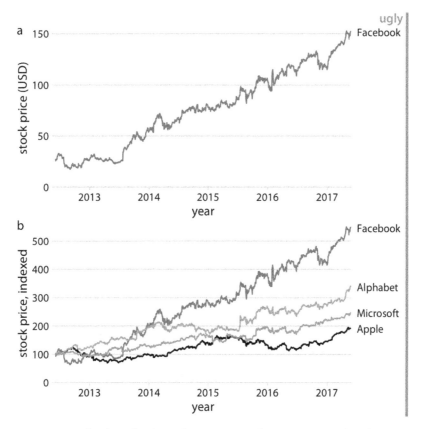

Figure 29-11. Growth of Facebook stock price over a five-year interval and comparison with other tech stocks. (a) The Facebook stock price rose from around $25/share in mid-2012 to $150/share in mid-2017. (b) The prices of other large tech companies did not rise comparably over the same time period. Prices have been indexed to 100 on June 1, 2012 to allow for easy comparison. This figure is labeled as "ugly" because parts (a) and (b) are repetitive. Data source: Yahoo! Finance.

I would recommend to leave part (a) as is but replace part (b) with a bar plot showing percent increase (Figure 29-12). Now we have two distinct figures that each make a unique point and that work well in combination. Part (a) allows the reader to get familiar with the raw, underlying data and part (b) highlights the magnitude of the effect while removing any tangential information.

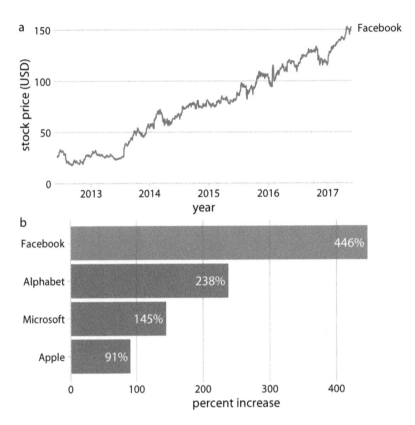

Figure 29-12. Growth of Facebook stock price over a five-year interval and comparison with other tech stocks. (a) The Facebook stock price rose from around $25/share in mid-2012 to $150/share in mid-2017, an increase of almost 450%. (b) The prices of other large tech companies did not rise comparably over the same time period. Price increases ranged from around 90% to almost 240%. Data source: Yahoo! Finance.

Figure 29-12 highlights a general principle that I follow when preparing sets of figures to tell a story: I start with a figure that is as close as possible to showing the raw data, and in subsequent figures I show increasingly more derived quantities. Derived quantities (such as percent increases, averages, coefficients of fitted models, and so on) are useful to summarize key trends in large and complex datasets. However, because they are derived they are less intuitive, and if we show a derived quantity before we have shown the raw data, our audience will find it difficult to follow. On the flip side, if we try to show all trends by showing raw data, we will end up needing too many figures and/or being repetitive.

How many figures should you use to tell your story? The answer depends on the publication venue. For a short blog post or tweet, make one figure. For scientific papers, I recommend between three and six figures. If there are many more than six figures for a scientific paper, then some of them may need to be moved into an appendix or supplementary materials section. It is good to document all the evidence we have collected, but we must not wear out our audience by presenting excessive numbers of mostly similar-looking figures. In other contexts, a larger number of figures may be appropriate. However, in those contexts, we will usually be telling multiple stories, or an overarching story with subplots. For example, if I am asked to give an hour-long scientific presentation, I usually aim to tell three distinct stories. Similarly, a book or thesis will contain more than one story, and in fact may contain one story per chapter or section. In those scenarios, each distinct story line or subplot should be presented with no more than three to six figures. In this book, you will find that I follow this principle at the level of sections within chapters. Each section is approximately self-contained and will typically show no more than six figures.

Annotated Bibliography

No single book can cover everything there is to know about a topic. I encourage you to read other texts on data visualization to deepen your understanding and to develop your technical skills in making figures. Here, I provide a limited selection of books that I have personally found interesting, thought-provoking, or helpful. Books listed in the first section are the most similar in scope to the present book, and may provide complementary or alternative perspectives on the topics I have covered. Books listed in "Programming Books" on page 352 address the important topic of how to make visualizations using programming approaches and available software libraries. The remaining sections list other books that will expand your knowledge of data visualization and help you communicate with visuals and data.

Thinking About Data and Visualization

The following books discuss the thought processes and decision making required for turning data into visualizations. They serve as introductory texts on how to choose what visualizations to make and what pitfalls to look out for:

Alberto Cairo. The Truthful Art. *New Riders, 2016.*
> An excellent all-around introduction to data visualization, in particular for journalists. The book covers many important concepts of data visualization, such as how to visualize distributions, trends, uncertainty, and maps. In many chapters, it also serves as an introduction to basic statistical principles, explaining concepts such as populations, samples, and confidence levels.

Stephen Few. Show Me the Numbers. *Analytics Press, 2012.*
> A book about data visualization for the business professional. It is similar in scope and target audience to the following reference but contains more material and covers many topics in more depth. However, it is not as well written or carefully produced as the following book.

Cole Nussbaumer Knaflic. Storytelling with Data. *John Wiley & Sons, 2015.*
> A well-written and carefully produced book on how to turn data into visuals. The book's primary audience is people making business graphics, and it's an excellent reference for the topics it covers. However, it does not cover many topics of importance to scientists, such as the visualization of distributions, trends, or uncertainty.

Programming Books

The following references are all how-to books that teach programming approaches to data visualization:

Kieran Healy. Data Visualization: A Practical Introduction. *Princeton University Press, 2018.*
> An introduction to using ggplot2 for data visualization. Recommended as follow-up after Wickham and Grolemund's *R for Data Science* (mentioned later in this list).

Scott Murray. Interactive Data Visualization for the Web: An Introduction to Designing with D3. *2nd ed. O'Reilly Media, 2017.*
> An introduction to making interactive online visualizations with D3, using HTML, CSS, JavaScript, and SVG.

Jake VanderPlas. Python Data Science Handbook: Essential Tools for Working with Data. *O'Reilly Media, 2016.*
> An introduction to using the programming language Python for data science. Has extensive material on data visualization using Python's Matplotlib and Seaborn.

Hadley Wickham, Garrett Grolemund. R for Data Science. *O'Reilly Media, 2017.*
> An all-around introduction to using the programming language R for data science. Contains several chapters on using ggplot2 for data visualization.

Statistics Texts

Introductory texts in statistics will generally contain material on data visualization, covering topics such as scatterplots, histograms, boxplots, and line graphs. There are many such texts that could be listed. Here, I mention just a few recent additions that are worth a look:

David M. Diez, Christopher D. Barr, Mine Çetinkaya-Rundel. OpenIntro Statistics. *3rd ed. OpenIntro, Inc., 2015.*
> An open source introductory statistics text book. The entire book is freely available, as are the LaTeX files and R code used to compile the book and make the figures.

Susan Holmes, Wolfgang Huber. Modern Statistics for Modern Biology. *Cambridge University Press, 2018.*

> A statistics text that emphasizes computational tools needed for modern biology. The entire book is freely available, and R code for all examples is provided.

Chester Ismay, Albert Y. Kim. Modern Dive—An Introduction to Statistical and Data Sciences via R. *https://moderndive.com.*

> An online-only introductory textbook that teaches basic statistics and data science. The book covers both theoretical concepts and practical approaches using R.

Historical Texts

The books in this section are of interest primarily for historical reasons. They were influential at the time of their publication, but similar material can now be found elsewhere or in more modern form:

William S. Cleveland. The Elements of Graphing Data. *2nd ed. Hobart Press, 1994.*

> One of the first books about information design written for statisticians. The book contains many examples of scatterplots, line graphs, histograms, and boxplots, and it discusses them in the context of data analysis and statistical modeling. It also popularized the Cleveland dot plot.

William S. Cleveland. Visualizing Data. *Hobart Press, 1993.*

> Companion book to *The Elements of Graphing Data* by the same author. This one is more mathematical and doesn't talk about human perception.

Edward R. Tufte. Envisioning Information. *Graphics Press, 1990.*

> This book popularized the concept of the small multiple.

Edward R. Tufte. The Visual Display of Quantitative Information. *2nd ed. Graphics Press, 2001.*

> First published in 1983, this book has been highly influential in the field of data visualization. It introduced concepts such as chart junk, data–ink ratio, and sparklines. The book also showed the first slopegraph (but didn't name it). However, it does contain several recommendations that have not stood the test of time. In particular, it recommends an excessively minimalistic plot design.

Books on Broadly Related Topics

The following books are all broadly related to the topics of data visualization and effective communication:

Joshua Schimel. Writing Science. *Oxford University Press, 2011.*
Teaches how to write about scientific and other technical topics in an engaging way, by telling a story. While not primarily a book about data visualization, this is an indispensable text for anybody who needs to write technical articles and/or proposals.

Jonathan Schwabish. Better Presentations. *Columbia University Press, 2016.*
A short and informative guide for making presentations. A must-read for anybody who routinely uses slides to give talks or presentations.

Maureen C. Stone. A Field Guide to Digital Color. *A K Peters, 2003.*
A comprehensive guide to how colors are captured, processed, and reproduced by computers.

Colin Ware. Information Visualization. *3rd ed. Morgan Kaufmann, 2012.*
A book about principles of visualization, specifically addressing topics such as how the human visual system works and how different graphical patterns are perceived. The book covers many different visualization scenarios, including user interfaces and virtual worlds, but it puts comparatively less emphasis on visualizing data in the form of 2D figures.

Technical Notes

The entire book was written in R Markdown, using the bookdown, rmarkdown, and knitr packages. All figures were made with ggplot2, with the help of several add-on packages including cowplot, geofacet, ggforce, ggmap, ggrepel, ggridges, hexbin, patchwork, sf, statebins, tidybayes, and treemapify. Color manipulations were done with the colorspace and colorblindr packages. For many of these packages, the current development version is required to compile all parts of the book.

The source code for the book is available at *https://github.com/clauswilke/dataviz*. The book also requires a supporting R package, dviz.supp, whose code is available at *https://github.com/clauswilke/dviz.supp*.

The book was last compiled using the following environment:

```
## R version 3.5.0 (2018-04-23)
## Platform: x86_64-apple-darwin15.6.0 (64-bit)
## Running under: macOS Sierra 10.12.6
##
## Matrix products: default
## BLAS: /Library/Frameworks/ ... /libRblas.0.dylib
## LAPACK: /Library/Frameworks/ ... /libRlapack.dylib
##
## locale:
## [1] en_US.UTF-8/en_US.UTF-8/ ... /C/en_US.UTF-8/en_US.UTF-8
##
## attached base packages:
## [1] stats   graphics  grDevices utils   datasets  methods   base
##
## other attached packages:
##  [1] nycflights13_1.0.0   gapminder_0.3.0   RColorBrewer_1.1-2
##  [4] gganimate_1.0.0.9000 ungeviz_0.1.0     emmeans_1.3.1
##  [7] mgcv_1.8-24          nlme_3.1-137      broom_0.5.1
## [10] tidybayes_1.0.3      maps_3.3.0        statebins_2.0.0
## [13] sf_0.7-1             maptools_0.9-4    sp_1.3-1
## [16] rgeos_0.3-28         ggspatial_1.0.3   geofacet_0.1.9
## [19] plot3D_1.1.1         magick_1.9        hexbin_1.27.2
```

```
## [22] treemapify_2.5.0      gridExtra_2.3       ggmap_2.7.904
## [25] ggthemes_4.0.1        ggridges_0.5.1      ggrepel_0.8.0
## [28] ggforce_0.1.1         patchwork_0.0.1     lubridate_1.7.4
## [31] forcats_0.3.0         stringr_1.3.1       purrr_0.2.5
## [34] readr_1.1.1           tidyr_0.8.2         tibble_1.4.2
## [37] tidyverse_1.2.1       dviz.supp_0.1.0     dplyr_0.8.0.9000
## [40] colorblindr_0.1.0     ggplot2_3.1.0       colorspace_1.4-0
## [43] cowplot_0.9.99
##
## loaded via a namespace (and not attached):
##  [1] rjson_0.2.20          deldir_0.1-15
##  [3] class_7.3-14          rprojroot_1.3-2
##  [5] estimability_1.3      ggstance_0.3.1
##  [7] rstudioapi_0.7        farver_1.0.0.9999
##  [9] ggfittext_0.6.0       svUnit_0.7-12
## [11] mvtnorm_1.0-8         xml2_1.2.0
## [13] knitr_1.20            polyclip_1.9-1
## [15] jsonlite_1.5          png_0.1-7
## [17] compiler_3.5.0        httr_1.3.1
## [19] backports_1.1.2       assertthat_0.2.0
## [21] Matrix_1.2-14         lazyeval_0.2.1
## [23] cli_1.0.1.9000        tweenr_1.0.1
## [25] prettyunits_1.0.2     htmltools_0.3.6
## [27] tools_3.5.0           misc3d_0.8-4
## [29] coda_0.19-2           gtable_0.2.0
## [31] glue_1.3.0            Rcpp_1.0.0
## [33] cellranger_1.1.0      imguR_1.0.3
## [35] xfun_0.3              strapgod_0.0.0.9000
## [37] rvest_0.3.2           MASS_7.3-50
## [39] scales_1.0.0          hms_0.4.2
## [41] yaml_2.2.0            stringi_1.2.4
## [43] e1071_1.7-0           spData_0.2.9.4
## [45] RgoogleMaps_1.4.3     rlang_0.3.0.1
## [47] pkgconfig_2.0.2       bitops_1.0-6
## [49] geogrid_0.1.1         evaluate_0.11
## [51] lattice_0.20-35       tidyselect_0.2.5
## [53] plyr_1.8.4            magrittr_1.5
## [55] bookdown_0.7          R6_2.3.0
## [57] generics_0.0.2        DBI_1.0.0
## [59] pillar_1.3.0          haven_1.1.2
## [61] foreign_0.8-71        withr_2.1.2.9000
## [63] units_0.6-1           modelr_0.1.2
## [65] crayon_1.3.4          arrayhelpers_1.0-20160527
## [67] rmarkdown_1.10        progress_1.2.0.9000
## [69] jpeg_0.1-8            rnaturalearth_0.1.0
## [71] grid_3.5.0            readxl_1.1.0
## [73] digest_0.6.18         classInt_0.2-3
## [75] xtable_1.8-3          munsell_0.5.0
## [77] concaveman_1.0.0
```

References

Bateman, S., R. Mandryk, C. Gutwin, A. Genest, D. McDine, and C. Brooks. 2010. "Useful Junk? The Effects of Visual Embellishment on Comprehension and Memorability of Charts." *ACM Conference on Human Factors in Computing Systems*, 2573–82. doi:10.1145/1753326.1753716.

Becker, R. A., W. S. Cleveland, and M.-J. Shyu. 1996. "The Visual Design and Control of Trellis Display." *Journal of Computational and Graphical Statistics* 5: 123–55.

Bergstrom, C. T., and J. West. 2016. "The Principle of Proportional Ink." *http://calling bullshit.org/tools/tools_proportional_ink.html*.

Borgo, R., A. Abdul-Rahman, F. Mohamed, P. W. Grant, I. Reppa, and L. Floridi. 2012. "An Empirical Study on Using Visual Embellishments in Visualization." *IEEE Transactions on Visualization and Computer Graphics* 18: 2759–68. doi:10.1109/TVCG.2012.197.

Brewer, Cynthia A. 2017. "ColorBrewer 2.0. Color Advice for Cartography." *http://www.ColorBrewer.org*.

Carr, D. B., R. J. Littlefield, W. L. Nicholson, and J. S. Littlefield. 1987. "Scatterplot Matrix Techniques for Large N." *Journal of the American Statistical Association* 82: 424–36.

Clauset, A., C. R. Shalizi, and M. E. J. Newman. 2009. "Power-Law Distributions in Empirical Data." *SIAM Review* 51: 661–703.

Cleveland, R. B., W. S. Cleveland, J. E. McRae, and I. Terpenning. 1990. "STL: A Seasonal-Trend Decomposition Procedure Based on Loess." *Journal of Official Statistics* 6: 3–73.

Cleveland, W. S. 1979. "Robust Locally Weighted Regression and Smoothing Scatterplots." *Journal of the American Statistical Association* 74: 829–36.

———. 1993. *Visualizing Data*. Summit, New Jersey: Hobart Press.

Dua, D., and E. Karra Taniskidou. 2017. "UCI Machine Learning Repository." University of California, Irvine, School of Information; Computer Sciences. *https://archive.ics.uci.edu/ml*

Fisher, R. A. 1936. "The Use of Multiple Measurements in Taxonomic Problems." *Annals of Eugenics* 7: 179–188. doi:10.1111/j.1469-1809.1936.tb02137.x.

Haroz, S., R. Kosara, and S. L. Franconeri. 2015. "ISOTYPE Visualization: Working Memory, Performance, and Engagement with Pictographs." *ACM Conference on Human Factors in Computing Systems*, 1191–1200. doi:10.1145/2702123.2702275.

———. 2016. "The Connected Scatterplot for Presenting Paired Time Series." *IEEE Transactions on Visualization and Computer Graphics* 22: 2174–86. doi:10.1109/TVCG.2015.2502587.

Hullman, J., P. Resnick, and E. Adar. 2015. "Hypothetical Outcome Plots Outperform Error Bars and Violin Plots for Inferences About Reliability of Variable Ordering." *PLOS ONE* 10: e0142444. doi:10.1371/journal.pone.0142444.

Kale, A., F. Nguyen, M. Kay, and J. Hullman. 2018. "Hypothetical Outcome Plots Help Untrained Observers Judge Trends in Ambiguous Data." *IEEE Transactions on Visualization and Computer Graphics* 25: 892–905. doi:10.1109/TVCG.2018.2864909.

Kay, M., T. Kola, J. Hullman, and S. Munson. 2016. "When (Ish) Is My Bus? User-Centered Visualizations of Uncertainty in Everyday, Mobile Predictive Systems." CHI Conference on Human Factors in Computing Systems, 5092–5103. doi:10.1145/2858036.2858558.

Marcos, M. L., and J. Echave. 2015. "Too Packed to Change: Side-Chain Packing and Site-Specific Substitution Rates in Protein Evolution." *PeerJ* 3: e911.

McDonald, Ian. 2017. "DW-NOMINATE Using ggjoy." *http://rpubs.com/ianrmcdonald/293304*

Molyneaux, L., S. K. Gilliam, and L. C. Florant. 1947. "Differences in Virginia Death Rates by Color, Sex, Age, and Rural or Urban Residence." *American Sociological Review* 12: 525–35.

Okabe, M., and K. Ito. 2008. "Color Universal Design (CUD): How to Make Figures and Presentations That Are Friendly to Colorblind People." *http://jfly.iam.u-tokyo.ac.jp/color/*.

Paff, M. L., B. R. Jack, B. L. Smith, J. J. Bull, and C. O. Wilke. 2018. "Combinatorial Approaches to Viral Attenuation." bioRxiv, 29918. doi:10.1101/299180.

Schimel, J. 2011. *Writing Science: How to Write Papers That Get Cited and Proposals That Get Funded.* Oxford: Oxford University Press.

Sidiropoulos, N., S. H. Sohi, T. L. Pedersen, B. T. Porse, O. Winther, N. Rapin, and F. O. Bagger. 2018. "SinaPlot: An Enhanced Chart for Simple and Truthful Representation of Single Observations over Multiple Classes." *Journal of Computational and Graphical Statistics* 27: 673–76. doi:10.1080/10618600.2017.1366914.

Stone, M., D. Albers Szafir, and V. Setlur. 2014. "An Engineering Model for Color Difference as a Function of Size." 22nd Color and Imaging Conference, 253–258.

Telford, R. D., and R. B. Cunningham. 1991. "Sex, Sport, and Body-Size Dependency of Hematology in Highly Trained Athletes." *Medicine and Science in Sports and Exercise* 23: 788–94.

The Economist online. 2011. "Corrosive Corruption." *https://www.economist.com/graphic-detail/2011/12/02/corrosive-corruption*.

Tufte, E. R. 1990. *Envisioning Information*. Cheshire, Connecticut: Graphics Press.

———. 2001. *The Visual Display of Quantitative Information*. 2nd ed. Cheshire, Connecticut: Graphics Press.

Wehrwein, A. 2017. "It Brings Me ggjoy." *http://austinwehrwein.com/data-visualization/it-brings-me-ggjoy/*.

Wickham, H. 2016. *ggplot2: Elegant Graphics for Data Analysis*. 2nd ed. New York: Springer.

Wikipedia, User:Schutz. 2007. "File:Piecharts.svg." *https://en.wikipedia.org/wiki/File:Piecharts.svg*.

Yates, F. 1935. "Complex Experiments." *Supplement to the Journal of the Royal Statistical Society* 2: 181–247. doi:10.2307/2983638.

Index

Symbols

2D bins, 41
2D error bars, 43
2D histograms, 222-225
2D, projection of 3D objects into, 305, 309
3D plots, 305-314
    appropriate use of, 313-314
    avoiding 3D position scales, 307-313
    avoiding gratuitous 3D, 305-307
    distortion from projecting objects into 2D, 305
    problems with 3D bars, 306, 312

A

absolute number vs. percentages, 101
accent color scales, 33
Action–Background–Development–Climax–Ending story format, 334
aesthetics, 7-12, 328
    applied to maps of geospatial data, 171
    commonly used in data visualizations, 7
    encoding single variable in multiple aesthetics, legends and, 253
    mapping data onto with scales, 10-12
    representing continuous or discrete data, 8
    types of data in visualizations, 8
age pyramids, 68
Albers projection, 167
amounts, visualizing, 37, 45-58
    bar plots, 45-50
        grouped and stacked bars, 50-53
    dot plots and heat maps, 53-58
    on log scales, problems with, 212
anticorrelated variables, 121

associations, visualizing, 117-129
    correlograms, 121-124
    dimension reduction, 124-127
    paired data, 127-129
    scatterplots, 117-121
automation, xiii
    programmatically generated figures, 327
axes, 16-24
    axis ranges in small multiples, 257
    coordinate systems with curved axes, 22-24
    nonlinear, 16-22
    omitting in plots, 272
    titles, 270-272
        example plot with appropriate titles, 270
        omitting, 270
        overdoing, 272
    visualizing many distributions along the horizontal axis, 88-91
    visualizing many distributions along the vertical axis, 81-87
axis labels, 270
    (see also axes, titles)
    larger, using, 291-295

B

background grids, 279, 282-287
    along both axes, in scatterplots, 287
    for figures about change in y axis values, 284
    grid lines running perpendicular to key variable of interest, 286
    horizontal reference lines, 284
    in bar plots, 286
    in ggplot2 software, 282

using nonmonotonic color scales to encode data values, 237-238

encoding categorical variable by bar color, 52

fundamental uses in data visualizations, 27

in photographic images, 322

line drawings and, 297

manipulations, packages used, 355

mapping data values onto colors in heatmaps, 56

redundant coding, 243

(see also redundant coding)

using gray background for figures, 283

using in visualizations of geospatial data, 42

color scales, 12, 27-34

accent, 33

diverging, 30

qualitative, 27

sequential, 29

color-vision deficiency, 238-242, 243-253

deuteranomaly/deuteranopia, 238, 244

protanomaly/protanopia, 238, 244

tritanomaly/tritanopia, 238, 244

ColorBrewer color scales, 27, 30

compound figures, 255, 260-264

alignment of individual figure panels, 264

how individual panels fit together, 261

labeling of individual panels, 260

compression, lossless and lossy, of bitmap graphics, 321-322

lossy compression in JPEGs, 324

confidence bands, 44, 181, 197

graded, 199

confidence interval, 194

confidence levels, 199

confidence strips, 43

as alternative to error bars, 193

conformal projection, 163

connected scatterplots, 42

visualizing high-dimensional time series using PCA, 141

visualizing time series with two or more response variables, 139

consistency, achieving without being repetitive, 345-349

content and design, separation of, 330-331

context in figures, 277

(see also balancing data and context)

continuous data, 8

contour lines, 41, 225-231

drawing each in its own panel, 230

drawing multiple sets in different colors, 228

coordinate systems and axes, 13-24

Cartesian, 13-16

coordinate systems with curved axes, 22-24

nonlinear axes, 16-22

coordinates, 7

correlated or anticorrelated variables, 121

correlation coefficients

calculating, 121

plotting as correlograms, 41

correlograms, 41

drawback of, 124

visualizing associations among quantitative variables, 121-124

credible intervals, 194

cumulative densities, 38

cumulative distribution, 72

(see also empirical cumulative distribution functions)

curve fits, visualizing uncertainty of, 197-201

CVD (see color-vision deficiency)

D

data

categories of, 8

in figures, 277

(see also balancing data and context)

too much data in figures, 338

data exploration vs. data presentation, 327-330

data source statements, 268

data transformations (for 3D visualizations), 309

data values, using color to represent, 29-32, 42

data visualization software

autogeneration of legends, 248

choosing, 325-331

data exploration vs. data presentation, 327-330

reproducibility and repeatability, 326-327

separation of content and design, 330-331

smoothing features, 150

thoughts on graphing software and figure preparation pipelines, xii

data–ink ratio, 277

About the Author

Claus O. Wilke is a professor of Integrative Biology at The University of Texas at Austin. He holds a PhD in theoretical physics from the Ruhr-University Bochum, Germany. Claus is the author or coauthor of over 170 scientific publications, covering topics in computational biology, mathematical modeling, bioinformatics, evolutionary biology, protein biochemistry, virology, and statistics. He has also authored several popular R packages used for data visualization, such as cowplot and ggridges, and he is a contributor to the package ggplot2.

Colophon

The animal on the cover of *Fundamentals of Data Visualization* is a western rosella parakeet (*Platycercus icterotis*), a small species of parrot in southwestern Australia. The name *icterotis* is derived from ancient Greek for "yellow ear," referring to the yellow spot on each of the bird's cheeks. The rosella is very colorful indeed—it has a red head and neck, a barred green, black, and red back, blue wing feathers, and a blue-green tail. They average about 10 inches in length.

This parakeet is found in forests, farmland, and parks. It usually has a diet of grass, seeds, and fruit, but requires more protein in breeding season so it also eats insect larvae at that time. The birds forage on the ground, gathering in groups of around 20 individuals where food is plentiful. Mating pairs nest in hollows of trees (eucalyptus trees are often preferred) and lay between 2–7 eggs in each brood.

Western rosella parakeets are popular in aviaries, and they can live 15 years or more.

Many of the animals on O'Reilly covers are endangered; all of them are important to the world. To learn more about how you can help, go to *animals.oreilly.com*.

The cover illustration is by Karen Montgomery, based on a black and white engraving from Shaw's *Zoology*. The cover fonts are Gilroy Semibold and Guardian Sans. The text font is Adobe Minion Pro; the heading font is Adobe Myriad Condensed; and the code font is Dalton Maag's Ubuntu Mono. The figure fonts are Adobe Myriad Pro and Adobe Myriad Condensed.